THE FRANCISCAN TRADITION

SPIRITUALITY IN HISTORY SERIES

The Franciscan Tradition

Regis J. Armstrong

Ingrid J. Peterson

Phyllis Zagano, Series Editor

LITURGICAL PRESS
Collegeville, Minnesota

www.litpress.org

Cover design by Ann Blattner. Cover art: Saint Francis of Assisi by the Maestro di Frate Francesco in the Capella di San Gregorio at the Monastero di San Benedetto near Subiaco. Photo by David Manahan, O.S.B.

1	2	3	4	5	6	7	8	9

Library of Congress Cataloging-in-Publication Data

Armstrong, Regis J.
   The Franciscan tradition / Regis J. Armstrong, Ingrid J. Peterson ;
   Phyllis Zagano, series editor.
       p. cm. — (Spirituality in history series)
   Includes bibliographical references.
   ISBN 978-0-8146-3030-3 — ISBN 978-0-8146-3922-1 (e-book)
   1. Franciscans.   2. Spiritual life—Catholic Church.   I. Peterson, Ingrid J.,
   1935–   II. Title.

BX3602.3.A76 2010
271'.3—dc22   2010001254

Contents

Acknowledgments   vii

Preface   ix

Introduction   xi

The Franciscan Tradition   xvii

  Francis of Assisi (c. 1182–1226)   1

The First Order of the Lesser Brothers   9

  The Rule of the Friars Minor   11

  Anthony of Padua (1195–1231)   17

  Bonaventure of Bagnoregio (c. 1217–1274)   23

  Felix of Cantalice (1515–1587)   30

  Junípero Serra (1713–1784)   37

  Maximilian Mary Kolbe (1894–1941)   50

  Solanus Casey (1870–1957)   57

The Second Order of the Poor Ladies   65

  The Form of Life of Clare of Assisi   67

  Clare of Assisi (1194–1253)   78

  Colette of Corbie (1381–1447)   89

  Catherine of Bologna (1413–1463)   95

  Veronica Giuliani (1660–1727)   99

The Third Order of the Brothers and Sisters of Penance   105

   An Exhortation of St. Francis to the Brothers and Sisters of Penance   107

   Angela of Foligno (1248–1309)   110

The Third Order Regular   119

   Mary of the Passion (1839–1904)   121

   Marianne Cope of Molokai (1838–1918)   128

The Third Order Secular   135

   The Marytrs of Nagasaki (1597)   137

   Jean-Marie Vianney (1786–1859)   143

   Matt Talbot (1856–1925)   149

New Rules   163

   The Secular Franciscan Order   165

      The Rule of the Secular Franciscan Order Approved by
         Pope Paul VI (1978)   167

   The Third Order Regular of St. Francis   173

      The Rule and Life of the Brothers and Sisters of the
         Third Order Regular of St. Francis Approved
         by Pope John Paul II (1982)   175

Notes   183

Bibliography   189

Acknowledgments

Texts from *Francis of Assisi: Early Documents: The Saint* and *The Founder* are used with permission. (Copyright 1999 and 2000, Regis J. Armstrong, O.F.M. Cap., J. A. Wayne Hellmann, O.F.M. Cap., William J. Short, O.F.M. Published by New City Press, 202 Cardinal Rd., Hyde Park, NY 12538 [www.newcitypress.com]).

Texts from *Clare of Assisi: Early Documents: The Lady* are used with permission. (Copyright 2006, Regis J. Armstrong, O.F.M. Cap. Published by New City Press, 202 Cardinal Rd., Hyde Park, NY 12538 [www.newcitypress.com]).

Seek First His Kingdom: An Anthology of the Sermons of the Saint, by a contemporary Franciscan. Translated by Fr. Livio Poloniato, O.F.M. Conv. Edizioni Messaggero Padova, 1988.

Excerpt from *Writings Concerning the Franciscan Order*, trans. Dominic Monti, vol. 5, Works of Saint Bonaventure (St. Bonaventure, NY: Franciscan Institute Publications, 1993). Reprinted by permission of Franciscan Institute Publications, St. Bonaventure University, St. Bonaventure, NY 14778. All rights reserved.

Excerpts from *Palou's Life of Fray Junípero Serra*, trans. Maynard Geiger (Washington, DC: Academy of American Franciscan History, 1955). Used with permission.

Michael H. Crosby, ed., *Solanus Casey: The Official Account of a Virtuous American Life*, copyright © 2000, published by Crossroad. By permission of the Provincial Archives of the Capuchin Province of St. Joseph.

Excerpts from Catherine of Bologna, *The Seven Spiritual Weapons*, trans. Hugh Feiss and Daniela Re (Toronto: Peregrina Translation Series, 1998). Used with permission.

Excerpts from Lazaro Iriate, "The Franciscan Spirit of St. Veronica Giuliani," trans. Edward Hagman, *Greyfriars Review* 7, no. 2 (1993): 193–227. Reprinted by

Preface

The worldwide explosion of interest in "spirituality" has sent inquirers in several directions. One of the more fruitful is toward the traditional spiritualities that have enriched and nurtured the church for many hundreds of years. Among the oldest Christian spiritualities are those connected to particular foundations, charisms, or individuals. This series of spiritualities in history focuses on five distinct traditions within the history of the church, those now known as Benedictine, Carmelite, Dominican, Franciscan, and Ignatian.

Each volume in the series seeks to present the given spiritual tradition through an anthology of writings by or about persons who have lived it, along with brief biographical introductions of those persons. Each volume is edited by an expert or experts in the tradition at hand.

The present volume of Franciscan spirituality has been coedited by Regis J. Armstrong, O.F.M. Cap., and Ingrid J. Peterson, O.S.F., both experts in Franciscan spirituality. Fr. Armstrong is the John and Gertrude Hubbard Professor of Religious Studies in the School of Theology and Religious Studies at The Catholic University of America. He is the acknowledged world expert on the writings of Clare and Francis and has written or edited nine books and countless articles on Franciscan spirituality. His books include *Francis and Clare: The Complete Works* (Paulist Press, 1986), *Francis of Assisi: Early Documents* (New City Press, 1999–2001), and *Clare of Assisi: The Lady* (New City Press, 2006). Sr. Ingrid served as an adjunct professor at the Franciscan Institute of St. Bonaventure University and author of several works on Franciscan spirituality, including *Clare of Assisi: A Biographical Study* (Franciscan Press, 1993).

Their compact presentation of the essentials of the Franciscan Tradition traces the living out of Francis's charism chronologically within the three parts of his family—the First Order, the Second Order, and the

Third Order—through the eight centuries since he laid down his belongings and went out of Assisi to rebuild the church.

The lives and writings of the Franciscan men and women in this volume demonstrate the adaptability of Francis's vision across cultures and throughout history. Each entry underscores the poverty at the crystal center of Francis's spirituality. If nothing material matters, then only the immaterial—the spirit living within each and every one of us—is what must be most revered and reverenced. Then and only then will the promise of Franciscan spirituality—universal brotherhood and peace—be recognized and received.

My own work on this book and for this series has continued with the able assistance of librarians, particularly the reference and interlibrary loan staff of Hofstra University, Hempstead, New York, who have tirelessly met so many of my research needs. I am grateful as well for the congenial staff of Liturgical Press, and especially for the professional support and encouragement of Colleen Stiller, Ann Blattner, Hans Christoffersen, and Peter Dwyer.

Phyllis Zagano
June 13, 2009
Feast of St. Anthony of Padua

Introduction

"Interpreters of that reality that begins with Baptism": this phrase of Pope Benedict XVI comes to mind when introducing someone to the Franciscan Tradition. With a penetrating simplicity, the Spirit of the Lord that enters the Christian soul at baptism seems the only explanation for the universality, the all-embracing character, and the joy Francis and his tradition brought to the religious life of the church. The Spirit, the Spirit alone, was needed by the thirteenth-century saint, perhaps the most popular saint in the church's two millennia history.

While the young Francis of Assisi began his journey of conversion encountering and embracing a leper, his formation in the spiritual life took place in the school of poverty where he learned he had nothing that he could call his own beyond his sin and his vice. In reading his life, it becomes clear how his biographers saw material poverty taking him by the hand and leading him through the world where he learned to call God's creatures brothers and sisters and that they—like him—groaned until set free by the firstfruits of the Spirit. In reading his writings chronologically, the Spirit's role becomes ever more influential, drawing him into the very inner life of the triune God. As the apostle Paul before him, Francis seemed overwhelmed at the meaning of his baptismal life, so much so that the eighth chapter of the letter to the Romans with its vision of a Christian's trinitarian life might appear as a blueprint for his vision of life.

What is it that makes Francis of Assisi such a popular figure, perhaps the most attractive saint of Christian living? The vast, ever-growing literature about him written in so many languages is as powerful a witness as the countless number of pilgrims who continue to come to Assisi. His is a universal language that all peoples seem to understand: therein seems to be the symbol that best expresses his appeal as the Spirit of

Pentecost draws people to him, bringing with it the promise of peace and universal brotherhood. In that light, Francis's repeated call becomes more intelligible: the call to desire only the Spirit of the Lord and his holy activity, the Spirit of holy prayer and devotion, the Spirit that unites us as brothers and sisters centered on the firstborn Son, Jesus, and the Spirit that impels us to see and proclaim all things through and in him. As he came to appreciate this, Francis realized that little else—nothing else—was needed. As he grew less and less dependent on things, he came to depend ever more on the Spirit and, understandably, the Spirit came to depend on him to bring about a new pentecost.

In that school of poverty created by those lonely years of repairing the churches of San Damiano, San Pietro, and Our Lady of the Portiuncula, Francis certainly had time to reflect on what God was asking of him. According to an insight provided by Clare of Assisi, he did have something of a prophetic intuition that San Damiano would become a "monastery for holy ladies." Beyond that, however, there is little evidence that he had any intention of founding a new religious group. Only when his first followers came did he struggle with that phenomenon and resolved it through the Lord "revealing" to him that he had to live the holy Gospel. When Clare and other women after her came to him, he provided them an extremely simple Gospel way of life that was to be lived, as he did, in poverty. And when other men and women came who were married or obliged in other ways, he offered them a similar pattern. The accounts of men and women who appear in this volume will do so in these three categories or orders, as the term emerged early in the tradition, and will do so with the appropriate ancient rule that forms that order. The Rule of the Third Order Regular religious communities that was approved by Pope John Paul II in 1982, a collaborative effort of Franciscan religious women and men in the Third Order tradition, will conclude this volume as it emerges from the resurgence of interest in the writings of Francis and Clare after the Second Vatican Council. A major challenge in preparing this volume was that of choosing those who would represent the multifaceted tradition begun by Francis of Assisi (c. 1182–1226).

The First Order obviously needed to consider Anthony of Padua (+1231) and Bonaventure of Bagnoregio (+1274), two of the outstanding early followers of Francis. There was a number of fourteenth- and fifteenth-century figures who could easily have appeared: John Duns Scotus (+1308), Bernardine of Siena (+1444), John of Capistrano (+1456), or James of the Marches (+1476). The Capuchin lay brother Felix of

Cantalice (+1587), however, represented a saint coming after the division of the First Order and the emergence of the reform movements of the sixteenth century. Junípero Serra (+1784) bridged the European and American worlds, especially Mexico and the United States, and reflected the strong influence of the Observant Friars. Maximilian Mary Kolbe (+1941) dramatically portrays the Conventual Friars in the most tragic period of the world history, and Solanus Casey (+1957) depicts the Capuchins in the twentieth-century United States. There were so many others who could have been included: a spiritual director of Teresa of Avila, Peter of Alcantara (+1562), Fidelis of Sigmaringen (+1622), Joseph of Cupertino (+1663), the mystic Padre Pio of Pietrelcina (+1968), the biblicist Gabriele Allegra (+1976), or the missionary Zenon Zebrowski (+1982).

One of the second-generation biographies of Francis, *The Legend of the Three Companions*, prompts imagining that, while rebuilding San Damiano, he was struck with his first inspiration to make it a "monastery of ladies through whose fame and life our heavenly Father will be glorified throughout the church."[1] Clare of Assisi (+1253) fulfilled Francis's prophecy and became his first female follower. Her Form of Life, the first written by a woman, envisions a hidden life devoted to the contemplative embrace of Christ, her beloved. Following a more monastic paradigm of stability, however, the tradition of the Second Order contains a variety of expressions that strive to follow the inspirations of both Francis and Clare. In addition to Clare, Colette of Corbie (+1447) remains a dominant figure who struggled to rekindle the love of the Form of Life written by Clare in 1253 and approved by Pope Innocent IV; she did this in France by accentuating the simplicity that was being lost in the tumultuous fourteenth century. At the same time in Italy, Catherine of Bologna (+1463) was attempting to do the same in the tradition emerging from Clare's inspiration by means of the Rule approved by Pope Urban IV in 1263; her means of reform was that of accentuating remembrance of Christ's passion. In the seventeenth and eighteenth centuries, moreover, Veronica Giuliani (+1727) became a model for those Sisters of Saint Clare trying to live Clare's vision of the Franciscan gospel in the spirit of the Capuchin reform. As with Francis's followers in the First Order, there are so many women in the Second Order who have been overlooked: Clare's own sister, Agnes of Assisi (+1253); the sister of St. King Louis IX of France, Isabelle (+1270); Agnes of Prague (+1282) with whom Clare corresponded; Beatrice de Silva (+ c.1492); Josephine Leroux (+1794), a martyr of the French Revolution; Mary Maddalena Bentivoglio (+1905) who brought the Poor Clares to the United States in 1875; Mary Francis of Roswell (+2006); and Veronica Namoyo of Lusaka.

Yet another insight comes from Thomas of Celano's *Life of Francis* when he writes of those "people of all ages and both sexes [who] hurried to behold the wonders which the Lord worked anew in the world through his servant. . . . To all," Thomas continues, "he gave a norm of life and to those of every rank he sincerely pointed out the way of salvation."[2] This became the Third Order composed of what we now call the Brothers and Sisters of Penance or the Secular Franciscans and the Third Order Regular, those who have embraced a religious way of life as priests, sisters, or brothers. Choosing representatives of this vast number of Francis's followers proved even more daunting as they came from exactly what Thomas of Celano suggests: "every rank" of society and, as his family grew, from all parts of the world. It seems appropriate to begin with Angela of Foligno (+1309) who leads the way among the countless women who embraced the Gospel vision of life of both Francis and Clare throughout the centuries. In a sense Angela is her own category as she could be considered representative of the entire penitential movement, both the secular and the regular.

Whom to choose from the litany of Third Order Regular religious women became more difficult, however. Angeline of Montegiove (+1435), the foundress of the first Third Order Regular community for women; Mary Alfred Moes (+1899), foundress of American foundations and a world-famous hospital; and Lurana White, cofoundress with Paul Francis Watson of the Franciscan Sisters of Atonement: all of these religious heroines would have been worthy subjects. For various reasons, the following women seem appropriate to highlight as both expressed different dimensions of that vision: Mary of the Passion (+1904) and Marianne Cope (1918).

Whom to chose from the Secular Franciscan Tradition was equally difficult. Elizabeth of Hungary (+1231) and Louis IX of France (+1270), patrons of the Secular Franciscans, typify in extraordinary ways the ideals of the Secular Franciscans, as does Thomas More (+1535). The unheralded Japanese Secular Franciscans and their literal "cojourners" (+1597) seem ideal subjects in their ability to express the evangelizing witness to the Franciscan vision of the Gospel: twenty-six Christians—six friars of whom four were Spanish, one Mexican, one Portuguese-Indian; three Japanese Jesuits, two of whom had been received into the Society a few days before; fourteen laymen, members of the Third Order or associates of the Franciscans; three young boys who were fourteen, thirteen, and twelve years old. Two final representatives of the Secular Franciscans, moreover, seemed at first out of place. On further reflection they both offer wonderful expressions of the hidden yet transparent Franciscan paradox: the diocesan priest Jean-Marie Vianney (+1859) and the layman Matt Talbot (+1925), both men whose examples are timeless in their relevancy.

The energy of the Spirit of the Lord that Francis and Clare encouraged his followers to have invigorated them after the Second Vatican Council and, prompted by the Decree on Religious Life (*Perfectae Caritatis*), inspired them to examine their lives in light of Francis's writings. Surprisingly the writings of both Francis and Clare were relatively unknown before then. The friars of the First Order and the sisters of the Second have since been wonderfully enriched by the vitality of the Franciscan Traditions. The Second Vatican Council, however, brought to the fore challenges for all Christians—for Franciscans as well: the recovery of tradition. In 1978, Pope Paul VI promulgated a new rule for the Secular Franciscans that now begins with the norm of life Francis left for them at the beginning. Four years later, Pope John Paul II promulgated a new rule for the Third Order Regular women and men, one that they struggled to compose in the spirit of the Second Vatican Council's encouragement to retrieve the charism of their founder.

We wish to give special thanks for the initiative, assistance, and patience of Phyllis Zagano, the series editor, and for all those men and women who have helped us with finding, translating, and affirming this introductory overview of the Franciscan Tradition especially John Ford, C.S.C.; Matthew Foley, O.F.M. Conv.; Anthony M. Lajato, O.F.M. Conv.; William J. Short, O.F.M.; the friars and staff of San Lorenzo Friary and Mission Santa Barbara; Alma Dufault, F.M.M.; Mary Laurence Hanley, O.S.F.; Iowans Shannon McAllister and Justin White; and, as usual, Noel Riggs.

The Franciscan Tradition

The Franciscan Tradition has its origins in the young man from Assisi, Francis, who was born in 1182 and died in 1226. From his writings, it might be concluded that he simply wanted to live the fullness of life he received at his baptism, but in a short period of time men and women began to follow his vision of a poor and simple trinitarian life. As does Jesus, so too his follower Francis continues to draw vast numbers of followers.

The Turbulent World of Francis

The history of Assisi at the end of the twelfth and the beginning of the thirteenth centuries shows how its geographical location was the envy of those lusting for power. This could not have been lost on the son of a cloth merchant whose business would have been dependent on access to the Via Franca, the principal highway linking Assisi with cities—and markets—to its north and south. Perched as it is on Monte Subasio, Assisi became increasingly strategic and, therefore, vulnerable. Its citizens were ever attentive to any threat to this vital artery and warded off any attempts to master them.

In 1198, when Francis was sixteen, the members of the Commune of Assisi attacked the Rocca Maggiore, the fortress of the feudal nobility, where only a year or so earlier Frederick II, the future emperor of the Holy Roman Empire, had been born. This was essentially an act of civil war that pitted members of Assisi's nobility against the newly powerful members of the rising merchant class. Ironically, the two sides represented not only Francis, son of the ambitious merchant Pietro di Bernardone, but also Clare di Favarone, the young daughter of an aristocratic family whose ancestry could be traced to Charlemagne himself. Buoyed by this act of defiance, the Assisiani looked beyond their city walls, so that the ebb and flow of war touched almost every family. In 1202, however, things changed. The Battle of Collestrada was an engagement of two ancient rivals, the Assisiani and their archenemies, the hated men of Perugia. As the Perugians overwhelmed their ambitious neighbors in what became the region's bloodiest skirmish, the Assisiani were literally beaten into the ground or dragged off to prison.

While there is no record of Francis's involvement in the uprising of 1198, we can easily imagine the sixteen-year-old joining in the destruction of the Rocca, that symbol of feudal tyranny, and in the beginning of a new social order. But there is some knowledge of the young man's role in the Battle of Collestrada; that is, his biographers write that he was one of those imprisoned in Perugia. At his release, Francis returned to Assisi in broken health. But dreams of military glory continued to fill his imagination so that the drudgery of working in his father's business made him increasingly restless.

Although there is little information of where the clergy of Assisi were on these issues, they may well have been suffering from the same turmoil as the clergy of the institutional church throughout Europe. Whether indifferent or ill-prepared, the clergy of the time came across as insensitive to the yearning of many Christians for the simplicity of Gospel living. Throughout Europe new expressions of lay spirituality and of consecrated life were emerging; so too, however, were those of the dualist approach of third-century Manichaeism promoted by the Cathars and Albigensians. Under the guise of freeing themselves from anything material, they rejected a sacramental approach to the spiritual life and, in its place, embraced a radical "other-worldly" asceticism. Confronted with an apathetic and poorly formed clergy, the laity of the twelfth and early thirteenth centuries left the institutional church in ever-growing numbers.

The Foundations of Francis's Vision of Life

In the conflicting currents of this Umbrian town, Francis encountered the presence of God who, in his own words, "led him to begin to do penance" by encountering a leper.[1] The remainder of his life would be a journey of an intense spirituality in which the gift of baptism, the Spirit of the Lord, would be the dynamism of his life, uniting him to the Father and to all creatures with the Son. His search to understand the mystery of baptismal life inspired him to live the unending pursuit to be like the perfect Son, Jesus, in order to remain in communion with the Father. Each day, therefore, brought a new dimension of entering more profoundly into Gospel life and, consequently, the challenge of a life of penance.

When he and his small group of brothers went to Pope Innocent III for approval of their simple proposal of Gospel life, the formula of the vows somehow made its way into the document. Francis obviously had no difficulty with that formula particularly when the pope himself in 1198 had interpreted the three vows of poverty, chastity, and obedience as expressing the essential elements of religious life. Years later, however, the memories of his youth seem to have prompted him to revisit his thoughts of the life of penance he had embraced and, as he attempted to encourage his followers in their own embrace of it, influenced his *Second Admonition*. This ever-so-simple writing expresses his understanding of human nature as he sees it burdened with the ravages of original sin:

> The Lord said to Adam: *Eat of every tree; you may not eat, however, of the tree of the knowledge of good and evil* [cf. Gen 2:16,17].
>
> He was able to eat of every tree of paradise because, as long as he did not go against obedience, he did not sin. For that person eats of the tree of the knowledge of good who makes his will his own and, in this way, exalts himself over the good things the Lord says and does in him. And so, through the suggestion of the devil and the transgression of the command, it became the apple of the knowledge of evil. Therefore it is fitting that he suffers the punishment.[2]

While Adam had received everything from the Creator, he turned from the only restriction given to him as a reminder of his dependency on the divine generosity. In that one act of disobedience, Francis perceived the two enduring tendencies of the human nature: to make its will its own and to exalt itself over that which really belongs to God. What he had experienced in his early years—and undoubtedly throughout his life— were the grasping and ambitious ways of sinful human beings who, like Adam, tended to be so easily deceived by passing pleasure. His program of holiness became quite simply that of following the poverty, humility, and consequent patient endurance of Jesus. Paradoxically, toward the end of his life the nearly blind, vulnerable Francis saw clearly that everything was pure gift as "The Lord gave me and gives me still . . ."[3] became the refrain of his dying recollections.

The Franciscan Family

"The Lord gave me brothers," Francis wrote, "and no one showed me how to live but the Most High himself revealed to me that I should live according to the pattern of the holy Gospel."[4] Not only were those who came to him personal gifts from God, learning how he was to live with them was also a gift. The words are reminiscent of John's gospel: "You gave me those who follow me . . . and I gave them the words you gave to me." For Francis life in brotherhood became fleshed out for him in the dimensions of the Gospel life: to grow in the one was to grow in the other. Therein lies the breath and variety of the Franciscan Gospel life, one that became quickly divided into three families or Orders.

The First Order, the Order of Friars Minor or Lesser Brothers, was from the beginning composed entirely of men—priests and lay— whose primary goal was to live the Gospel as brothers aiming to be the least of Christ's disciples. Even while he was alive, however, two strains emerged among his followers: one that tended to more itinerant or eremitical patterns of living, the other that was comfortable with more stability or urban life. These two currents gradually assumed characteristics that have endured to present time. The itinerant or eremitical expressions tended to encourage the brothers to bond according to their desired inspirations or emphases—itinerant preaching or missionary endeavors, hermitages—while those favoring stability or a more common way of life established *conventi* (convents or friaries) among the poor. The early centuries of Franciscan history are filled with attempts to bring these two strands together. Eventually a decree of Pope Leo X in 1517 officially recognized the two: the Order of "Observants"—into which some of the smaller clusters were brought—and the Order of "Conventuals." In this decisive period of the Reformation, the Capuchins emerged from the Observant strain in 1528 advocating a return to the dynamics of an authentic form of Gospel life. In 1897, Pope Leo XIII consolidated the smaller groups such as the Observants and the Reformers, into the Order of Friars Minor of the Leonine Union, while the Conventuals and Capuchins remained autonomous as they are today.

The Second Order is composed of women committed to living as poor, monastic contemplatives. It began when the eighteen-year-young Clare of Assisi came to Francis for advice about the Gospel life, embraced a contemplative life at San Damiano, the first church he rebuilt, and began to attract her own followers. In the beginning Francis provided them a simple way of life whose contours were fundamentally trinitarian: "Because by divine inspiration you have made yourselves daughters and servants of the most high King, the heavenly Father, and taken the Holy Spirit as your spouse, choosing to live according to the perfection of the Gospel."[5] Before his death, he asked and counseled them "to live this most holy life and poverty . . . and to never depart from this by reason of the teaching or advice of anyone."[6] In 1219 the pope's legate, Cardinal Hugolino dei Conti di Segni, gave her a form of life based on the Benedictine Rule that mitigated their observance of a life without anything of their own and set the stage for a struggle that was to continue until shortly before her death: the approval of a form of life based on the Gospel vision lived in poverty that she received through Francis. At her death, the Poor Ladies—as they were known—now spread throughout Europe were living three different patterns of life: that of Clare approved on the day before her death, that of Hugolino given in 1219, and that of Pope Innocent IV given and later rescinded in 1246. In 1264 Pope Urban IV, desiring to bring some uniformity, wrote yet another rule that permitted common ownership of property. Only those who wished to observe the "primitive rule" of Clare were obliged until the early fifteenth century when St. Colette of Corbie revived its observance. With the exception of the "Colettines," the Rule of St. Clare was overlooked until after the Second Vatican Council.

To those laywomen and laymen eager to follow him, Francis gave a simple form of life, *An Exhortation to the Brothers and Sisters of Penance*, which became their foundational document. Lay movements such as this had their beginnings in the earliest days of religious life; in fact, religious life may be seen as evolving from those women and men who, in their eagerness to follow the example of Jesus, went into the desert where they discovered the need for spiritual guides. Benedictine monasteries had oblates: laypersons wanting to live the monastic spirit who chose not to be formally professed but to be officially associated with a monastery of their choice. The landscape of the twelfth century is populated with such figures: the Canons Regular of Premontré and the Cistercians developed their own categories giving rise—among the men—to lay brothers; itinerant preachers attracted followers, among them the Waldensians or Vaudois of Peter Waldo, a wealthy merchant who chose to live as a poor beggar. The Humiliati were at this time a group of noblemen who were captured by Emperor Henry V (1081–1125) and brought to Germany where, some say, they "humiliated" themselves by doing penance. On the advice of Bernard of Clairvaux, many of them, with the consent of their wives, withdrew into a monastery founded at Milan and later adopted the Benedictine Rule tailored to their needs. This group spread rapidly and gave rise to two new branches, a "second order" composed of women, and a "third order" composed of priests. Pope Innocent III (1198–1216) initially censured this "third order" but eventually provided it with a juridical structure. In 1221 Pope Honorius III provided a similar juridical structure for those men and women who followed Francis, one that has been revised and renewed by a number of popes from Gregory IX to Pope Paul VI.

While many of these "tertiaries" remained living and working in secular pursuits, others left their homes to live in hermitages or in fraternities united by the religious vows of obedience, poverty, and chastity following Honorius III's rule as revised in 1289 by Nicholas IV. During the fourteenth century, confraternities of female penitents that had been absorbed into the Third Order began to recruit new members to assist them with their apostolic works. In 1324 Pope John XXII officially recognized the community of Angelina Montegiove. Hers was the first women's congregation with a *magistra* general overseeing many houses of vowed religious women. As the years passed the Third Order "Regular" continued to become increasingly regularized or even semi-cloistered. In doing so, these women and men fell back on a distinction that had its origins in the eleventh century: between the "secular" and the "regular." In 1521 Pope Leo X issued a rule specifically for vowed members and again, in 1927 Pope Pius X issued yet another.

In light of the profound changes in the theology of consecrated life after the Second Vatican Council and a new wave of scholarship in the Franciscan family, the women and men of this Third Order tradition proposed two new rules, one approved for the Secular Franciscans by Pope Paul VI in 1978, the other for the Third Order Regular Franciscans by Pope John Paul II in 1982.

The Franciscan Vision

At the very heart of Francis's understanding of his call and that of his followers is an awareness of "the Spirit of the Lord and His holy activity."[7] The Spirit is that which he perceives as receiving the primary attention in all activity: in shaping the contours of a Gospel life that is profoundly trinitarian, contemplative in its perception of reality, passionate in proclaiming Jesus as Lord, and reverent in embracing all creation. Since he possessed a poetic spirit, however, Francis was attentive to the Spirit's presence in the word, especially in the words spoken by the Word. As a result his life became a continuous process of allowing the words of the Gospel to enter profoundly into every fiber of his being: their sound, articulation, imagery, and meaning. Not surprisingly, he sees prayer not as an enterprise of the "Spirit of holy prayer and devotion" but also teaches that everything "must contribute to it."[8] Early on, his followers, in addition to establishing the rhythm of each day through the Eucharist and the Liturgy of the Hours, established two periods of intense mental prayer: one hour in the morning when they would listen to the Lord speaking to their hearts, another in the evening when they would reflect on how the Lord had revealed his presence in those they encountered who brought that word to life during the day. He was described as "praying so much that he became prayer,"[9] which might easily be interpreted as his entire life being transparent with the Spirit's activity of inspiring us to live as children of a loving God.

Franciscan spirituality has interpreted Francis's *Canticle of Brother Sun* as supremely characteristic of his Gospel vision, as a key to his inner self, or as revelatory of his entire personality. His followers provide the details of the tempestuous circumstances in which the dying poet at three different moments spontaneously sang God's praises: the first coming from his own struggle of faith, the second from the political struggles of Assisi, and the third from his struggle with his imminent death. If it is true that poets are people who surrender themselves to the inner journey, then they are indeed indispensable to society. In this light, no better text than Francis's *Canticle* reveals his vision of life.

This is the song of a man who is losing his sight, whose eyes burn at the sight of light, and whose body and spirit ache with fatigue and the discouragement that comes with it. In the middle of the night he twists and turns as at times everyone does, and the next morning he tells his companions what had been taking place.

> Feeling sorry for himself, he said: "Lord, help me in my infirmities so that I may have the strength to bear them patiently!" He then heard: "Tell me, brother: if, in compensation for your suffering and tribulations you were given an immense and precious treasure: the whole mass of the earth changed into pure gold, pebbles into precious stones, and the water of the rivers into perfume, would you not regard the pebbles and the waters as nothing compared to such a treasure? Would you not rejoice?" "Lord," he replied, "it would be a very great, very precious, and inestimable treasure beyond all that one can love and desire!" "Well, brother," the voice said, "be glad and joyful in the midst of your infirmities and tribulations. As of now, live in peace as if you were already sharing my kingdom."[10]

With that Francis burst into song as if, as Carl Jung once wrote of true genius, "to a temporal world out of a world eternal." His song is an echo of "the message of penance and peace" he proclaimed to the world after hearing the missionary mandate of the Gospel:

> Most High, all-powerful, good Lord,
>   Yours are the praises, the glory, the honor, and all blessing,
>   to You alone, Most High, do they belong,
>   and no human is worthy to mention Your name.
>
> Praised be You, my Lord, with all Your creatures,
>   especially Sir Brother Sun,
>   Who is the day and through whom You give us light,
>   and He is beautiful and radiant with great splendor,
>   and bears a likeness of You, Most High One.
> Praised be You, my Lord, through Sister Moon and the stars,
>   in heaven You formed them bright and precious and beautiful.
> Praised be You, my Lord, through Brother Wind,
>   and through the air, cloudy and serene, and every kind of weather,
>   through whom You give sustenance to Your creatures.
> Praised be You, my Lord, through Sister Water,
>   who is very useful and humble and precious and chaste.
> Praised be You, my Lord, through Brother Fire,
>   through whom You light the night
>   and he is beautiful and playful and robust and strong.
> Praised be You, my Lord, through our Sister Mother Earth,
>   who sustains and governs us,
>   and who produces various fruits with colored flowers and herbs.
> Praise and bless my Lord
>   and give Him thanks
>   and serve Him with great humility.[11]

The Fabric of Creation

The Franciscan vision flows ultimately from the realization that, in the words of the Jewish Scriptures, the beginning of wisdom is the fear of the Lord. The "most high, all-powerful, Lord" is above all "good": this is what Francis never tires of reiterating. It is this that liberates him from the petty moments of life, enabling him to rise above human frailty and to trust in God alone. It is this that impels him to struggle with his all too human temptation to reach out for what in reality belongs only to God: praise, glory, honor, and blessing. It is this that prompts the poet Francis to be focused on God's presence in the creation that enfolds him.

Without uttering a word the poetry of God's creation reminds him of his own poor performance and of his need for penance to reenter into its beauty and radiance. "No human is worthy to mention your name." The words introduce a shadow that hovers over him as a reminder of the indictment and punishment of the first inhabitants of paradise.

Immediately, however, the cloud passes. The brilliance of the sun, of the day resumes the hymn of praise gently reminding him of the words of the psalmist: "in your light we see light." The God who is beauty shines radiantly on all his creatures evoking from them nothing but praise, a praise that is his as well as theirs: "Praise be You, my Lord, with all Your creatures." The words seem to echo those of Paul: *the whole created world eagerly awaits the revelation of the children of God*. In the meanwhile, the poet Francis recognizes the Spirit's presence in creation as it sings by its sheer wonder the praises of the One who breathed upon it. What follows then is a paradoxically unified hymn of opposites in which the Creative Spirit and created being, the heavens and earth, the masculine and feminine join in one stanza after another. What is precious, playful, serene, radiant, humble takes on qualities enshrined in beauty itself prompting nothing but praise for goodness of the most high, all-powerful, good Lord of all. If it is true that the source of poetic genius is the deepest inner self, then this section of Francis's *Canticle* reflects the trinitarian traces of his spiritual life: the Father whom elsewhere he describes dwelling "in inaccessible light," the Son and the saints—precious, clear, and beautiful—shining like the moon and the stars in the night of sin, and the Spirit stirring the air and the clouds, bringing life humbly and without cost like water, burning with warmth and light like fire. Here too the *Canticle* suggests the Marian underpinnings of Francis's vision of the church—as does Assisi's cathedral, San Rufino, originally a Roman temple called "Mother Earth"—sustaining, governing, and producing fruit as "the virgin-made church" of whom he sings in his *Salutation* to her.

The Tranquility of Love

Acrimony prompted the second section of the *Canticle*: hostility that was probably brooding for a long while between Assisi's ecclesial and civil leaders. When he learned that it had erupted, Francis's companions tell us that he told them to go to Assisi, to sing the verses he had just composed, and to add these:

> Praised be You, my Lord, through those who give pardon for Your love,
>   and bear infirmity and tribulation.

> Blessed are those who endure in peace
> for by You, Most High, shall they be crowned.[12]

There is no evidence that the bishop, *podestà* (mayor), and the people had heard the first section of the *Canticle* before this, nor is there any indication that Francis had asked his brothers to read any other message of peace to them. The combination of both segments, however, may well have sufficed to bring the two men to peace as it did. For with these verses Francis envisions the human person now gently and unassumingly entering into the hymn of the universe. Those who give pardon out of love, bear infirmity and tribulation, and endure in peace are those who take on the qualities of the Word made flesh. They bring to the pursuit of peace more than "the tranquility of order" reflected in the first segment of the *Canticle*; they bring "the tranquility of love," as Bonaventure would later refine Augustine's concept of peace, the love shown by Jesus.

The Blessed Hope

Just before his death, Francis asked the brothers to sing once again the *Canticle* and the two segments he had already composed. Now, however, he added yet another:

> Praised be You, my Lord, through our Sister Bodily Death,
> from whom no one living can escape.
> Woe to those who die in mortal sin!
> Blessed are those whom death will find in Your most holy will,
> for the second death shall do them no harm.[13]

The canticle of creation and of reconciliation now becomes one of hope, of the certain hope for which he prayed from the earliest years of his conversion. Living a life without anything of one's own, that is, a life of radical poverty, instills profound hope as time after time it teaches the poor one that God is never outdone in generosity.

More than anything else, however, these verses chant the praises of the Gospel call Francis envisions: that of the baptized life. It is baptism that enables one to welcome bodily death as a sister, not as something to be dreaded but as part of life and as one whose embrace can be longed for as that of one's family. There is perhaps sadness in the failure not to have discouraged others from what prevents that warm embrace and causes death to be feared: greeting it mired in sin. At the same time, there is an echo of how simply Francis sees the demands of baptism. "Now that we have left the world," he encourages, "we have nothing else to do but to follow the will of the Lord and to please Him."[14] Baptism, the first death, frees one to love without fear and to be assured in hope.

The Wisdom of Simplicity

The earliest manuscript of Francis's *Canticle* comes from the mid-thirteenth century; all others follow it almost exactly. None of them, however, indicates whether Francis intended the following refrain to be sung after each verse or after each section. It appears without any directions at the very end but, in so many ways, summarizes the entire *Canticle*, each of its sections, as well as of its verses. Indeed, it captures the depths of the Franciscan spirit:

> Praise and bless my Lord and give Him thanks
>   and serve Him with great humility.[15]

In the wisdom of his simple Gospel vision, the lesser brother saw these as the operative verbs of his life: praise, blessing, giving thanks, and serving the Lord. It is as if the Franciscan vision sees these as the only ones that matter as they can only come from one who knows that everything comes from God and that all his brothers and sisters serve God better. To be a poor, humble, vulnerable brother—to be a lesser brother—that is the baptismal call of the Gospel.

A wonderful eucharistic mysticism took hold of Francis in the last days of his life. Consciousness of the sacrament of the Body and Blood of the Lord—the concrete, down-to-earth way in which he writes of the Eucharist—is present even in his earlier writings. Something prompted the deepening of this awareness in his *First Admonition*, an undated writing that clearly shows a maturing of his thought, and, above all, in his *Letter to the Entire Order*, which was written more than likely after the first two segments of the *Canticle*. Could it be that in the Eucharist Francis saw God choosing each day to use the gifts of creation to make present the love of His Son? "Daily" becomes a frequent refrain, as does the Lord's embrace of poverty, humility, and patient endurance as the Most High defines what it means to be a lesser one and shows the way to true brotherhood.

If this were so, Francis's *Canticle* may be understood as the quintessential expression of the tradition that bears his name and, if this were so, the culmination of the baptismal life that he strove to live with such intensity, one that leads to and learns from the daily self-giving of the Eucharist.

Francis of Assisi (c. 1182–1226)

It might well be argued that no saint in history has drawn more interest or so fired up the Christian imagination than he who was born in a small town in the Umbrian Valley of central Italy, Francis of Assisi. Not only has his appeal spanned eight centuries, it has also encompassed almost every corner of the globe. Ironically, the relatively few writings left to posterity were neglected by his followers until recently, possibly because they are so very simple and transparent. Thomas of Celano wrote Francis's first biography, *The Life of Saint Francis*, at the time of his canonization within two years of his death. Twenty years later Francis's followers commissioned him to write another, which Thomas called *The Remembrance of the Desire of a Soul*, and, three years later, yet another devoted solely to his miracles. Francis's followers then turned to their newly elected leader, the Parisian theologian Bonaventure, to compile these portraits of Thomas into two companion portraits, in which Francis's life is described as an unfolding of grace. Unwittingly, Bonaventure may have unleashed a wave of later biographies of Francis as the restless imagination of his followers attempted to build on the comparatively sparse facts of his life.

Toward the end of his life, Francis wrote of how the Lord had worked in his life: "a remembrance, admonition, and exhortation," he described it, "[his] testament."[1] He begins the document quite simply with a description of how the Lord guided him to begin to do penance and provided insights that led to what was the decisive moment in his life: overcoming himself by embracing a leper and, in doing so, finding God. In order to appreciate the depths of that seemingly impulsive moment, however, it is helpful to reflect upon what sort of life he lived prior to it.

The role of Pietro di Bernardone, Francis's father, overshadows those early years of the young man's life. It was Pietro, a clothier who regularly

1

made business trips between Assisi and France, who dubbed his newly born son Francesco, the "Frenchman." Like every proud father, he undoubtedly dreamed of the day when his son would inherit his business, was unconcerned when he neglected his studies, and accepted his impulsiveness when he joined his adolescent friends in enjoying life. When his son dreamed of achieving glory as a knight and fought with his townsmen against neighboring Perugia, Pietro supported him; when the dream unraveled by his capture and imprisonment, Pietro probably interpreted this turn of events as a simple confirmation that his son was destined to follow in his footsteps.

A leper intervened, however, when Pietro's unsettled, still-recuperating son encountered this most scorned piece of humanity whose ravaging sickness signified a divine curse. Francis's initial response may have been one of revulsion but he overcame it and, in his own words, "showed him *misericordiam* [a heart sensitive to misery]."[2] Years later he saw that as the decisive moment of grace, the Lord's gift. It was the beginning of a series of events that led him into the abandoned church in which he heard the crucified Lord call him to rebuild it, set about using what he had at hand—his father's goods—to do so, and, understandably, incurred his father's wrath.

In a manner similar to the leper, Pietro became God's instrument causing Francis to confront his interior struggles. When he dragged his young son before the civil and then the ecclesiastical authorities, he set him free as the naked Francis dramatically placed his clothing—all his belongings—at the feet of Pietro and declared: "You, Pietro Bernardone, are no longer my father! No, my father is 'Our Father Who art in heaven!'" It was this far-reaching assertion that paradoxically gifted Francis with the freedom to trust completely in God's providence and the constraint of following his heavenly Father's will in ways he never imagined. Since that momentous day in Assisi's Piazza Vescovile, spiritual writers and historians have attempted to define the inner drive of Francis in the hope of expressing it anew. While the embrace of penance and poverty may well have ignited the flame, it was undoubtedly the gift of baptism, the gift of the Spirit, that set the process in motion. With nothing else to claim as his own, Francis disciplined his spirit to be guided by the Spirit of Christ, *the Son*, in order to follow the heavenly Father's will and to please him alone. Poverty freed him to live out his baptismal call just as it gifted him with a transparency that drew others—women as well as men—to follow his lead. "The Lord gave me brothers," Francis wrote at the end of his life, "and no one showed me what to do. The Most High revealed to me that I should live according to the pattern of the holy Gospel."[3] It was as simple as that.

A few years after that day in Assisi, Francis found himself with brothers. Together they set off to seek approbation from the pope for a simple Gospel life without anything of their own. Paradox again entered the life of the young man as he was ushered into the presence of the charismatic Pope Innocent III who, in some ways, was the apogee of the hierarchical church of the Middle Ages. Once it was granted, the small group of twelve returned to Assisi from where they embarked on living the Gospel life and mission and, like that earlier group of twelve, experienced the Spirit's power in adding more to their number. Among those drawn to his example was the beautiful woman, Clare, who was twelve years his younger.

In 1215 Innocent III convened the Fourth Lateran Council and set in motion two initiatives: the renewal of the church and the freeing of the Holy Land. While it is uncertain that he was present at the council, Francis certainly imbibed its spirit as he encouraged his brothers to renew their catholicity, reach out to the followers of Islam and nonbelievers, and to place the Eucharist at the heart of their lives. The council also deepened his own desire to lay down his life after the example of the beloved Son, whom he was always trying to emulate, by embarking on a mission of peace to the Islamic world.

Francis had set out twice before finally reaching Egypt in 1221. While the Christian forces of the Fifth Crusade had captured and occupied Damietta since 1219, by August 1221 the Muslim army had regrouped and surrounded a city that was strategic for controlling the Nile. The ever peace-minded Francis crossed the enemy lines eager to speak with the Islamic leaders. Captured, insulted, and beaten, he was eventually escorted into the presence of the Sultan Malil al-Kamil who was impressed with his courage and perhaps more by his trust in God that inspired his poverty. It was an amazing encounter during which two men, one comfortably surrounded by his powerful army and the other armed intrepidly with his faith, dialogued about the God of Abraham that united them both. Some forty years later, Bonaventure would write: "When [Francis] saw he was making no progress in converting these people and that he could not achieve his purpose, namely martyrdom, he returned to the land of the faithful."[4] God had other things in mind for him among which was the need for him to articulate clearly the Gospel life God has revealed to and through him to his followers.

After being away from his brothers for a while, Francis returned to find them in chaos. Those whom he left in charge during his absence had imposed practices taken from the religious rules of St. Augustine and St. Benedict or the Cistercian reform. In front of the church's representative, Cardinal Hugolino, Francis responded: "My brothers! My brothers! God has called me by way of simplicity and showed me the way of simplicity. I do not want you to mention to me any rule, whether of Saint Augustine, or of Saint Bernard, or of Saint Benedict. The Lord has told me what He wanted! He wanted me to be a new fool in the world. God did not wish to lead us by any other than this knowledge."[5] In this simple statement, Francis may well have provided what he intuitively understood as being a Lesser Brother or a Friar Minor: to be simply a brother to those whom the Lord gave to him and to consider himself always lesser than them.

Shortly thereafter, however, Francis began rewriting the description of life that he had presented to Pope Innocent III in 1209—basically a simple collection of gospel passages to which he added and clarified as the circumstances in which he and his brothers found themselves between then and 1223 demanded. Thanks to the help of the cardinal and one or two of his brothers who may have been knowledgeable in ecclesiastical law and Latinists, the result was a more abbreviated and concise document. "The rule and life of the Lesser Brothers is this: to live the Holy Gospel of our Lord Jesus Christ."[6] At its very heart was a simple statement: "let them pay attention to what they must desire above all else: to have the Spirit of the Lord and His holy activity."[7] In their simplicity these two statements have challenged the Lesser Brothers throughout the centuries to a profound experiential mystagogy in which they simply live out their baptismal commitment.

As if by way of confirming the blessings to which their way of life would lead, shortly afterward the Lord granted Francis two extraordinary mystical experiences. The first was at the midnight celebration of Christmas at Greccio when the Infant appeared in Francis's arms; the second was when the Crucified appeared to him on LaVerna and left the imprint of his passion on his hands, feet, and side. It was after this last experience that Francis left to posterity the first two sections of what some see as one of the greatest hymns of the mystical experience, the *Canticle of Brother Sun*, the conclusion of which he composed just before his death.

Surrounded by his brothers and laying naked on the ground, Francis passed on the evening of October 3. In less than two years, his friend and confidant, Pope Gregory IX, whom Francis knew as Cardinal Hugolino, canonized him. In doing so, he undoubtedly acclaimed one of the most trinitarian of all saints whose secret of holiness was as simple as clinging only to the gift of every Christian, that of baptismal life.

***

The trinitarian imprint of the writings of Francis may be most clearly recognized in this twenty-second chapter of his *Earlier Rule*. There is a temptation to read over the Scripture passages—especially those from the parable of the sower and the seed and those from the Prayer at the Last Supper—without recognizing the nuances Francis adds to them, nuances that flow from his memorization of these passages and the ease with which they flow from his heart.

From *Earlier Rule*

Now that we have left the world, however, we have nothing else to do but to follow the will of the Lord and to please Him. Let us be careful that we are not earth along the wayside, or that which is rocky or full of thorns, in keeping with what the Lord says in the Gospel: *The word of God is a seed.* What *fell along the wayside and was trampled underfoot, however, are those who hear the word* and do not understand it. *The devil comes immediately and snatches what was planted in their hearts and takes the word from their hearts that they may not believe and be saved.* What *fell on rocky ground, however, are those who, as soon as they hear the word, receive it at once with joy. But when tribulation and persecution come because of the word, they immediately fall away.* These have no roots in them; they last only for a time, because *they believe only for a time and fall away in time of trial.* What *fell among thorns, however, are those who hear the word of God and the anxiety and worries of this world, the lure of riches, and other inordinate desires intrude and choke the word and they remain without fruit. But what was sown in good soil are those who hear the word with a good and excellent heart,* understand *and preserve it and bear fruit in patience.* Therefore, as the Lord says, brothers, let us let *the dead bury their own dead.* . . .

But, in the holy love which is God, I beg all my brothers, both the ministers and the others, after overcoming every impediment and putting aside every care and anxiety, to serve, love, honor and adore the Lord God with a clean heart and a pure mind in whatever way they are best able to do so, for that is what He wants above all else.

Let us always make a home and a dwelling place there for Him Who is the Lord God Almighty, Father, Son and Holy Spirit, Who says: *Be vigilant at all times and pray that you have the strength to escape the tribulations that are imminent and to stand before the Son of Man. When you stand to pray say: Our Father in heaven.* And let us adore Him with a pure heart, *because it is necessary to pray always and not lose heart; for the Father seeks such* people who adore Him. *God is Spirit and those who adore Him must adore Him in Spirit and truth.* Let us have recourse to Him as *to the Shepherd and Guardian of our souls,* Who says: "I am the Good Shepherd Who feeds My sheep and I lay down My life for my sheep."

All of you are brothers. Do not call anyone on earth your father; you have but one Father in heaven. Do not call yourselves teachers; you have but one Teacher in heaven. If you remain in me and my words remain in you, ask for whatever you want and it will be done for you. Wherever two or three are gathered together in my name, there am I in the midst of them. Behold I am with you until the end of the world. The words I have spoken to you are spirit and life. I am the Way, the Truth, and the Life. Let us, therefore, hold onto the words, the life, the teaching and the Holy Gospel of Him Who humbled Himself to beg His Father for us and to make His name known saying:

Father, glorify Your name and glorify Your Son that Your Son may glorify You. Father, *I have made Your name known to those whom You have given me. The words You gave to me I have given to them, and they have accepted them and truly have known that I came from You and they have believed that You sent me. I pray for them, not for the world, but for those You have given me, because they are Yours and everything of mine is Yours.* Holy Father, *keep in Your name those You have given me that they may be one as We are. I say this while in the world that they may have joy completely. I gave them Your word, and the world hated them, because they do not belong to the world as I do not belong to the world. I do not ask you to take them out of the world but that you keep them from the evil one. Glorify them in truth. Your word is truth. As You sent me into the world, so I sent them into the world. And I sanctify myself for them that they also may be sanctified in truth. I ask not only for them but also for those who will believe in me through them, that they may be brought to perfection as one, and the world may know that You have sent me and loved them as You loved me. I shall make known to them Your name, that the love with which You loved me may be in them and I in them. Father, I wish that those whom You have given me may be where I am that they may see Your glory in Your kingdom.*[8]

***

In light of this biblical spirituality, this letter of Francis to a struggling unknown brother called to minister to his all too human confreres expresses wonderfully the depths of his awareness of *misericordia* (a heart sensitive to misery).

From *A Letter to a Minister*

To Brother N., minister: May the Lord bless you.

I speak to you, as best I can, about the state of your soul. You must consider as grace all that deters you from loving the Lord God and whoever has become an impediment to you, whether brothers or others, even if they lay hands on you. May you want it to be this way and not otherwise. Let this be for you the true obedience of the Lord God and my true obedience, for I know with certitude that it is true obedience. Love those who do those things to you and do not expect anything different from them, unless it is something the Lord God shall have given you. Love them in this and do not wish that they be better Christians. Let this be more than a hermitage for you.

And in this way I wish to know that you love the Lord and me, His servant and yours, if you do this: may there not be any brother in the world who has sinned—however much he could have sinned—who, after he has looked into your eyes, would ever depart without your mercy, if he is looking for a heart sensitive to misery. And if he is not looking for a heart sensitive to misery, ask him if he wants mercy. And if he sins a thousand times before your eyes, love him more than me that you may draw him to the Lord; and always be merciful with brothers such as these. You may announce this to the guardians, when you can that, for your part, you are resolved to act in this way.

With the help of God and the advice of our brothers during the Chapter of Pentecost, we shall make one chapter such as this from all the chapters of the Rule that treat of mortal sin:

If any one of the brothers, at the instigation of the enemy, shall have sinned mortally, let him be bound by obedience to have recourse to his guardian. Let all the brothers who know that he has sinned not bring shame upon him or slander him; let them, instead, show great mercy to him and keep the sin of their brother very secret because *those who are well do not need a physician, but the sick do.* Let them be bound by obedience, likewise, to send him to his custodian with a companion. And let that custodian provide for him with a heart full of mercy as he would wish to be provided for were he in a similar position. If he falls into some venial sin, let him confess to his brother who is a priest. If there is no priest there, let him confess to his brother until he has a priest who may canonically absolve him, as it is said. And let them not have the power to impose any other penance on them except this: *Go and sin no more.*[9]

The First Order of
the Lesser Brothers

The Rule of the Friars Minor[1]

Honorius,

Bishop, Servant of the servants of God,

to His Beloved Sons,

Brother Francis and the other brothers

of the Order of the Lesser Brothers:

Health and Apostolic Benediction.

The Apostolic See is accustomed to grant the pious requests and favorably to accede to the laudable desires of its petitioners. Therefore, beloved sons in the Lord, attentive to your pious prayers, We confirm with Our Apostolic Authority, and by these words ratify, the Rule of your Order, herein outlined and approved by Our predecessor, Pope Innocent of happy memory, which is as follows:

[Chapter I]
In the Name of the Lord!
The Life of the Lesser Brothers Begins

The Rule and Life of the Lesser Brothers is this: to observe the Holy Gospel of Our Lord Jesus Christ by living in obedience, without anything of one's own, and in chastity. Brother Francis promises obedience and reverence to our Lord Pope Honorius and his successors canonically elected and to the Roman Church. Let the other brothers be bound to obey Brother Francis and his successors.

[Chapter II]
Those Who Wish to Adopt This Life,
and How They Should Be Received

If there are any who wish to accept this life and come to our brothers, let them send them to their provincial ministers, to whom alone and not to others is permission granted to receive the brothers. Let the ministers examine them carefully concerning the Catholic faith and the sacraments of the Church. If they believe all these things, will faithfully profess them, and steadfastly observe them to the end; and if they have no wives, or if they have wives who have already taken a vow of continence and are of

11

such an age that suspicion cannot be raised about them, and who have already entered a monastery or have given their husbands permission by the authority of the bishop of the diocese, let the ministers speak to them the words of the holy Gospel that they go and sell all they have and take care to give it to the poor. If they cannot do this, their good will may suffice. Let the brothers and the minister be careful not to interfere with their temporal goods that they may dispose of their belongings as the Lord inspires them. If, however, counsel is sought, the minister may send them to some God-fearing persons according to whose advice their goods may be distributed to the poor. Then they may be given the clothes of probation, namely, two tunics without a hood, a cord, short trousers, and a little cape reaching to the cord, unless, at times, it seems good to these same ministers, before God, to act otherwise. When the year of probation has come to an end, they may be received to obedience promising always to observe this rule and life. On no account shall it be lawful for them to leave this Order, according to the decree of our Lord the Pope, for, according to the Gospel: *no one who puts a hand to the plow and looks to what was left behind is fit for the kingdom of God.* Those who have already promised obedience may have one tunic with a hood and another, if they wish, without a hood. And those who are compelled by necessity may wear shoes. Let all the brothers wear poor clothes and they may mend them with pieces of sackcloth or other material with the blessing of God. I admonish and exhort them not to look down upon or judge those whom they see dressed in soft and fine clothes and enjoying the choicest food and drink, but rather let everyone judge and look down upon himself.

[Chapter III]
The Divine Office, Fasting
and How the Brothers Should Go About in the World

Let the clerical [brothers] recite the Divine Office according to the rite of the holy Roman Church excepting the psalter, for which reason they may have breviaries. The lay [brothers], however, may say twenty-four *Our Fathers* for Matins, and five for Lauds; seven for each of the Hours of Prime, Terce, Sext, and None, twelve for Vespers, and seven for Compline. Let them pray for the dead.

Let them fast from the feast of All Saints until the Lord's Nativity. May those be blessed by the Lord who fast voluntarily during that holy Lent that begins at the Epiphany and lasts during the forty days which our Lord consecrated by His own fast; but those who do not wish to keep it will not be obliged. Let them fast, however, during the other [Lent] until the Lord's Resurrection. At other times they may not be bound to fast except on Fridays. During a time of obvious need, however, the brothers may not be bound by corporal fast.

I counsel, admonish, and exhort my brothers in the Lord Jesus Christ not to quarrel or argue or judge others when they go about in the world; but let them be meek, peaceful, modest, gentle, and humble, speaking courteously to everyone, as is becoming. They should not ride horseback unless they are compelled by an obvious need or an infirmity.

Into whatever house they enter, let them first say: "Peace be to this house!" According to the holy Gospel, let them eat whatever food is set before them.

[Chapter IV]
Let the Brothers Never Receive Money

I strictly command all my brothers not to receive coins or money in any form, either personally or through intermediaries. Nevertheless, the ministers and custodians alone may take special care through their spiritual friends to provide for the needs of the sick and the clothing of the others according to places, seasons and cold climates, as they judge necessary, saving always that, as stated above, they do not receive coins or money.

[Chapter V]
The Manner of Working

Those brothers to whom the Lord has given the grace of working may work faithfully and devotedly so that, while avoiding idleness, the enemy of the soul, they do not extinguish the Spirit of holy prayer and devotion to which all temporal things must contribute. In payment for their work they may receive whatever is necessary for the bodily support of themselves and their brothers, excepting coin or money, and let them do this humbly as is becoming for servants of God and followers of most holy poverty.

[Chapter VI]
Let the Brothers Not Make Anything Their Own;
Begging Alms; the Sick Brothers

Let the brothers not make anything their own, neither house, nor place, nor anything at all. As pilgrims and strangers in this world, serving the

Lord in poverty and humility, let them go seeking alms with confidence, and they should not be ashamed because, for our sakes, our Lord made Himself poor in this world. This is that sublime height of most exalted poverty which has made you, my most beloved brothers, heirs and kings of the Kingdom of Heaven, poor in temporal things but exalted in virtue. Let this be your portion which leads into the land of the living. Giving yourselves totally to this, beloved brothers, never seek anything else under heaven for the name of our Lord Jesus Christ.

Wherever the brothers may be and meet one another, let them show that they are members of the same family. Let each one confidently make known his need to the other, for if a mother loves and cares for her son according to the flesh, how much more diligently must someone love and care for his brother according to the Spirit! When any brother falls sick, the other brothers must serve him as they would wish to be served themselves.

[Chapter VII]
The Penance To Be Imposed on the Brothers Who Sin

If any brother, at the instigation of the enemy, sins mortally in regard to those sins concerning which it has been decreed among the brothers to have recourse only to the provincial ministers, let him have recourse as quickly as possible and without delay. If these ministers are priests, with a heart full of mercy let them impose on him a penance; but, if the ministers are not priests, let them have it imposed by others who are priests of the Order, as in the sight of God appears to them more expedient. They must be careful not to be angry or disturbed at the sin of another, for anger and disturbance impede charity in themselves and in others.

[Chapter VIII]
The Election of the General Minister of This Fraternity
and the Chapter of Pentecost

Let all the brothers always be bound to have one of the brothers of this Order as general minister and servant of the whole fraternity and let them be strictly bound to obey him.

When he dies, let the election of his successor be made by the provincial ministers and custodians in the Chapter of Pentecost, at which all the provincial ministers are bound to assemble in whatever place the general minister may have designated. Let them do this once in every three years, or at other longer or shorter intervals, as determined by the aforesaid minister. If, at any time, it appears to the body of the provincial ministers and custodians that the aforesaid general minister is not qualified for the service and general welfare of the brothers, let the aforesaid brothers, to whom the election is committed, be bound to elect another as custodian in the name of the Lord.

Moreover, after the Chapter of Pentecost, the provincial ministers and custodians may each, if they wish and it seems expedient to them, convoke a Chapter of the brothers in their custodies once in the same year.

[Chapter IX]
Preachers

The brothers may not preach in the diocese of any bishop when he has opposed their doing so. And let none of the brothers dare to preach in any way to the people unless he has been examined and approved by the general minister of this fraternity and the office of preacher has been conferred upon him. Moreover, I admonish and exhort those brothers that when they preach their *language be well-considered and chaste* for the benefit and edification of the people, announcing to them vices and virtues, punishment and glory, with brevity, because our Lord when on earth kept his word brief.

[Chapter X]
The Admonition and Correction of the Brothers

Let the brothers who are the ministers and servants of the others visit and admonish their brothers and humbly and charitably correct them, not commanding them anything that is against their soul and our rule. Let the brothers who are subject, however, remember that, for God's sake, they have renounced their own wills. Therefore, I strictly command them to obey their ministers in everything they have promised the Lord to observe and which is not against their soul or our Rule.

Wherever the brothers may be who know and feel they cannot observe the Rule spiritually, they can and should have recourse to their ministers. Let the ministers, moreover, receive them charitably and kindly and have such familiarity with them that these same brothers may speak and deal with them as masters with their servants, for so it must be that the ministers are the servants of all the brothers.

Moreover, I admonish and exhort the brothers in the Lord Jesus Christ to beware of all pride, vainglory, envy and greed, of care and solicitude for the things of this world, of detraction and murmuring.

Let those who are illiterate not be anxious to learn, but let them pay attention to what they must desire above all else: to have the Spirit of the Lord and Its holy activity, to pray always to Him with a pure heart, to have humility and patience in persecution and infirmity, and to love those who persecute, rebuke and find fault with us, because the Lord says: *Love your enemies and pray for those who persecute and calumniate you. Blessed are those who suffer persecution for the sake of justice, for theirs is the kingdom of heaven. But whoever perseveres to the end will be saved.*

[Chapter XI]
The Brothers May Not Enter the Monasteries of Nuns

I strictly command all the brothers not to have any suspicious dealings or conversations with women, and they may not enter the monasteries of nuns, excepting those brothers to whom special permission has been granted by the Apostolic See; and they may not be godfathers to men or women, so that scandal may not arise among the brothers or concerning them on account of this.

[Chapter XII]
Those Going Among the Saracens and Other Non-Believers

Let those brothers who wish by divine inspiration to go among the Saracens or other non-believers ask permission to go from their provincial ministers. The ministers, however, may not grant permission except to those whom they see fit to be sent.

In addition to these points, I command the ministers through obedience to petition from our Lord the Pope for one of the Cardinals of the Holy Roman Church, who would be the governor, protector, and corrector of this fraternity, so that, being always submissive and subject at the feet of the same Holy Church and steadfast in the Catholic Faith, we may observe poverty, humility, and the Holy Gospel of our Lord Jesus Christ as we have firmly promised.

> It is forbidden, therefore, for anyone to tamper with this decree which we have confirmed, or rashly dare to oppose it. If anyone presume to attempt this, let him know that he shall incur the anger of Almighty God and of His blessed Apostles Peter and Paul.
>
> Given at the Lateran, the twenty-ninth day of November, in the eighth year of Our pontificate.

Anthony of Padua (1195–1231)

For eight centuries Anthony of Padua was famous in the Catholic Church primarily as a worker of miracles whose popularity in many ways exceeded that of Francis of Assisi. Ferdinand Bulhoes was born in Lisbon, Portugal, in 1195, and raised in a world of privilege but one that was divided into two camps: Christian and Muslim. At the time of his birth, Lisbon—or Al-Usbuna as it was called by the Moors—was turbulent, as was typical of many cities of the Iberian Peninsula. Forty-one years earlier Portugal's King Alfonso I with the help of English, Flemish, German, and French crusaders had regained control of the city and brought with them the breed of tension that flourishes among rival cultures. At the same time, his birthplace became a cosmopolitan city in which the promising young man encountered an ever-changing variety of cultures and worldviews.

Ferdinand's education began at Lisbon's cathedral school under the direction of the Canons Regular of Saint Augustine where the liberal arts curriculum of the *trivium* and *quadrivium* undoubtedly shaped his intellectual character. At some time during his late teens, the young man entered the community of the Canons Regular at São Vicente just outside the walls of Lisbon where he began the formal program of study demanded of those called to the priesthood. The library at São Vicente boasted of a wide variety of manuscripts on the natural sciences, particularly medicine, which may well explain why his later sermons are filled with references to biology, anatomy, and medicine. A few years later he asked to be transferred to the Abbey of Santa Cruz in order to prepare himself more intensely for his ordination. Since Coimbra had become the intellectual center of the Portuguese kingdom, Ferdinand undoubtedly became deeply involved in the study of Scripture and the fathers of the church. Scholars continue to debate the details of Ferdinand's ordination to the presbyterate—the date, place, and, therefore, his status.

While he was studying in Coimbra, Ferdinand met the first followers of Francis of Assisi who came to Portugal in 1217. They had obtained permission to use a small hermitage at Olivais dedicated to Saint Anthony of Egypt. Following the teachings of the Gospel in the spirit of Francis, they would walk to Coimbra for alms and frequently went to the Canons. Among them may well have been six brothers—Berard, Peter, Adjute, Accurs, Odo, and Vitalis—who stopped in Coimbra on their way to Morocco. They were single-minded in their determination to proclaim the Gospel to the Muslims despite all the hardships they knew they would encounter, even the possibility of death. This simple desire seems to have sparked a Gospel idealism in the heart of the young Canon Regular. Its flame, however, was ignited when, a short time later, the bodies of these six brothers were brought back to the Abbey of Santa Cruz and honored as the first martyrs of the followers of Francis of Assisi. The martyrdom of these passionate evangelizers so inspired Ferdinand that he gained permission to join the brothers of Olivais, took the name of the patron of the hermitage, Anthony, and a short while later embarked on his own quest to proclaim the Gospel and achieve martyrdom.

Anthony had hardly arrived on the shores of North Africa when he became gravely ill and was persuaded to return to Portugal. He had not preached one sermon, converted one Moor, or lost even one drop of his blood at Saracen hands. It must have been a time of great disillusionment for the young, new friar. Providentially the ship transporting him back to Portugal was driven off course and brought him to Sicily instead. There he found his confreres and stayed with them until, in the spring of 1221, they made their way to Assisi for what became known as the "Chapter of Mats," the last gathering of *all* the friars during which they—together with Francis—added new insights and clarifications of the Gospel life. This was a turning point in the life of this newly professed young friar as he met and joined with Francis and his first brothers. At the chapter's conclusion, Anthony became a member of the Italian province of Romagna and was assigned to the hermitage of Monte Paola where he spent fifteen months or so living the intense eremitical life he had only tasted at Olivais. An ordination of Friars Minor and Friars Preacher in nearby Forli changed the direction of the hidden life he had eagerly embraced. It was then that his gift for preaching became evident as the knowledge of Scripture and the liberal arts he had acquired as a Canon Regular came to the fore. His provincial sent him throughout Romagna using his skills for the people and eventually for the friars themselves.

The request made of Anthony to teach theology to the friars in Bologna, however, changed not only his life but also that of the fledgling Order of Friars Minor. In November of 1223, Pope Honorius III placed the papal seal of approval on what became the definitive rule of the friars. Francis had written in its tenth chapter "[the brothers] not knowing letters should not strive to learn them,"[1] a passage that effectively discouraged the sort of ministry of teaching that Anthony was asked to assume. A brief letter from Francis himself to Anthony calmed the young friar's hesitancy: "Brother Francis to Brother Anthony, my Bishop: greetings. I am pleased that you read sacred theology to the brothers, as long as in studying of this sort you do not extinguish the spirit of prayer and devotion, as it is contained in the Rule."[2] Effectively Francis gave the study of theology the same challenge as that of manual labor: to contribute or—to express it negatively—to be subservient to prayer and to the spiritual life.

The sedentary life of a professor, however, did not keep Anthony in Bologna for very long. Within a year he began preaching in France, first in Toulouse, then in Limoges. In 1227 he became the provincial minister of Romagna and spent the next three years of his life ministering to and, in Padua, teaching his brothers, while never relinquishing preaching to ever-growing audiences especially to the people of Le Marche di Treviso. The eremitical call, however, never seemed to leave him as he set aside long stretches of time at the hermitage of Camposampiero outside Padua to rest in the Lord until, on June 13, 1231, he rested in him for eternity.

***

Of the many sermons of Anthony, this captures not only his profound love of Mary, the Mother of God, but also the depth of his knowledge of Scripture and his marvelous use of images.

From *Seek First His Kingdom*

Blessed Are You, Mary!

"While he was saying this, a woman from the crowd called out, 'Blessed is the womb that bore you and the breasts that nursed you!'" (Lk 11:27)

Speaking of his bride in the Song of Songs, the groom exclaimed: "Let me hear your voice, for your voice is sweet." (Sg 2:14) How sweet is the voice that praises the Blessed Virgin! It rings most sweetly in the ears of the groom, Jesus the Virgin's Son. Let us, therefore, raise our voices together and individually to praise the Blessed Virgin, and let us say to her Son: "Blessed is the womb that bore you and the breasts that nursed you."

Etymologically, "blessed" signifies "well increased." Blessed is the person who has whatever he or she desires, wanting nothing evil. Blessed is the person who has obtained all that he or she desires. Blessed, therefore, is the womb of the glorious Virgin who for nine months was worthy to carry all goodness, the highest goodness, the bliss of angels and the reconciliation of sinners. This is why St. Augustine wrote: "We were reconciled by means of the only Son according to the flesh and not by the only Son simply according to the divinity. The Trinity reconciled us to itself in that the same Trinity made the only Word into flesh."

Blessed, therefore, is the womb of the glorious Virgin, of whom St. Augustine said: "Except for the Holy Virgin Mary, about whom, for the honor of the Lord, I want there to be no doubt when sin is mentioned, for concerning her we know that more grace for conquering sin in every way was given to her who merited to conceive and give birth to him who certainly had no sin whatsoever. This Virgin excepted, if we could ask . . . all saints whether they were without sin, what do we think they would answer if not repeat with John, "If we say we have no sin, we deceive ourselves, and the truth is not in us" (Jn 1:8).

The glorious Virgin was filled with singular grace to the point of having as the fruit of her womb the One whom she had from the beginning as the Lord of the Universe. Blessed, therefore, is the womb about which, in praise of his Mother, the Son says in the Song of Songs: "Your womb is a heap of wheat encircled with lilies" (Sg 7:3). Yes, the womb of the Virgin was truly a "heap of wheat." It was a "heap" because in her were gathered all privileges of merits and rewards. It was a "heap of wheat" because in it, as in a granary, grain was stored so that Egypt would not die of hunger. This was done out of Joseph's foresight (Gn 41:56-57).

Grain is called *triticum* because it is stored very purely in a granary or because it is finely ground. White on the inside and ruddy on the outside, it symbolizes Jesus Christ, who was stored for nine months in the granary of the blessed womb of the Virgin and then ground for us in the mill of the cross. He was spotlessly white in the innocence of his life and red in the blood that he shed.

This blessed womb was "surrounded by lilies." The lily was given this name because it is almost *latea* [milky]. Its candor symbolizes the virginity of Mary, whose womb was surrounded by lilies, that is, she was fortified by the wall of humility. This is why St. Augustine wrote: "When he was conceived, God the only Son took true flesh of the Virgin and at his birth conserved intact his mother's virginity."

Truly blessed is the womb that carried you who are God and the Son of God, Lord of Angels, Creator of heaven and earth, Redeemer of the world. O Cherubim, Seraphim, Angels and Archangels, with your faces lowered and your heads bowed, reverently venerate the temple of the Son of God, the sanctuary of the Holy Spirit, the Blessed Virgin surrounded by lilies, and say: "Blessed is the womb that bore you."

And you, sons of Adam, to whom such a grace, such a special privilege was granted, with faithful devotion and penitent hearts, prostrate yourselves to the ground and venerate "the great ivory throne" of the true Solomon (1 Kgs 10:18), the high and lofty throne mentioned by Isaiah (Is 6:1). "Blessed is the womb that bore you!" "How beautiful you are, how pleasing my love, my delight! Your very figure is like a palm tree and your breasts are like its clusters" (Sg 7:7-8). This is how her Son praised her in the Song of Songs.

How beautiful you are in spirit and how gracious in body, my mother, my spouse . . . filled with delights, that is, with the rewards of eternal life! "Your very figure is like a palm tree." The bark of the palm tree is rough near to the ground but closer to the sky is pleasant in its appearance and in its fruit. Even at a hundred years it gives fruit.

The same can be said of Mary. In this world, she was rough in the bark of poverty but in heaven she was beautiful and glorious because she was the queen of angels and deserved to receive the "hundredfold fruit" which is given to virgins. The king's cupbearer appeared to Joseph in a dream and said: "I saw a vine in front of me, and on the vine were three branches. It had barely budded when its blossoms came out, and its clusters ripened into grapes" (Gn 40:9-10).

Seven things are mentioned in this passage: vine, three branches, buds, blossoms, grapes. Let us see how well they all point to Mary.

Vines sink roots quicker than other plants and can be easily tied to nearby plants. Mary can be called a vine because sooner and deeper than other people she rooted herself in God's love and inseparably tied herself to the true vine, that is, to her Son, who said, "I am the true vine" (Jn 15:1). The words of Sirach can be attributed to her: "I bud forth delights like the vine, my blossoms become glorious and abundant fruit" (Sir 24:17).

Christ's birth from the Virgin knows no equal among women, but it is mirrored in nature. Someone may ask how the Virgin gave birth to the Savior. She begot him like a blossom emanates perfume. The blossom of the vine remains incorrupt after it has given off its perfume, and likewise, faith leads us to believe that the modesty of the Virgin—the modesty with which she gave birth to the Savior—was not violated. What else is the flower of virginity if not a sweet perfume?

The three branches of the vine were the angel's greeting, the overshadowing of the Holy Spirit, the glorious conception of the Son of God.

The buds of the vine are Mary's humility and virginity. Its blossoms are her incorrupt fruitfulness and her painless giving birth to Christ. The three clusters of grapes are her poverty, patience and chastity. These are the grapes that produce a ripe and fragrant wine which, as it inebriates, at the same time makes sober the minds of the faithful. The Book of Proverbs wisely admonishes: "Her love will invigorate you always, through her love you will flourish continually" (Prv 5:19). Thus, through her love, you can look down on the false pleasures of the world and crush the lust of your flesh.

We pray to you, our Lady, our hope. We are tossed about by the storm of life's seas. May you, Star of the Sea, enlighten and guide us to our safe harbor. Assist us with your protective presence when we are about to depart from this life so that we may merit to leave this prison fearlessly and reach happily the Kingdom of endless joy. We hope to receive these favors from Jesus Christ, whom you bore in your blessed womb and nursed at your most holy breast. To him all honor and glory, forever and ever.[3]

Bonaventure of Bagnoregio (c. 1217–1274)

Bagnoregio is a small, out-of-the-way town not far from Viterbo, Italy. It was here that, in 1217, Giovanni de Fidanza was born. Years later he wrote that as a young boy he was "snatched from the jaws of death by the invocation [of St. Francis]," an invocation made by his mother that brought about his miraculous cure. A fifteenth-century legend maintains that when the infant was brought to Francis, he exclaimed, *"O buona ventura* [O blessed coming]" and, from that moment, Giovanni was called Bonaventure. In 1235 he traveled to the University of Paris where students in its Faculty of Arts, such as the young Bonaventure, embarked on a course of studies that was primarily seen as preparing them for higher studies in the faculties of theology, medicine, or law. Although he left no writings from this period of his life, his later writings suggest that even as a young man he excelled in his studies. The earliest of these writings reveal his masterful, artistic use of grammar and rhetoric as well as a thorough awareness of both the secular and religious classical tradition that preceded him; those of his higher studies and beyond show quite clearly that he became a master dialectician.

After successfully fulfilling the required courses for a bachelor of arts in 1243, Bonaventure entered the Order of Lesser Brothers. In the same year a similar young man joined the Order of Preachers, Thomas Aquinas. (Between 1245 and 1248, 1252 and 1257, and 1268 and 1272, the lives of both men would overlap at the University of Paris, as they sat at one another's feet and dialogued in the presence of other Parisian masters.) Some authors have argued that Bonaventure may well have been inspired by the friars of his native Bagnoregio; others suggest that it was in fulfillment of his debt he owed Francis of Assisi for his cure. In his *Letter on Three Questions to an Unknown Master*, however, he offers a more compelling reason:

I confess before God that the reason that made me love most of all the life of blessed Francis is the fact that it resembles the beginning and growth of the Church. The Church, indeed, began with simple fishermen, and was later enriched with the most illustrious and learned doctors. Thus you may understand that the religious of blessed Francis was established, not by the prudence of men, but by Christ, as shown by God Himself. And because the works of Christ do not fail but ceaselessly grow, it is God who has accomplished this work, since scholars have not been reluctant to join the company of simple men, heeding the word of the Apostle: *If any one of you thinks himself wise in this world, let him become a fool that he may come to be wise* (1 Cor 3:18).[1]

As a follower of Francis at the University of Paris, Bonaventure came to know and live with some of these "simple men" who became outstanding liturgists, theoreticians, and biblicists, among them the brilliant Alexander of Hales in whom the young brother found an ideal mentor. Alexander's writings, however, suggest that the "mentor" only asked questions to which his promising student later responded before asking his own.

In 1248 the young friar was licensed as a biblical bachelor and began his teaching career commenting on the literal sense of Scripture. Five sets of commentaries seem to come from this period: on the gospels of Luke and John and on the books of Wisdom and Ecclesiastes. Three years later, Bonaventure began his commentary on Peter Lombard's *Book of Sentences*, a compilation of patristic and authoritative quotations that had become the official textbook of the faculty of theology in the University of Paris. He became regent master of the *Couvent des Cordeliers* and began a prolific period of theological writing: the *Disputed Questions* on the knowledge of Christ, Gospel perfection, and the mystery of the Trinity. Throughout all of these works, we find an answer to a question in his commentary on *Sentences*: "Is theology a grace of contemplation, that we may become good, or a speculative science that is practical?"[2] It becomes clear that Bonaventure, like Anthony of Padua, was eager to follow Francis's counsel to be a theologian for no other reason than to form saints, that is, not to teach a theology that is mere science, but to teach "holy theology" or the theology of holiness.

Abruptly, however, the life of the regent master changed when the friars gathered in Rome for an extraordinary chapter, on February 2, 1257, and elected the forty-year-old friar general minister of the order, a position he held until the chapter of Lyons, Pentecost, May 19, 1274. It is difficult to determine when Bonaventure received the news of his election as minister general. He made his way to La Verna, the site of Francis's reception of the stigmata, in the autumn of 1259, moved, as he writes, by a divine impulse "to satisfy the yearnings of my soul for peace."[3] The *Itinerarium mentis in Deum* is the mystical masterpiece that was the result of Bonaventure's stay on the mountain where Francis had been graced with the stigmata. It is the work of the pilgrim who had made his way to this Franciscan shrine in order to intensify his knowledge of the saint of Assisi and to deepen his spirit within himself. While expressing Franciscan spirituality from the perspectives of the Christian mystics—Pseudo-Dionysius, Augustine, Bernard of Clairvaux, the Victorines—the *Itinerarium* was essentially a statement of the response to the divine call to live the mystical life and to taste of God's goodness in ecstatic union according to the example of the saint of Assisi.

In preparation for the next chapter of the friars in 1260, Bonaventure collated the bits and pieces of legislation enacted since the death of their founder. While adopting these "Constitutions," the chapter of Narbonne commissioned their general to compile the existing portraits of St. Francis. The finished products, *Major Legend* and the *Minor*, display Bonaventure's theological and literary skills at underscoring the directive in Francis's Rule to desire always "the Spirit of the Lord and His holy activity" as the dynamism of the Gospel life. A phrase from Saint Paul's letter to Titus, "The grace of God our Savior," begins both portraits providing the leitmotif that subtly unfolds as the historical and the virtuous strands of the saint's life unfold. When his portraits are read in light of his *Itinerarium*, it becomes clear that Bonaventure had struggled to understand Francis's stigmata and understood them as symbolic expressions of the working of the Spirit. When understood properly, both texts provide a remarkable *vademecum* of the trinitarian spirituality that the friars approved at their next chapter in 1263 and three years later accepted as the official portrait of Francis.

The remaining years of Bonaventure's life revolve around that Franciscan axis as he tirelessly dedicated most of his efforts to promoting an understanding of the Gospel vision of Francis, especially among his brothers. While he delivered most of his sermons in Paris, others, especially those delivered after the summer of 1268, suggest that he traveled extensively throughout France, Italy, Spain, and Germany. In 1269, however, Gerard of Abbeville of the University of Paris attacked the academic rights of the Friars Minor and the Friars Preacher, as William of Saint Amour had done in 1256. At that time, both Thomas Aquinas and Bonaventure responded to William's allegations that the mendicants not only had no right to teach but also no right to exist. Now it was left to Bonaventure to defend the mendicant right to profess poverty and to continue their obligations at the university. He did so in his *Apologia Pauperum*, a defense that was so thorough that it silenced his opponents.

Three sets of "collations" come from these years. A monastic tradition that was revived in 1231 at the University of Paris by the Dominican Jordan of Saxony, these theological conferences presented opportunities to respond to the provocative issues of the time. In 1267 Bonaventure delivered the briefest of these, *The Collations on the Ten Commandments*, which treat the goal of life and a way of achieving it. Although a commentary on Matthew 19:17 ("If you wish to enter into life, keep the commandments"), these collations offered Bonaventure the opportunity to address the errors of those using Aristotle to undermine Christian faith. The following year, the *Collations on the Gifts of the Holy Spirit* were delivered, nine brilliantly thought out reflections, which some consider a high point in the theological development of this much-overlooked teaching. During the Easter season of 1273, Bonaventure began what has been called "the last testament of a theologian concerned only with bringing minds and hearts to the knowledge and love of the Master of wisdom, Christ"[4]: the *Collations on Hexaemeron or on the Illuminations of the Church*. The work was abruptly interrupted on May 28, 1273, when envoys arrived in Paris informing Bonaventure that Pope Gregory X had named him Cardinal-Archbishop of Albano.

The next fourteen months of his life were taken up with bringing his ministry as general of his brothers to a close and with collaborating with Gregory X on preparation for the fourteenth ecumenical council to be held in Lyons, which was scheduled to begin on May 7, 1274. While the two men were preparing the agenda, word reached them that another theological genius had died after setting out to join them. Thomas Aquinas died at the Cistercian Abbey of Fossanova on March 7, 1274. Historians credit Bonaventure and the friars he sent to Constantinople as having major roles in achieving the reunion of the Greek Church, which was celebrated July 6, 1274. Nine days later on July 15, 1274, however, the Lord called Bonaventure of Bagnoregio to himself. The Fourth Session of the Council of Lyon was still in session.

Bonaventure was canonized by Pope Sixtus IV on April 14, 1482; on March 14, 1557, Pope Sixtus V gave him the title of Doctor of the Church. He is traditionally called the "Seraphic Doctor," a title given to him in 1333 by a Dominican, Raynor of Pisa, in the prologue to his *Pantheologia*.

***

As young Italian men discovering the wonders of Christian revelation, accomplished Parisian professors united in defending their mendicant traditions and articulating the *symbolum fidei* in academia, and passing into eternal rewards while accomplishing their ecclesial mandates, the writings of Bonaventure of Bagnoregio and Thomas Aquinas have always absorbed the attention of believing and nonbelieving scholars. While each enjoyed theological perspectives as different as their Franciscan and Dominican callings, each excelled in the gifts God had given them and, in a sense, complemented one another. Even those who vigorously claim that Bonaventure does not attain the heights of scholastic refinement and precision achieved by Thomas admit that Thomas's writings lack the mystical sensitivity and depth of Bonaventure's. The Spirit of Truth uses the writings of Thomas to continue to enlighten the mind and those of Bonaventure to enkindle the heart; the Spirit's flame burns in Thomas's love of theology while the same Spirit consumes in Bonaventure's theology of love.

The following example of Bonaventure's exhilarating and uplifting mystical poetry is taken from the fourth chapter in *The Journey of the Mind into God*. After reflecting in the first two chapters how the vestiges of God can be found through and in creation, he proceeds to take the same approach by reflecting on the human person in whom he discovers the image of God. At this point, however, Bonaventure pauses to ask rhetorically why humans are unable to perceive this and, in light of the Fall of the first human, reflects on the need for the divine-human and the restoration achieved in him.

From *Itinerarium mentis in Deum*

Just as when one has fallen,
he must inevitably remain there
until someone draw near and live close to him,
in order to raise him up.
Our soul could not perfectly be lifted up
from these things of sense
to a contuition of itself
and of the Eternal Truth in itself
unless the Truth, assuming a human form in Christ,

became a ladder, repairing the first ladder
that had been broken in Adam.
Therefore, no matter how enlightened one may be
by the light of natural and acquired knowledge,
he cannot enter into himself
to delight in the Lord in his very self,
unless by the mediating Christ who says:
I am the door.
Whoever enters through me will be saved,
and will go in, will go out,
and will find pastures.
We do not come near this door
unless *we believe in, hope in, and love* Him.
Therefore, if we wish to re-enter
into the enjoyment of Truth as into paradise,
we must embark
through *faith in, hope in and love of* Jesus Christ,
the mediator between God and humanity,
who is like
the tree of life in the middle of paradise.

The image of our soul, therefore, should be clothed-over with the
three theological virtues by which the soul is purified, enlightened,
and perfected. Thus the image is reformed and made to conform
to the heavenly Jerusalem and part of the Church Militant which,
according to the Apostle, is the offspring of the heavenly Jerusalem.
For he says: *That Jerusalem which is above is free, which is our mother.*

The soul, then, is
believing in, hoping in, and loving
Jesus Christ,
who is the incarnate, uncreated and inspired Word,
that is the *way, the truth, and the life.*
When through faith
[the soul] believes in Christ
as the uncreated Word and Splendor of the Father,
it recovers its spiritual hearing and sight:
hearing for receiving the words of Christ,
sight for viewing the splendors of His Light.
When by hope
[the soul] longs to receive the inspired Word,

it recovers through desire and affection
the spiritual sense of smell.
When by charity
[the soul] embraces the incarnate Word,
as one receiving delight from Him
and as one passing over into Him through ecstatic love,
it recovers taste and touch.
After recovering these senses,
as long as it sees, hears, smells, tastes, and embraces
its Spouse,
[the soul] can sing like the bride of the Song of Songs,
which was composed for the exercise of contemplation
according to this fourth step,
which *no one* grasps *except him who receives*,
because it is greater
in affective experience than in rational consideration.
For on this step,
when the interior senses are repaired
for sensing [what is] the most highly beautiful,
for hearing [what is] the most highly harmonious,
for smelling [what is] the most highly fragrant,
for tasting [what is] the most highly sweet,
for embracing [what is] the most highly delightful,
the soul is disposed for mental ecstasy
through devotion, admiration, and exultation
according to those three exclamations in the Song of Songs.
The first of these flows
through the fullness of devotion
through which the soul becomes
like a column of smoke from aromatic spices of myrrh and frankincense;
the second through the excellence of admiration
through which the soul becomes
like the dawn, the moon and the sun
according to the process of illuminations
lifting up the soul to admire [its] considered Spouse;
the third through the superabundance of exultation
through which the soul becomes
overflowing with the delights of the sweetest pleasure,
leaning completely *upon her beloved*.[5]

Felix of Cantalice (1515–1587)

In his *Remembrance of the Desire of a Soul,* Thomas of Celano sings the praise of the virtue of simplicity that Francis "demanded in his brothers, learned and lay." "It was not just any kind of simplicity that he approved," Thomas writes, "but only that which, content with her God, scorns everything else."[1] There may be no better expression of that virtue than in the Capuchin lay brother, Felice Porri of Cantalice, Italy, who spent most of his public life on the streets of Rome begging bread for his brothers and his hidden life lost in prayer. When he died just shy of his eightieth birthday, those who used to seek his counsel and prayers—the pope, cardinals, and religious leaders such as Charles Borromeo and Philip Neri, ordinary Roman citizens, and, above all, the poor—acclaimed him a saint.

The seeds of the simplicity that was the secret of his holiness were undoubtedly sown and took root in the farming family of six in which he was the next to the youngest. Appropriately it would seem the names of his parents, Santi and Santa, bore a premonition of his future. He had an older sister, Potenza, two older brothers, Biaggio and Carlo, and one younger, Peter Martin. Like members of any farming family, they all worked long hours simply to survive. Early on Felix tended the family sheep; later, however, he was hired out to a nearby family where he helped on their farm. Both occupations fostered two dimensions of his character: a love of solitude and of being close to the earth. It may well have been a cousin who inspired the young boy's religious imagination by reading to him the lives of the early monks of the Desert Fathers. Their heroic embrace of asceticism and that of the Franciscan "hermits" living near Cantalice, the Capuchins, shaped his resolve to follow their examples. Nonetheless, Felix's response to that inspiration, according to his telling, took a threefold Samuel-like happenstance. Twice he heard an angelic voice calling him and directing him to the Franciscans in Leonessa and Rieti, that is, to the Capuchins. Nothing came of those visits. After each one, Felix returned to his simple chores until one day he attempted to yoke two oxen to plow when they bolted, turned on him, and dragged the sharp plow over his body. Although his clothes were in tatters, there was not a scratch on his body prompting him to go to the Capuchin friary where he was welcomed by the saintly Bernardine of Asti. Together they would become pivotal in ensuring the continuing character of the Capuchin reform. The year was 1543. Felix was twenty-eight years old.

If Bernardine of Asti taught his Capuchin confreres that the love of contemplative prayer and the cultivation of genuine poverty were the benchmarks of Franciscan life, Felix of Cantalice demonstrated their impact on the disillusioned, misguided, or simply searching Roman people. From the outset, his daily life was characterized by the rhythm of prayer, liturgical as well as personal, nourished by a deepening awareness of God's loving heartache toward sinners, and purified by a heroic poverty that resonated with his memories of the tradition of the Desert Fathers he had learned as a boy. His initial formation ended, Felix was sent to Rome where he was assigned the task of begging food for his brothers. For the next forty years—until a few days before his death—Brother Felix of Cantalice was a familiar figure on the Roman streets begging, engaging in conversations with rich and poor, visiting their sick, and sharing the fruits of his questing with the marginalized.

The stories of his Roman "encounters" reveal perhaps more than anything else that his simple love of people prompted them to love him simply. While there is always a tendency to begin recounting how those hurting and needy people came to him—which was natural for someone who treated everyone equally—his legendary exchanges with aristocrats, the influential, and even the hierarchy reveal how beloved by all he was. In a conversation with his fellow Franciscan, Conventual Friar Felice Peretti, he predicted his election to the papacy and told him: "When you are elected pope, be pope for the glory of God and the good of the Church. Otherwise it would be better that you remain a simple friar." One day the newly elected Pope Sixtus V met Felix as he was begging, asked for some of his bread, and, as he felt how hard and stale it was, heard Felix apologize: "Sorry, Holy Father, but after all, you are a friar."[2] In a similar vein, Felix happened to meet Cardinal Julius Anthony Satori, the cardinal protector of the friars, who frequently and inappropriately interfered in their internal affairs so that he became for them a heavy burden. "My dear Lord Cardinal," Felix told him, "you were appointed to protect us not to meddle in our Order's affairs. Those are what our superiors are supposed to handle!"[3] Neither pope nor cardinal took offense.

Nor did the aristocratic woman of questionable virtue who asked Felix for a gift from the garden that would make her respectable, and received this response: "First change your way of life"[4]; nor did the lawyer who took umbrage when a client, in the presence of the holy brother, came to him accompanied by a lowing heifer. "Do you understand what [this heifer] is telling you?" Felix asked. "She is telling you to take good care of the interest of your client."[5] None took offense for they knew that none was intended.

Ordinary people, especially those in need, were the special focus of his attention. Were he alive today, Felix might well be described as an ardent promoter of life. Couples eager to have children frequently came to him asking for prayers. Women having difficulties in childbirth or fearing miscarriages came to him for simple blessings. Parents with children facing life-threatening diseases called "the saint" before they called the doctor. It was the children themselves, moreover, who nicknamed him "*Fra Deo Gratias* [Br. Thanks be to God]" as they mimicked how he would respond to those who donated to him. It was the children who also brought to everyone's attention one of his most endearing qualities: his sense of humor, which won him the reputation for being "the saint of joy." As Felix walked the streets of Rome begging bread for his confreres, he seemed unable to overlook the poor, the starving, the sick, those whose quality of life he felt compelled to improve. Many times he came back to his brothers empty-handed: the result of giving to those he met the very food he had been given to feed his brothers.

These brothers, those with whom he lived each day, were the very ones who revered his holiness. Felix's novice master, Br. Boniface of Fiuggi, stayed in touch with him for the remainder of his life and, since he outlived him, was able to testify before the commission investigating his holiness. Because he was always wrestling with his sinfulness, Boniface narrated how his daily meat and drink were manual labor, penance, vigils of prayer, and privations of every sort. Shortly after his death, on May 18, 1587, his confreres began collecting their recollections about his life. This was how they described his life of penance:

> Brother Felix slept barely two or three hours, on his knees or on bare boards. He chastised his innocent body with the discipline and hair shirt. He ate only a small portion of stale bread, and on rare occasions took a little soup.

He observed several fasts a year. From Holy Thursday until Easter Sunday he observed a total fast. His habit was of the coarsest material more suited to torment his body than to protect it from the elements.[6]

It may have been this grappling with his humanity that made the simple Capuchin so transparent and attractive to all he met as, after Mass each morning, Felix would walk the streets of Rome begging. Therein is also an irony. In the spirit of the Fathers of the Desert who had inspired him early on, Felix vowed never to eat bread. As an old man reflecting on his years of begging bread for his brothers, he joked about this twist of fate: "I never wanted to touch bread again, but the Lord sent me into every bakery in Rome, and I have done nothing else but lug bread on my shoulders day-after-day."[7]

He was in the eyes of his confreres a natural contemplative who spent whatever free time he had in the church or in the solitude of his room. How profound was this dimension of his call became most clear, however, after his brothers had gone to bed. Felix would sleep for a few hours after Evening Prayer and would then go to the chapel where he prayed until midnight when he would ring the bell for Matins. Once he was assured that all the brothers had left, he would spend the remainder of the morning hours alone with his eucharistic Lord in whose presence some of his confreres caught him in ecstasy or levitating. "I live with such joy," he once said, "that it seems I am already in heaven. May God never grant me any reward in this life for the little good I may do!"[8] One of those who saw him observed the Blessed Mother appear to him shortly before Christmas. At Felix's request, she gently handed him the Infant Jesus she held in her arms.

On April 30, 1587, Felix fell seriously ill, the first time he had ever been so, beyond a bout with an unusual fever when he was a novice and another with colitis in 1572. "The donkey has fallen down," he told one of his brothers. "He won't get up again!"[9] Sick as he was, he would not stay in bed but went to the chapel where he frequently collapsed. When his confreres insisted that he follow the doctor's orders by staying in bed, he responded: "Pardon me, brothers, but I don't dare stay far from the church. I would gladly obey the doctor and infirmarian, if I could obey God at the same time."[10] On the morning of May 18, he asked the brother staying with him to leave and to shut the door. "I see the Blessed Virgin Mary surrounded by a marvelous company of angels."[11] Shortly afterward he asked for the sacrament of the sick and at the final words—"Depart, O Christian soul, from the world"—he obediently did so.

That very day hoards of Romans began coming to pay their respects. One of those observing them was Felix's novice master who was still living and quite feeble. "Great judgments of God are seen!" he commented. "Brothers of great holiness have been in this friary, men who have done marvelous things during life! Many were seen praying in church lifted up from the earth higher than you could imagine, and other awesome things! We have said nothing about them. But the Lord God in all of these things has now deigned to exalt so greatly this simplicity that he has never given such special signs of such great grace!"[12]

Shortly thereafter Sixtus IV, the pope who had received stale and hard bread from Felix, encouraged the Capuchins to begin the process of his canonization. While the process officially came to an end two years later, it was delayed by the pope's death in 1590 and not resumed until 1614. Pope Urban VIII beatified Felix in 1625; Pope Clement XI canonized him in 1712.

***

Attempting to capture the wonderful heritage of the lay brothers of the Franciscan Tradition becomes challenging because of the absence of their writings, be they personal letters or, far less, essays or books. The famous saying that Johannes Jørgensen put on the lips of St. Francis aptly describes a lay brother such as Felix: "Preach the Gospel; if necessary, use words!" In Felix's case, his *madrigaletti* or ditties have endured and were incorporated into his process of canonization. It is impossible to capture their charm in English; hence some of the more well known are presented in both the Italian and English.[13]

From *Processus Sixtinus*

Giesú, Giesú, Giesú,	Jesus, Jesus, Jesus,
figliolo di Maria,	little son of Mary,
hor chi ti possede	now whoever possesses you,
quanto bene havria.	what good he would have!
Giesú, somma letitia,	Jesus, highest happiness,
non casca mai in tristizia	may the heart that has tasted You
il cor che t'ha assaggiato.	never fall into sadness.

———

Hoggi, in questa terra	Today on this earth
è nata una rosella,	a little rose was born,

Maria verginella	the virgin Mary,
ch'è Madre d'Iddio	who is Mother of God.

Se tu non sai la via	If you do not know the way
d'andare in paradise,	to go to Paradise,
vattene a Maria	hurry off to Mary
con pietoso viso,	with a kind expression,
ch'è clemente e pia:	who is merciful and kind:
t'insegnerà la via	she will show you the way
d'andare in paradise.	to go to Paradise.

Shortly after Felix was terminally stricken, the Spanish ambassador sent an aide to learn of his condition. As he was leaving the sickroom, Felix told him to have the ambassador say this *canzone* frequently:

Giesù, Giesù, Giesù,	Jesus, Jesus, Jesus,
pigliate lo mio cuore:	take my heart:
non me'l rendete piú.	no more give it back to me!

***

Tales of how Felix and St. Philip Neri enjoyed one another's friendship are numerous. Romans who watched the two of them told stories of practical jokes they played on one another or of the banter that frequently took place between them. "When will I see you killed, when burned?" one would ask. "You should be beaten and dragged through the streets of Rome!" or, "You should be thrown into the Tiber with a millstone around your neck!" would be the reply. As the amused crowd laughed, one or the other would cry out: "All of this you would endure for the love of Christ!"[14] Thus the point was made.

***

It was Philip who introduced Cardinal Charles Borromeo to Felix.[15] How this took place was recorded in Felix's process of canonization:

After the archbishop of Milan had composed a rule for oblates, he asked canonists and others known for piety to review it, one of whom was Philip Neri. The holy cardinal asked Philip to accompany him in the carriage to discuss the rule together, which he agreed to do provided he could direct the carriage. Philip then told the coachman to go directly to the Capuchins, where he had them call Brother Felix, and Philip gave him the rule to review and amend.

Felix excused himself, saying that he did not even know how to read, and that it was no task for him. But Philip accepted no excuse, ordered him in virtue of holy obedience to review and correct it anyway, and where he did not know how to read to have someone else read it to him, so that he should make a note of corrections on another paper of anything in the rule that did not please him. This happened to the surprise of the cardinal who, not knowing the virtue nor the person of the blessed man, was amazed that the review was entrusted to such an uneducated person.

Blessed Felix carried out everything; in fact, he amended two of these rules. When they finally arrived in the hands of Saint Charles, they caused him great wonder, realizing only then that they needed to be corrected in ways that neither he nor many men of learning and spirit had ever noticed, but that had been noticed by this unlettered man.

Junípero Serra (1713–1784)

"*Siempre adelante! ¡Nunca para atrás!*"[1] ("Always go forward! Never turn back!") These words of Blessed Junípero Serra of the Order of Friars Minor say a great deal about the character and spiritual prowess of one of the most dynamic individuals in the settlement of what is now the state of California. Always going forward and never turning back on his mission to bring the Gospel to women and men wherever the "Apostle of California" encountered them: this was the legacy of the one-time professor of theology whose zeal for souls knew no bounds!

Miguel Serra y Abram was born on November 24, 1713, in a small farming village of Petra, on the island of Majorca, Spain. His parents sent him to a nearby school run by the Friars Minor where they cultivated his intellectual abilities and undoubtedly encouraged his vocation. When he was only fifteen, Miguel expressed his desire to be a friar and a priest, and made his way to Palma to begin his formation. On September 14, 1730, he entered the novitiate where, according to the custom of receiving a new name, he adopted the name Junípero, an early follower of St. Francis known for his simple and frequently comical ways. The year of probation was not easy for him. Because he was so small—like Francis only five feet, two or three inches—and so slight, he was initially denied entrance. "In the novitiate," he later recalled, "I was almost always ill and so small of stature that I could not reach the lectern, nor could I help my fellow novices in the necessary chores of the novitiate."[2] Yet it was during this difficult time of initiation into Franciscan life that the undaunted spirit of his life became evident to his confreres. He threw himself into his study of philosophy and theology and so excelled that after his ordination to the priesthood in 1739 he was appointed a lector of philosophy, three years later became a doctor of sacred theology, and in 1743 was offered the Chair of the Prince of the Subtle Master, Duns Scotus, at the prestigious Lullian University, the Pontifical, Imperial, Royal, and Literary University of Majorca.

During the next six years Junípero developed a reputation as being an excellent teacher, scholar, and preacher. Secretly, though, he was struggling with a call to be a missionary and was quite surprised when one of his classmates, Francisco Palou, came to him asking for advice about his own struggle. Palou later recalled:

> I did not want to decide the latter without first consulting my beloved father, master, and lecturer, Fray Junípero Serra. One day when he came to my cell, and when I was alone, I seized the occasion and unburdened the feeling of my heart, asking him to give me his opinion. When he learned of my intention, he began to shed tears, not of affliction as I first thought, but of joy. Then he said to me: "I am the one who intends to make this long journey and I have been sorrowful because I would have no companion for so long a journey, but I would not on that account turn back from my purpose . . . and just now resolved to speak to you and invite you to go along on the journey."[3]

Once again, Junípero suffered a setback when he and his companion were denied permission to work in "New Spain," the Spanish colony now known as Mexico. Nonetheless, in 1749 Junípero—and Palou—set sail for Mexico where they landed in Veracruz on December 6, 1749, and began the two-hundred and seventy mile walk to Mexico City. It was then that Junípero's feet began to swell with fatigue and mosquito bites. As a result he suffered a leg affliction that was to bother him for the rest of his life.

After five months in Mexico City, he was sent to the rugged, mountainous region of Sierra Gorda, several hundred miles north, where he remained for nine years ministering to the Pame Indians, learning their language in order to teach them the fundamentals of the faith and to improve their agricultural skills. In 1758 Junípero was brought back to Mexico City where he asked to take the place of one of the two missionaries who had been martyred by the Apaches in the San Saba River missions in Texas. His hope for a similar martyrdom was dashed by an assignment to use his teaching skills in Mexico City's College of San Fernando. Even then, however, he walked miles to minister to and teach the Indians beyond the city limits. He was away on one of those missions when in 1767 Junípero was chosen to be the *custos*, or caretaker, of the thirteen missions established by the Jesuits in Baja California that had to be abandoned when the king of Spain banished them from his dominions. The following year Spanish Inspector General Jose de Galvez organized an expedition to explore and found missions in Alta California, what we now know as the state of California, an expedition intended to serve Spain's strategic interest by preventing Russian explorations and to christianize the Indian population. The plan was to have the soldiers and settlers colonize the land while the missionaries would convert—and civilize—the Indians. Don Gaspar de Portolá was to supervise the civil operation; Junípero Serra and Francisco Palou were to care for the spiritual.

Junípero was in his fifty-sixth year as these events were unfolding. It was Portolá who expressed his concern about his companion's health who knew from years of friendship that once set on a course Junípero would stay the course. "Despite the fact that I remonstrated with [Serra]," Portolá wrote to Palou, "and pointed out the delay it would cause the expedition if he should become incapacitated along the road, I was unable to convince him to remain and have you go in his place. . . . His consistent answer was that he trusted in God to give him the strength to enable him to reach San Diego and Monterey."[4] The asthmatic, anemic, and crippled friar was, as always, undaunted living by his guideline: "*¡Siempre adelante! ¡Nunca para atrás!*" ("Always go forward! Never turn back!")

He arrived in San Diego on July 1, 1769, and established there the first of the twenty-one California missions of which he was personally responsible for founding: San Carlos (June 3, 1770); San Antonio (July 14, 1771); San Gabriel (September 8, 1771); San Luis Obispo (September 1, 1772); San Francisco de Asis (October 8, 1776); San Juan Capistrano (November 1, 1776); Santa Clara (January 12, 1777); San Buenaventura (March 31, 1782). While the other missions were founded by his confreres, Junípero Serra oversaw the planning, construction, and staffing of each mission from the friary in Carmel. From there he traveled on foot to visit each one and to help his confreres with their work. Walking thousands of miles through dangerous terrain with an ulcerated and infected leg would have exhausted even a healthy man. Junípero never gave in.

It was a difficult period of history in which the Spanish colonists used antiquated methods to exert their influence. Confronting the furor that arose in 1987 over the imminent beatification of Junípero, Pope John Paul II reminded the native peoples of the Americas: "The early encounter between your traditional cultures and the European way of life was an event of such significance and change that it profoundly influences your collective life even today. That encounter was a harsh and painful reality for your peoples. The cultural oppression, the injustices, the disruption of your life and of your traditional societies must be acknowledged." The pope then singled out Junípero as one who "worked to improve living conditions, set up educational systems, learning your languages in order to do so, and above all, proclaimed the Good News of salvation in our Lord Jesus Christ, an essential part of which is that all men and women are equally children of God and must be respected and loved as such."[5] He then acknowledged:

> [Junípero Serra] had frequent clashes with the civil authorities over the treatment of Indians. In 1773 he presented to the Viceroy in Mexico City a *Representación*, which is sometimes termed a "Bill of Rights" for Indians. The Church had long been convinced of the need to protect them from exploitation. Already in 1537, my predecessor *Pope Paul III proclaimed the dignity and rights of the native peoples of the Americas by insisting that they not be deprived of their freedom or the possession of their property* (Pauli III, *Pastorale Officium*, 29 maggio 1537: Denz.-S. 1495). In Spain the Dominican priest, Francisco de Vitoria, became the staunch advocate of the rights of the Indians and formulated the basis for international law regarding the rights of peoples.[6]

As a result of his persistence, animosity arose between Junípero and Governor Philipe de Neve who, among other things, obstructed Junípero's administration of the sacrament of confirmation, prevented him from locating the mission of Santa Barbara at its presidio, and attempted at every turn to stem the "¡*Siempre adelante!*" spirit of the physically frail but spiritually indefatigable old missionary.

During the last three years of his life, Junípero made one final visit to each of the missions from San Diego to San Francisco in order to confirm all of those who had been recently baptized. At the journey's end, however, his strength gave out and, on August 28, 1784, he went forward to the Lord not as a martyr as he had hoped but as his faithful servant. His statue now adorns Statuary Hall in the Capitol Building in Washington DC, as does another in Golden Gate Park in San Francisco. On September 25, 1988, the "Apostle of California" was enrolled among the blessed by Pope John Paul II who praised him as "an exemplary model of one proclaiming the gospel full of self-denial, a glory of the entire Franciscan Family."[7]

***

> Two letters were written by Father Junípero Serra to his cousin, Father Francisco Serra, O.S.F., a friar living in the Convento of San Bernardino in Petra, Spain. Junípero wrote the first, a farewell letter, before sailing from Cadiz, Spain, to Veracruz, Mexico. The second was written in Veracruz, Mexico, upon his arrival.

From *The Tidings*

Long live Jesus, Mary and Joseph!

My Dearest Friend in Christ Jesus, Father Francisco Serra!

This is a farewell letter, since we are ready to leave this city of Cadiz and sail to Mexico. We do not yet know the day of our departure, but we are packing our trunks and getting things ready. They say, however, that in three or four days our ship, called Villasota, will leave the bay of Cadiz. We thought at first that we would leave sooner; this is why I told you in my preceding letter that we would probably depart on Saint Bonaventure's day; however, it has been postponed until this present.

My dear friend, words cannot express the feelings of my heart, while I bid you farewell; I reiterate my request that you be the stay, comfort, and consolation of my aged parents in their sorrow and affliction at my departure. I wish I were able to make them partakers of the joy of my heart. I think that if they knew it they certainly would encourage me always to go forward and never fall backwards. Let them remember that the office of an apostolic preacher, especially in a young man like myself is the most exalted position they could ever have wished for me. Let them, likewise, remember that their life, they being already well up in years, must needs be brief, and if they compare it with eternity they will realize it to be but a fleeting instant. This being the case, it will be most proper and in harmony with God's will that they should not miss the insignificant help I could have given them, but rather praise God, because they can obtain so much better from His bounty that, should we fail to see each other in this world, we may meet all together in Heaven. Tell them how sorry I feel that hereafter I will not be so close to them, as I have been, to assist, cheer, and console them; but let them remember that the will of God should come first and should be placed before, over, and above all things. It was for the love of God that I left them; now, since I, for the love of God, and with the help of his grace, have left them, it is but just and right that they also, for God's sake, should be glad to be deprived of my company.

Again, let my dear parents listen to what their spiritual adviser and confessor will say to them, and they will see then how true it is that God's blessing has entered their home. It is in patience and conformity to the will of God that they shall possess their souls and obtain life eternal. Let them attribute to none but God what they now lament, and then and not till then will they experience how light and sweet is the yoke of the Lord; and what they endure as a great tribulation will be changed into exceedingly great joy. This is no time in which to muse and worry or be bowed in grief over the happenings of life, but to be resigned to the will of God, and prepare ourselves for a holy and happy death. This is, indeed, the all-important business in life; this one attained, all the rest fall into insignificance. Should we attain to Heaven, it will be of little moment to lose the whole world, but should we lose Heaven, all the rest will be of no profit. They should feel proud to have a son priest, though a poor and unworthy one, and a sinner who every day prays for them in the Holy Sacrifice of the Mass, and a great many times offers it especially for them, that the good Lord may assist them and grant them sufficient means for their decent support, patience in their trials, resignation to the will of God, peace, union and harmony with the whole world, strength to resist the temptations and attacks of the devil, and finally, when the last summons comes, a holy and peaceful death, in the loving embrace of God. Should I happen to be a good religious, through the grace of God, then my prayers would be more efficacious and you would not be the least in sharing in the profits thereof.

I wish to convey the same feelings to my beloved sister in Christ, Juana, and to my dear brother-in-law, Miguel. Let them remember me only in their prayers, that I may be a good priest and a worthy minister of God; because in this we are all interested, and it is, after all, what really is worthwhile. I remember well when my father was so sick, that fearing for his life he was anointed. Then being a professed religious, I attended him. One day, thinking he was going to die soon, he called me apart and said to me: "My dear son, this is my earnest request, that you be always a good religious of our Holy Father Saint Francis." Now, my beloved father, I wish you to understand that these words are still ringing in my ears, and furthermore, it is in order to be a good religious that I have taken this course of a missionary life. Do not be sorry that I do your own good will and pleasure, which is, indeed, also God's. I know full well that my mother has never failed to pray for me that I may be a good religious. Now, my beloved mother, it may be that it is due to your prayers that the good Lord has given me this vocation. Be glad, therefore, of what God has disposed, and in all your trials say from the bottom of your heart, "Praised be God! Let His holy will ever be done!"

My beloved sister Juana will remember that it is not very long ago that she was at the point of death, and that God restored her to health, through the merits and intercession of our Blessed Lady. If she were now dead, she would not worry over my being in or away from Majorca. Let her praise and thank the Lord for all He has ordained and disposed, because whatever He sends us that is exactly what is convenient for our temporal and spiritual welfare. And it is very likely that God spared her in order that she might be, in my absence, the stay and comfort of our good, dear old parents. Let us praise and love God who loves and sustains us all! I most earnestly request Miguel, my brother-in-law, and Juana, my sister, not to forget what I have told them on other occasions, namely, that they both continue to live in peace, union, and harmony, that they honor, forbear, and console our old dear father and mother, that they be diligent in bringing up their children, educating them, and to all I entreat to attend church regularly, to frequent the holy sacraments of Penance and Holy Eucharist, to walk the stations of the cross frequently, in a word, to be good and fervent Christians. I hope that, as heretofore they have prayed for me, so they will continue. Thus mutually praying to the Lord—I for them and they for me—He will assist us all and give us His grace here and the life of glory hereafter.

Farewell, my dear father! Farewell, my dear mother! Farewell, my sister Juana! Good-bye Miguel, my brother-in-law! Mind you that little Miguelito be a good Christian and a good school boy and so the two little girls. Trust in God that your uncle may be yet of some service to you. Adios! Adios!

My beloved brother, Fattier Francisco Serra, farewell! As I told you before, it will now be seldom that you will receive letters from me. Still, concerning the love and gratitude I owe you, my cousin, and other relatives of mine, and then, Father Vicar, Father Gordian, and Father Master of Novices, et al., I say and hope that *epistola mea nines vos estis* [you are included in my letter]. Should Father Vicars and Master of Novices deem it proper, I wish this letter to be read in the presence of my father, my mother, my sister, and my brother-in-law. If it should be read to anyone else, let it be to my cousin, Juana, and her husband, to whom, you will please convey my best wishes. Send my best regards also to my aunt Apolonia Boronada, Xurxa, and other relatives. Send my regards to Dr. Fiol, his brother, Señor Antonio, his father, and his entire household. Present my warm regards to Raphael Moragues Costa and his wife; to Dr. Moragues, his brother, and his wife; as also to Dr. Serralta; to Señor Vicar Perello; to Señor Alzamora; to Señor Juan Nicolau and to Regidor Barthomeu, his brother and his household. In a word, remember me to all my friends. My final word: let the Lord gather us all in glory and keep your reverence for many years. This is my earnest prayer in this house of holy Mission in the city of Cadiz.

August 20, 1749

Father Palou sends to your reverence his loving regards.
Your cordial friend in Christ,
Fr. Junípero Serra, a most unworthy priest.

***

Long live Jesus, Mary and Joseph!

My dearest Friend in Christ, Father Fray Francisco Serra:

My Lord and Master! Thanks be to God! I am at the most desired end of a long and tedious navigation in the city of Vera Cruz and ready to start my journey to the City of Mexico which is situated eighty leagues from the port of Vera Cruz. We shall leave tomorrow or day after tomorrow. Our hazardous crossing of the Atlantic Ocean is a long story. However, let me say in a few words that our voyage, though a long one, has been a happy one. We all had our little share in suffering and hardship, but the greatest trial to me has been my lack of patience to endure those little disappointments and privations. We embarked on the 29th of August, late in the evening, and we left the bay of Cadiz on August 30th, which fell this year on Saturday. On the 8th of September, the Feast of the Nativity of the Blessed Virgin, we were facing the Canary Islands. Then we continued our voyage, without encountering any contrary wind, and we went, on the whole, prosperously except for some dead calms. Only on Michaelmas and its vigil the sea became pretty rough and unruly; so much so that the pilot began to be much concerned for our safety. Yet this alarming beginning passed without assuming the proportions of a storm.

On the Feast of Our Lady, the Queen of the most Holy Rosary, fearing that we would run short of water, they cut down our supply for drinking. So poorly measured was it that only one small glass of water—and not full—like those of the refectory of the convento at Petra, was served to every one of the passengers at each of the two daily meals. We could not take chocolate, though we had a good supply of it, for want of water to cook it. This lasted fifteen days, till at length we reached Porto Rico, which is twelve or thirteen hundred leagues distant from Cadiz. The want and famine of water was the greatest tribulation we had. We were, at times, so thirsty that we would gladly have drunk from the stagnant holes and rain-pools which are found in the streets and along the roads. However, a sailor from Majorca was, at times, of great service to us, Father Palou and myself, giving us some drinking water which he obtained for us, or which he denied to himself in order that we might be comfortable. While we were in this adversity, which borne with patience might have been a source of spiritual joy to us, we arrived and landed in the city of Porto Rico, on October 18th—Feast of the Apostle and Evangelist St. Luke, which fell this year on Saturday. Our lodging here was at the Sanctuary of the Immaculate Conception, which is located within the city limits. Upon our arrival at night we said the Rosary with a fairly good attendance of people. At the evening services of the second day I recited the mysteries; and delivered a short instruction inviting the people to the Mission, which was to be given the following days according to the orders I had from the Father President. The next day we went out to preach on the streets and public squares. The commotion was simply great. Then, seeing that the Sanctuary of the Immaculate Conception, which is more or less like the Church of the Convent of Jesus, at Palma, was too small even for one-third of the attendance, the Vicar General asked us to hold the mission in the Cathedral. So the wish of the Vicar General was at once complied with. The Cathedral soon was unable to hold the crowds.

The following was the order of the mission: In the Cathedral the doctrinal sermons were in charge of a missionary from Sahagun; the mission proper was preached by Father President, who is a missionary from Sancti Spiritus, and myself. Thus it went, I having the first sermon in the Cathedral, and then Father President and I taking turns. Doubtless those good Fathers delighted in honoring me; but here I found my own confusion and humiliation, because at once I sorrowfully recognized in my heart the vast difference that existed between my sermons and the sermons of those good Fathers. Mine were chaff, theirs grain and gold; mine cold as snow, theirs warm and ardent as fire; mine were dark as night, theirs clear and cheerful as the day. When Father President preached there was such a commotion in the audience, such was the abundance of tears and cries, the striking of breasts, that even long after the sermon was over the lingering clamor could be heard. Thus moved and crying, the people returned to their homes. The same happened at times when the Father Missionary from Sahagun preached in the

Sanctuary of the Immaculate Conception, after the mission of the Cathedral, during those days we were obliged to remain in Porto Rico. But when I preached nothing could be heard, no tears, no moaning; even when I preached on those subjects naturally apt to move the audience, and that in spite of my strenuous efforts in delivering my sermons. So, it was made clear enough to everyone, which indeed should be sufficient to subdue my pride, that I was the only one lacking that interior fire which inflames the words of the preacher and moves and fires the audience.

I hope your reverence will have pity on me and will pray for me that I may love God with all my heart and with all my strength, and that He may deign to make me a fit and worthy minister of His Word. The mission, through the efforts of said missionaries and the zeal displayed by the others in the confessional which was truly a luminous example to all, was so fruitful that I was hearing confessions every day, morning, afternoon and evening. I used to go to the confessional at three or four o'clock in the morning, and heard confessions in the evening until midnight. The people were very good to us and grateful. They brought to us food, refreshments and so many presents that our house was too small to hold them.

Let me tell you a little incident. We had made arrangements with our sea captain to provide board and lodging for us during our stay in Porto Rico. But lo! he failed to fulfill his word, and refused to provide the least thing for us. So we all landed, twenty religious and three servants without one single penny wherewith to buy anything to eat. And yet, for eighteen days we ate better than in any convent, all drinking chocolate every day, and having tobacco to smoke and to snuff, lemonade and refreshments in the afternoons, and everything we could wish to have; and after that one of the brothers had yet forty pesos which had been given for the missionaries; and of food, fruit, and groceries we had as much as we could carry, which was sufficient for the rest of the journey. And all this came when we were assuring the people that we did not want any presents and luxury for ourselves.

As soon as we landed in Porto Rico two or three gentlemen who appeared to be men of wealth and distinction, came to us and asked whether in the mission were any fathers from Majorca, and seeing two of them, Father Palou and myself, they at once made various and splendid offerings. And when they found out that we did not accept anything for ourselves, they sent to the community, fruit, preserves, money to buy meat and candles for lighting purposes because here there was no olive oil, and great many other things. They honored us greatly and treated us royally. In addition to these two gentlemen who gave to me and to Father Palou such special marks of benevolence and affection so that the whole mission greeted the Fathers from Majorca, there came another gentleman, Juan Ferrer, nephew of Padre Definitor Botellas. He is the superintendent and manager of the Royal Warehouse, and treated us, likewise, very splendidly, and gave us numberless gifts.

Finally, we re-embarked on October 31st, and struggling to leave the port we simply could not. We were then in imminent danger of striking against a reef which was only two braces from us. At the same time we fired our cannons and gave the alarm. The people in the city thought we were all drowned, so that cries and lamentations could be heard everywhere. The Governor ordered that all the available boats should go to the scene at once, to rescue the people and the religious, and bring them ashore. We disembarked, though not all. The good people, thinking that we would not have food and beds that night, as we were arriving in the Sanctuary of the Immaculate Conception, some came with these; so that in a few minutes the Plaza in front of the Sanctuary was crowded with people. We had everything in abundance that night, chocolate in the morning, and a good supply for the rest of the journey.

That night, after the Rosary, we preached and heard confessions and next morning, the Feast of All Saints, we celebrated a High Mass in honor of the Blessed Virgin and in thanksgiving to God. On the same day, which was Saturday, we very happily left the port and proceeded across the gulf to Vera Cruz. At the end of this second part of our navigation which was extremely long, as the first, on account of the ponderous weight of our vessel, we fell again in imminent danger of losing our lives. On the second day of December we faced Vera Cruz. We thought surely that if we could not land that evening we could do it next day early in the morning. Now, as the sun was setting, a strong north wind began to blow which is very bad on this coast. As we tacked the boat moved from the coast, and for several days we were tossed to and fro by a furious storm. Thus receding from the shore, the boat began to leak and the main mast could stand only with great difficulty. In those perilous moments the twenty religious of our Order, and the Dominican Fathers, who were seven, en route to Guadalajara, held a meeting, and a proposition was brought up whether it would be advisable to make some vow or promise, that the good Lord might have mercy on us and spare our lives. It was determined that each should write secretly on a slip of paper the name of the saint of his especial devotion and veneration, and that all the slips or cards should be likewise secretly placed in a box, and after a fervent prayer and invocation to the Holy Spirit, and a prayer to all the saints, they should draw one, and this one should be, together with all the saints, our especial patron and protector, and that once we landed we should celebrate a High Mass with sermon in thanksgiving to God.

I wrote on my card the name of San Francisco Solano, and Father Palou that of Saint Michael. None of them, however, was drawn but Santa Barbara, which had been written by a priest from Valencia, Father Ferrer. As soon as the name of the saint was called out, we all suddenly exclaimed: 'Long live Santa Barbara!' All this happened on Saint Barbara's day, in the evening, December 4, 1749. The ship veered to the port, and all rejoiced with exceeding great joy trusting in God's paternal Providence. The wind ceased and thus we sailed till we arrived at the port of Vera Cruz and cast anchor on Saturday, December 6, 1749. It is on Saturday that we have always experienced the maternal protection of the Blessed Mother of God. So we firmly believe that it was through the powerful intercession of Mary and that of Saint Barbara, our patron saint, that we were all delivered from imminent death off the coast of Vera Cruz. As soon as we landed at Vera Cruz the ship was found to be cracked and the main mast fallen, so that it was utterly unsafe to travel on it any longer without endangering the lives of the passengers. On the 10th of December we celebrated the Feast of Thanksgiving in this Convento of Our Holy Father Saint Francis, Father Prior of the Dominicans officiating and both communities being present, though they were all still seasick. The sermon on the occasion was entrusted to my insufficiency. Let all now help me to thank God for so many benefits, and pray for me in order that I may always show myself grateful to Him.

Kindly convey my loving regards to my father and mother, to my sister and brother-in-law, et al. Tell them to rejoice in the Lord for I never forget them, but remember them always in the Holy Sacrifice of the Mass. I have been free from accident and I am in good health. Among our religious brethren, and the Dominicans and servants of both, I am the only one that never was seasick, and when all the rest were half dead I was thoroughly well. Remember me to Father Guardian; to the Vicar, to the Rector, and to all. I send to your reverence a thousand embraces.

I hope you will pray for me and this is my loving request that we may meet again, if not here, hereafter.

Vera Cruz, December 14, 1749.
Your servant and friend in Christ,
Fr. Junípero Serra, a most unworthy priest[8]

Maximilian Mary Kolbe (1894–1941)

In one of those typical moments of frustration a young boy's mother asked him: "Whatever will become of you?" The boy, in this instance, was Raymond Kolbe, born on January 8, 1894, in Zdunska Wola, Poland, of Julius Kolbe of German descent and Marianne Dabrowska of Polish origins, both devout Catholics and both ardent Polish nationalists at another difficult period of Russian occupation that so often scarred the history of that country. His mother's question obviously hit its mark, as years later then Maximilian Mary Kolbe recalled it:

> That night I asked the Mother of God what was to become of me. Then she came to me holding two crowns, one white, the other red. She asked if I was willing to accept either of these crowns. The white one meant that I should persevere in purity, and the red that I should become a martyr. I said that I would accept them both.[1]

His could not have been a carefree youth. He had an older brother, Francis, and two others who both died at early ages: Joseph who died when Raymond was three and Andrew when he was ten. His parents moved to Pabianice where they both worked as basket weavers. Later his father worked at the two different mills and on rented land where he grew vegetables, and then joined Józef Piłsudski's Polish Legions and was captured by the Russians for fighting for the independence of a partitioned Poland. His mother, meanwhile, worked as a midwife and sold groceries and household goods in part of their rented house, which she used as a shop.

When he was only thirteen, Raymond and his older brother, Francis, decided to join the Conventual Franciscans. They had to cross the border between Russia and Austria-Hungary illegally where they entered a junior seminary in Lwów. Three years later Raymond was allowed to enter the novitiate; when he professed his first vows in 1911 he took the religious name of Maximilian, and three years later, at his final vows he asked to be professed as Maximilian Mary as a sign of his dedication to the Mother of God.

In 1912 he was sent to Kraków and later to Rome where he studied philosophy at the Gregorian University in Rome from 1912 to 1915, and theology at the Franciscan Collegio, the "Seraphicum," from 1915 to 1919. While still in seminary, he and six of his friends founded the *Militia Immaculatae* devoted to spreading devotion to Mary Immaculate. It was at this time, however, that the young friar was stricken with tuberculosis, which left him in frail health the rest of his life. When he was twenty-four Maximilian Mary Kolbe was ordained. Four years later, he received his *Doctorare* in theology from the "Seraphicum."

The following year, he returned to Poland where he taught history in the Conventual seminary and began publication of the *Knight of the Immaculate*, a magazine aimed at fighting religious apathy. Although his recurring tuberculosis forced him to take a medical leave from September 1926 to April 1927, his work for the *Militia Immaculatae* continued. In 1927 Polish Prince Jan Drucki-Lubecki gave him land at Teresin near Warsaw where he founded a new monastery of Niepokalanow, the City of the Immaculate, which was consecrated on December 8 of that year. At its peak the *Militia of the Immaculate* had a pressrun of 750,000 copies a month. Eight years later, the new friary began printing a daily Catholic newspaper, *The Little Daily*, with a pressrun of 137,000 on work days and 225,000 on Sundays and holy days.

By this time in his life three strong currents of the Spirit's activity could be discerned in the friar's life. From the first there was his intense devotion to the Immaculate Virgin Mary that prompted him to be called "The Apostle of Consecration to Mary." Closely allied to this was his ever-deepening love of the Eucharist that he expressed in words such as these: "You come to me and unite Yourself intimately to me under the form of nourishment. Your Blood now runs in mine, Your Soul, Incarnate God, compenetrates mine, giving courage and support. What miracles! Who would have ever imagined such!"[2] Both of these provided an increasingly strong desire to make known the love of God as his indefatigable writing and publishing attest.

Not content with his work in Poland, Maximilian went to his immediate superior, Father Cornelius Czupryk, in January 1930 to ask for permission to go to the Orient. "Where will you live?" his stunned confrere asked. "What will you do?" To both questions, Maximilian answered quite simply: "The Blessed Mother has her plan ready!"[3] Maximilian and four brothers left for Japan later that year. Within a month of their arrival, penniless and knowing no Japanese, Maximilian was printing a Japanese version of the *Knight* and within a year had founded a monastery in Nagasaki, Japan, one comparable to Niepokalanow. By 1936 the magazine, *Seibo no Kishi* grew to a circulation of 65,000. Within a short while, that is in mid-1932, he left Japan for Malabar, India, where he attempted to found a third Niepokalanow. A lack of manpower and the growing tensions throughout the world, however, did not enable it to survive. Poor health forced him to curtail his dedicated missionary outreach and, in 1936, to return to Poland.

By 1939 the City of the Immaculate housed a religious community of nearly eight hundred men. At the time of the Nazi invasion of Poland on September 1, 1939, it was completely self-sufficient with its own medical facilities—an infirmary as well as a pharmacy—and its own fire brigade. Niepokalanow was, therefore, viewed by the Third Reich as a threat. The forty-five-year-old friar was realistic in knowing that the friary would be taken over and so he sent most of the friars home, warning them not to join the underground resistance. Shortly afterward, the friary was ransacked. Maximilian and about forty of his confreres were transported to a holding camp in Germany and later to one in Poland.

Surprisingly, they were released and allowed to return on December 8, 1939. Quietly, the City of the Immaculate became a refugee camp for thousands of Poles and Jews of the Poznan district fleeing from Nazi persecution. Once again Kolbe and his confreres soon came under suspicion by the Gestapo. As a journalist, a publisher, and an intellectual who had refused German citizenship, Kolbe was considered a threat to what the Nazis wanted most: absolute domination. To incriminate him, the Gestapo permitted one final printing of the *Militia of the Immaculate* in December of 1940. They were delighted when they found this passage:

> No one in the world can change Truth. What we can do and should do is to seek truth and to serve it when we have found it. The real conflict is inner conflict. Beyond armies of occupation and the catacombs of concentration camps, there are two irreconcilable enemies in the depth of every soul: good and evil, sin and love. And what use are victories on the battlefield if we ourselves are defeated in our innermost personal selves?[4]

As a result, on February 17, 1941, Maximilian Kolbe was again arrested on charges of aiding Jews and the Polish underground. He was sent to Pawiak prison in German-occupied Warsaw where he was singled out for special ill-treatment.

On May 28, 1941, Maximilian and four of his companions were deported to Auschwitz. Upon being arrested he implored and encouraged the friars, as he had said before: "Courage, my sons. Don't you see that we are leaving on a mission? They pay our fare in the bargain. What a piece of good luck! The thing to do now is to pray well in order to win as many souls as possible. Let us, then, tell the Blessed Virgin that we are content, and that she can do with us anything she wishes."[5] Upon their arrival that infamous welcome sign greeted them as it would millions after them: *Arbeit macht frei* (Work makes you free), and the *SS-Hauptsturmführer* Karl "Butcher" Fritzsch, the deputy camp commander, told them that Jews had the right to live only two weeks, and Roman Catholic priests one month. Cruelly, they were told that the only way out of the camp was through the chimneys of the crematorium. Maximilian received the striped convict garment and the tattoo 16670. He was put to work immediately carrying blocks of stone for the construction of a crematorium wall. He was harassed and taunted for his faith; his priesthood prompted an even more rigorous hatred. He was frequently beaten to the point of death, was revived, and brought to the infirmary bunker where he would quietly encourage the weak, bless the dead, and absolve sinners all while reminding them to forgive and pray for the Nazis captors. Nonetheless, Maximilian Mary Kolbe struck awe in his Nazi captors. Physician Francis Wlodarski learned from a Nazi patient, the penal bunker chief, that Kolbe was "a psychic trauma, a shock!" "I overheard the SS talking about him among themselves," he told the physician. "We've never had a priest here like this one. He must be a wholly exceptional man!"[6]

In late July or early August 1941, a prisoner escaped from this Nazi death camp. As punishment, ten men were chosen from the same barracks, Block 11, to die of starvation. The prisoners were lined up in the blistering hot sun, while the commandant chose life or death for each of the men. The last man chosen, Francis Gajowniczek, let out a cry that he had a wife and children. Prisoner 16670 broke rank and volunteered to take his place. When "Butcher" Fritsch asked him who he was to make such a request, his answer was quite simple: "'I am a Catholic priest. I wish to die for that man. I am old; he has a wife and children.'"[7] The condemned man and Maximilian never spoke, but that momentary glance changed Gajowniczek forever. (After his release from Auschwitz, Gajowniczek made his way back to his hometown with the dream of seeing his family again. He found his wife but his two sons had been killed during the war. For the next five decades he made a pilgrimage to Auschwitz on August 14 to pay homage to the man who took his place.)

Maximilian and the other nine men went to a slow death of torture and starvation in the notorious Block 13. After three weeks, only four remained alive: among them was Maximilian. On August 14, the commandant decided the bunker was needed and ordered the prisoners to be injected with carbolic acid. Still conscious, Maximilian looked at the doctor and offered his arm. The body of Prisoner 16670 was removed to the crematorium, and without dignity or ceremony was disposed of, like hundreds of thousands who had gone before him, and hundreds of thousands more who would follow.

The heroism of Prisoner 16670—Maximilian Kolbe—went echoing through Auschwitz. In that desert of hatred he had sown love. A survivor, Jozef Stemler, later recalled: "There was nothing artificial in his behavior, he was serious but happy and he had the smile of a youth—these qualities attracted many people to him. I was coming back from the evening roll-call, half-dead from work and hunger, when I was ordered by an SS guard to carry the dead bodies to the crematorium. The sight of the body of a young man almost made me faint. . . . I realized it was Father Kolbe."[8] Another survivor, Jerzy Bielecki, declared that Father Kolbe's death was "a shock filled with hope, bringing new life and strength. . . . It was like a powerful shaft of light in the darkness of the camp."[9]

Maximilian Mary Kolbe was beatified as a confessor by Paul VI in 1971 and called him "that martyr of love." "History cannot forget these frightful and tragic pages," Paul VI declared on that occasion. "And so it cannot but fix its horrified gaze on the luminous points that reveal, but at the same time overcome, their inconceivable darkness. One of these points, perhaps the one glowing most brightly, is the calm, drained figure of Maximilian Kolbe. A serene hero, always pious and sustained by a paradoxical, yet reasonable confidence! His name will remain among the great; it will reveal what reserves of moral values lay among those unhappy masses, petrified by horror and despair."[10]

Eleven years later, Pope John Paul II, Maximilian's Polish compatriot, canonized him not as a confessor but as a martyr. "Maximilian prepared for this definitive sacrifice by following Christ from the first years of his life in Poland," John Paul proclaimed. "From these years comes the mysterious vision of two crowns—one white and one red. From these our saint does not choose. He accepts them both. From the years of his youth, in fact, Maximilian was filled with the great love of Christ and the desire for martyrdom. Men saw what happened in the camp at Auschwitz. Maximilian did not die but 'gave his life . . . for his brother.' In that death, terrible from the human point of view, there was the whole definitive greatness of the human act and of the human choice. He spontaneously offered himself up to death out of love. And in this human death of his there was the clear witness borne to Christ: the witness borne in Christ to the dignity of man, to the sanctity of his life, and to the saving power of death in which the power of love is made manifest."[11]

***

The following is an excerpt from notes for a book Maximilian Kolbe was intending to write, notes that are the fruit of his Franciscan formation but above all the expression of his prayer and lived experience. The idea for this work can be traced to his early days in Japan about which he wrote in a letter to his Provincial Cornelius Czupryk in 1932. The majority of the notes came from about 1938 to 1941; interrupted by his arrest by Gestapo and subsequent (final) internment in Auschwitz. They made their way into a conference or meditation given to the friars at Niepokalanow dated August 1940. For Maximilian, theology was not merely speculative, but a plan of life; the dogma of the Immaculate Conception became for him a blueprint for his entire spirituality and mission.

From *The Kolbe Reader*

The aim of creation, the end of man himself, is the love of God, Creator and Father—an ever greater love, the divinization of man, his return to God from whom he came, union with God, a fruitful love.

So that love for the Father might become even more perfect, infinitely more perfect, the love of the Son, Jesus, made itself manifest. He came down to earth, died on the cross and remains in the Holy Eucharist in order to arouse love for himself in hearts.

But so that the love for the Son might burn more intensely, and so that in this way love for the Father might be ever more mightily inflamed, help came to us from the Holy Spirit, from the Immaculate, the mother full of mercy, the Mediatrix of all graces, an earthly creature like ourselves, who strongly attracts hearts to herself and to her motherly heart. And as the love of God for creation descends to earth from the Father through the Son and the Holy Spirit, so, too, through the Holy Spirit and the Son the response to his love arises, the reaction, the love of creatures for the Father.

The love of the Father, the Son, and the Holy Spirit flames eternally; the love of the Father, of Jesus, and of the Immaculate knows no imperfection. Only man (not always and not in all things) responds imperfectly to this love with his own love. To arouse that love for the Immaculate, therefore, by enkindling it in one's own heart, to communicate this fire to those who live close to us, to set on fire with this love all souls and each one in particular, those who live now and those who will live in the future, to make this flame burst forth ever more intensely and without restrictions in ourselves and all over the earth—such is our purpose. Everything else is just a means.

An effect resembles the cause that produced it. Consequently every creature shows in itself some resemblance to God; and the more perfect the creature is, the more evident is this resemblance.

God the Holy Trinity is love. So the reciprocal love of persons who come together in a family is an authentic echo of divine love . . . the mutual love of father, mother, children, etc.

Much more evidently does this love show itself in the spiritual field, which joins together the intellect, the will and the being itself. Any representation of this love, even the most spiritual and perfect, will always remain infinitely far removed from the very fount of love, which is God.

Even if we could establish thousands and thousands of degrees, each more perfect, each more spiritually pure than the last, there would still remain an infinite distance between even the most elevated of these degrees and the source of love itself.

God brings himself down towards his own creature and joins himself to it in a love which annihilates that whole infinite space; he makes it part of his own family, makes of it one of his own children. The soul is regenerated in the sacred waters of baptism and thus becomes God's child.

Water, which purifies everything over which it runs, is a symbol of her who purifies every soul that draws near to her. It is a symbol of the Immaculate, of her who is without stain; upon whoever is washed in this water the grace of the Holy Spirit descends. The Holy Spirit, the divine Spouse of the Immaculate, acts only in her and through her; he communicates supernatural life, the life of grace, the divine life, the sharing in divine love, in the divinity itself.

The child of God, as a member of the divine family, has the Father for his father, and the mother of God for his mother. He has the Son of God for brother; he becomes God's heir, and is joined to the other members of this divine family through love. Nor is this all: the Son of God selects spouses from among souls; he unites himself with them in a "spousal" love, and through him they become the mothers of many, many other souls.

O soul! Abandon yourself into the hands of your Father![12]

Solanus Casey (1870–1957)

Bernard Francis Casey was born on November 25, 1870. His father, Bernard James Casey, was born in Castleblaney, County Monohan, in 1840, immigrated to the United States in 1857, and settled in Boston, Massachusetts. His mother, Ellen Elizabeth Murphy, was born in Camlough, County Armagh, in 1844 and immigrated to the United States in 1852. They were married in Salem, Massachusetts, in 1863, moved to Philadelphia, and, in 1865, moved to an eighty-acre farm near Prescott, Wisconsin. Barney Casey Jr., the sixth child in a family of ten boys and six girls, was born at Oak Grove and baptized at St. Joseph's Church, Hudson, Wisconsin. Eight years later, two of his sisters, Mary Ann and Martha, died of diphtheria, a disease that he also contracted but survived, although his throat and voice were affected. He received his primary education in the rural schools near his home but, as was typical of many farm boys, his education was uneven at best and graduation from primary school did not take place until he was sixteen. At that time, too, his young brothers and sisters began teasing him about a girl from the neighborhood, Rebecca Tobin, not knowing that their brother had told the young woman that he wanted to marry her. Rebecca's parents had other ideas and sent her to St. Paul, Minnesota, to complete her education.

When he was seventeen, Barney moved to Stillwater, Minnesota, where he hoped to find a job to help support his family. His mother's brother was a priest there, Father Maurice Murphy, after whom his older brother was named. At first Barney worked in a lumberyard, then as a part-time prison guard, and as one of Stillwater's first streetcar operators, a position he also held in Appleton and Superior, Wisconsin. In this last situation, he came upon a murder that had just taken place. The anger on the murderer's face and the fear frozen on that of his victim revived a thought in Barney that he had been nurturing since he was thirteen years old: that he might have a calling to be a priest, helping others to avoid evil and to do good. Barney made his way to his parish church, Sacred Heart, and spoke with Father Edmund Sturm who suggested that he enter Saint Francis de Sales Seminary in Milwaukee.

In January 1892, he began his secondary education as a young seminarian. Despite all his persistence, he could not keep up and, four years later, was told that he had to leave. Before doing so, however, the young man visited the Capuchins who, he had heard, were always praying for vocations. Initially he was not impressed with what he experienced. In the mysterious ways of God's Providence, however, something prompted him to write to the Capuchin provincial and, on December 24, 1896, he arrived at St. Bonaventure Monastery in Detroit where on January 14, 1897, he was invested as a novice and given the religious name Francis Solanus.

Solanus professed his temporary vows on July 21, 1898. On the day before, however, he was asked to write the following statement, an unusual step in the process of admission:

> *I,* Frater *[Brother] Solanus Casey, declare that I joined the Order of the Capuchins in the Province of Saint Joseph with the sure intention to follow thus my religious vocation. Although I would wish and should be thankful to be admitted to priestly ordination, considering my lack of talents, I leave it to my superiors to judge my faculties and to dispose of me as they think best.*
>
> *I will therefore lay no claim whatsoever if they consider me unworthy or incapable of becoming a priest and I always will humbly submit to their appointments.*

Studies were extremely difficult for the young friar and questions continually arose among his professors as to his qualifications for ordination. An entry in his notebook provides an insight into how he overcame what must have been continual discouragement: "Traits of Saintly Characters" he described as "(1) Eagerness for the glory of God; (2) Touchiness about the interests of Jesus; and (3) Anxiety for the salvation of souls."[1] His religious example eventually persuaded his Capuchin superiors to permit his ordination and Solanus was ordained on July 24, 1904. The young priest, however, was not given faculties to preach formal sermons or to administer the sacrament of penance.

His first assignment as a simple priest was to Sacred Heart Parish in Yonkers, New York, where he was given the responsibilities of sacristan and porter, as well as other nonsacramental positions, director of the Young Ladies Sodality and of the altar boys. During the fourteen years in which he discharged these responsibilities in Yonkers, Solanus continued to be known for his deep life of prayer, his example of simplicity and humility, and especially for his charity toward the sick and the poor, and for his attentiveness to non-Catholics. Shortly after his arrival in Yonkers, for example, he befriended the Friars and Sisters of the Atonement in Garrison, New York. Solanus was present when Paul Francis Watson was ordained and preached at his first Mass on July 3, 1910. During these years in Yonkers, moreover, two of Solanus's gifts became obvious: those of healing and of prophecy. Both of these continued when he was moved to the Capuchin parish of Our Lady Queen of Angels in Harlem and later Our Lady of Sorrow in Manhattan's Lower East Side. The advice he gave to those who came to him for help was simple: he would encourage them to make a sacrifice for the foreign missions and would then tell them to thank God ahead of time for granting the favor they had requested. Just as with his Capuchin confrere, Saint Felix of Cantalice, *Deo Gratias* (Thanks be to God) became a phrase identified with Father Solanus. There was a significant difference: this Irish-American Capuchin added "ahead of time" expressing his confidence that God would indeed take care of things. "Confidence in God," he would say, "is the very soul of prayer."

After twenty years on the East Coast, Solanus was sent to the Capuchin friary, the "monastery," of Saint Bonaventure in Detroit, Michigan, on August 1, 1924. He ministered there until April 25, 1946. Throughout those twenty-two years, Solanus became known for his charity to the poor whose numbers were daily increasing as the Great Depression of 1929 and the Second World War approached. The image of him in the soup kitchen offering to the poor food, clothing, or simple advice was quite well known. During the war years, 1941 to 1945, much of his time was taken up consoling and strengthening the faith of those who had a family member or loved one in service.

Because of his failing health, Solanus was sent on July 23, 1945, back to New York, this time to Saint Michael's friary in Brooklyn. His reputation for healing had literally exhausted him as people came to him in droves asking for time or for blessings or for prayers. Sending him to Saint Michael's where he had very few responsibilities was seen as a way of relieving him during what were thought to be his waning years. It was not. As his biographer, Michael Crosby notes, "the superiors' best intentions were subverted by people's needs, which did not recognize boundaries or state lines." Nine months later he was sent to the quiet and relative isolation of the Capuchin novitiate in Huntington, Indiana, where he remained for ten years until his return to Detroit on May 10, 1956.

Surprisingly much of the contemporary literature about Solanus Casey passes over the intense devotion to the Eucharist that characterized much of his life. Present day authors may perhaps have taken it for granted. Nonetheless, Francis of Assisi's *First Admonition* and *Letter to the Entire Order*, both of which seem to come from the last years of his life, may well have inspired Solanus's wonder at the Eucharist and at the priesthood. For someone whose lifetime mantra was *Deo Gratias* (Thanks be to God), the celebration of thanksgiving—the Eucharist—was a defining activity of his daily life. The altar boys in Yonkers may have been the first to observe this as they grumbled about the length of his devotion-filled Masses. The Capuchin novices in Huntington commented about the hours Solanus would spend before the Blessed Sacrament.

If, however, Francis had encouraged his brothers to mold their lives on the continuing revelation of God in the Eucharist as the Lord daily embraces the minority of humility and poverty, Solanus came to recognize that he was being encouraged to do the same and, in a special way, to embrace the eucharistic Lord's patient suffering. During these months the erysipelas and eczema with which he had been struggling for years intensified. Every other week, the aging friar would visit a hospital in nearby Fort Wayne. As the condition worsened, however, he was brought back to Detroit where much of the following year was spent in Detroit's St. John's Hospital. On July 31, 1957, as two nurses were attending him, Solanus suddenly sat up, lifted up his arms, and said: "I give my soul to Jesus Christ!" Fifty-three years after the celebration of his first Mass—to the very hour—Solanus's personal Eucharist had come to an end. When he died, he was eighty-seven years old.

Shortly after Solanus's death, the process of gathering information about his life, work, and the favors granted through his intercession was begun. The data was presented to John Cardinal Dearden, archbishop of Detroit, who presented it along with four volumes of Solanus's writings to the Congregation for the Causes of the Saints. On June 19, 1982, Pope John Paul II gave his official approval to introduce Solanus's cause in the Archdiocese of Detroit. On July 11, 1995, the congregation, together with the pope, promulgated the Decree of Heroic Virtue, a recognition of his great holiness.

***

The Capuchins of Switzerland capitalized on an inspiration
of a lady eager to support financially their foreign missions.

The Seraphic Mass Association became a resource for individuals asking for prayers for special intentions. Its members formed an international spiritual family in which each one prayed and sacrificed for the other and relied on the Capuchins to offer prayers and Masses for their intentions. Their donations—the enrollment fee was fifty-cents—could be, although did not need to be, added. All funds, however, went to the support of the foreign missions. The following is a letter written to Sister Cecilia Eagen about an enrollment that took place on March 12, 1925.

From *Solanus Casey*

From a Letter to Sister Cecilia Eagen

I hardly think I ever told you about our enrolling companies and projects in the Seraphic Mass Association. The following, first of several similar to it since, I am sure will please you.

The slump of the 1925–26 winter was a tough one on Detroiters. Every auto factory in the city shut down for at least a week at Christmas, without a word when they would start up again. Only a day or two before New Years it was announced that Ford would start up again, on such and such a day after New Year's Day and would continue at three days a week till further notice. That was quite a "beam of hope" for perhaps millions. The other auto companies followed lingeringly, but most of them just worked one and two days each week. One of the slowest seemingly was Chevrolet. As we learned only a year or two later, it had already started negotiations toward bankruptcy.

On the 12th of February, Thursday after 9:00 p.m. John McKenna, who had become enthusiastic about the SMA the first months after my arrival back from New York, August 1, 1924, came to the Office. He was evidently discouraged, notwithstanding his otherwise wonderful faith.

"Father," he began, "I don't know what to do. I can't support a wife and family with the hours I've been working. I haven't had a full day now in two weeks. Today I had only two hours. They're always finding an alibi to send the men home." All at once, as though by inspiration, he said, "Father! Enroll the Company!"

"That's new," thought I. Twenty times quicker than I could tell it, however, so that it seemed absurd to hesitate, [something] flashed on my mind: "If a single Holy Mass must help any legitimate cause, why should not five hundred Masses daily in connection with the holy foreign Missions help?" "All right, John," I answered. "Yes, Father; I'll give them fifty cents" [for an annual membership in the SMA].

That same night the company received an astounding order. Two nights later McKenna waved triumphantly: "Father! We had overtime yesterday and today and we heard this afternoon that the company has an order for 45,000 machines, wanted in thirty days." It was believed that order also saved Detroit itself from bankruptcy.[2]

***

From a Letter to Miss Mildred Maneal Written around 1945

My Dear Madam: M.M.M.: God bless you and yours.

I hope this finds your outlook brightening. I just read your letter of the 11th—pathetic indeed. And [I] surely do sympathize with you. Perhaps I ought rather to congratulate you on the unusual experience [from which] you are of course inclined to learn and which the unbelieving world must look upon as a sad indication of failure.

But Oh! Why discouragement as long as we have a spark of faith left? What [a] different view we get by exercising and by fostering the "triune virtue—FAITH, HOPE, CHARITY!" In the first place "life" here in this world is so short—comparatively so momentary—that in regard to its success or failure one is inclined to think: "After all, what is the difference?" "Life" so short, that worldlings are so inclined to worship [it] as the only LIFE—as everything [of] worth.

How is it possible that man can be so shallow-minded and still be considered "rational"?

Your failure, yes, is an indication of weakness of some kind, somewhere. But if "the weak thing[s] of this world hath God chosen to confound the strong . . ." as St. Paul so wonderfully assures us (and the history of religion abounds in examples and all creation says Amen), then why ever be discouraged, unless it be that our faith more or less weakens?

Why dear sister, you ought to rather thank God for having given you such an opportunity to humble yourself and such a wonderful chance to foster humility—and by thanking Him ahead of time for whatever crosses He may deign to caress you with, [having] CON-

FIDENCE in His wisdom. Confidence in God—the very soul of prayer hardly comes to any poor sinner like we all are without trials and humiliations. And your failure, though simple and possibly single, has no doubt been quite a little cross, at least for a "little soul" to carry. There is a little verse I am sure will profit you to keep in mind and ought [to] help you foster confidence in God: "God condescends to use our powers if we don't spoil His plans by ours." God's plans are always for the best, always wonderful.

But most especially for the patient and the humble who trust in Him are His plans unfathomably holy and sublime.

Let us, therefore, not weaken. Let us hope when darkness seem[s] to surround us. Let us thank Him at all time[s] and under whatever circumstances. Thank Him for our creation and our existence. Thank Him for everything—for His plans in the past that our sins and our want of appreciation and patience have so often frustrated and that He so often found necessary to change. Let us thank Him for all His plans for the future—for trials and humiliations as well as for great joys and consolations; for sickness and whatever death He may deign to plan. And with the inspired Psalmist, let us call all the creatures of the universe to help us praise and adore Him Who is the Divine Beginning and the everlasting Good—the Alpha and the Omega."[3]

The Second Order of
the Poor Ladies

The Form of Life of Clare of Assisi

*Innocent, Bishop, Servant of the servants of God, to his beloved daughters
in Christ, Clare, Abbess, and the other sisters of the monastery of San
Damiano in Assisi, health and apostolic blessing.*

*The Apostolic See is accustomed to accede to the pious requests and to
be favorably disposed to grant the praiseworthy desires of its petitioners.
Thus, we have before Us your humble request that We confirm by our Apostolic authority the form of life that Blessed Francis gave you and which
you have freely accepted. According to [this form of life] you should live
together in unity of spirits and in the profession of the highest poverty. Our
venerable brother, the Bishop of Ostia and Velletri, has seen fit to approve
this way of life, as the Bishop's own letters on this matter define more fully,
and We have taken care to strengthen it with our Apostolic protection.
Attentive, therefore, to your devout prayers, We approve and ratify what
the Bishop has done in this matter and confirm it in virtue of our Apostolic
authority and support it in this document. To this end we include herein
the text of the Bishop, word for word, which is the following:*

*Rainaldo, by divine mercy Bishop of Ostia and Velletri, to his most dear
mother and daughter in Christ, the Lady Clare, Abbess of San Damiano in
Assisi, and to her sisters, both present and to come, greetings and a fatherly
blessing.*

*Beloved daughters in Christ, we approve your holy proposal in the
Lord and we desire with fatherly affection to impart our kind favor upon
your wishes and holy desires, because you have rejected the splendors and
pleasures of the world and, following the footprints of Christ Himself and
His most holy Mother, you have chosen to live bodily enclosed and to serve
the Lord in the highest poverty that, in freedom of soul, you may be servants of the Lord. Acceding to your pious prayers, by the authority of the
Lord Pope as well as our own, we, therefore, confirm forever for all of you
and for all who will succeed you in your monastery, and we ratify by the
protection of this document this form of life, the manner of holy unity and
of the highest poverty that your blessed Father Saint Francis gave you for
your observance in word and in writing. It is as follows:*

[Chapter One]
In the Name of the Lord Begins the Form of Life of the Poor Sisters

The form of life of the Order of the Poor Sisters that Blessed Francis
established is this: to observe the Holy Gospel of our Lord Jesus Christ,
by living in obedience, without anything of one's own, and in chastity.

Clare, the unworthy handmaid of Christ and the little plant of the most blessed Father Francis, promises obedience and reverence to the Lord Pope Innocent and his successors canonically elected, and to the Roman Church. And, just as at the beginning of her conversion, together with her sisters she promised obedience to the Blessed Francis, so now she promises to observe the same inviolably to his successors. And the other sisters shall always be obliged to obey the successors of Blessed Francis and Sister Clare and the other abbesses canonically elected who succeed her.

[Chapter Two]
Those Who Wish to Accept This Life and How They Are to Be Received

If, by divine inspiration, anyone should come to us desiring to accept this life, the abbess is bound to seek the consent of all the sisters; and if the majority have agreed, she may receive her, having obtained the permission of the Lord Cardinal Protector. If she judges she should be received, let [the abbess] examine her carefully or have her examined concerning the Catholic faith and the sacraments of the Church. And if she believes all these things and is willing to profess them faithfully and to observe them steadfastly to the end; and if she has no husband, or if she has one who has already entered religious life with the authority of the Bishop of the diocese and has already made a vow of continence; and if there is no impediment to her observance of this life, such as advanced age or some infirmity or mental disorder, let the tenor of our life be thoroughly explained to her.

If she is suitable, let the words of the holy Gospel be addressed to her that she *should go* and *sell* all that she has and take care to distribute the proceeds *to the poor*. If she cannot do this, her good will shall suffice. Let the abbess and her sisters take care that they be not concerned about her temporal affairs, so that she may freely dispose of her possessions as the Lord shall have inspired her. However, if some counsel be required, let them send her to some discerning and *God-fearing* persons, according to whose advice her goods may be distributed to the poor.

After her hair has been cut all around and her secular clothes set aside, she may be permitted three tunics and a mantle. Thereafter, she may not go outside the monastery except for a useful, reasonable, evident, and justifiable purpose. When the year of probation is ended, let her be received into obedience, promising to observe perpetually the life and form of our poverty.

Let no one receive the veil during the period of probation. The sisters may also have little mantles for convenience and propriety in serving and working. In fact, let the abbess, with discernment, provide them with clothing according to the diversity of persons, places, seasons and cold climates, as in necessity she shall deem expedient. Young girls who are received into the monastery before the age established by law may have their hair cut all around; and, after putting aside their secular clothes, let them be clothed in religious garb, as the abbess sees fit. However, when they reach the age required by law, let them, clothed in the same way as the others, make their profession. Both for these and the other novices, the abbess shall carefully provide a mistress from among the more discerning sisters of the entire monastery, who shall form them diligently in a holy way of life and proper behavior according to the form of our profession.

Let the form described above be observed in the examination and reception of the sisters who serve outside the monastery. These sisters may wear shoes. No one may live with us in the monastery unless she has been received according to the form of our profession.

Out of love of the most holy and beloved Child *wrapped in poor little swaddling clothes and placed in a manger* and of His most holy Mother, I admonish, beg, and encourage my sisters always to wear poor garments.

[Chapter Three]
The Divine Office and Fasting, Confession, and Communion

Let the sisters who can read celebrate the Divine Office according to the custom of the Lesser Brothers. They may have breviaries for this reason, reading without singing. Those who, for some reasonable cause, occasionally are not able to recite their hours by reading them, may, like the other sisters, say the *Our Father.*

Let those who do not know how to read say the *Our Father* twenty-four times for Matins; Lauds five times; seven times for each of the hours of Prime, Terce, Sext, and None; twelve times, however, for Vespers; seven times for Compline. For the dead let them also say the *Our Father* seven times with the *Eternal Rest* for Vespers; twelve times for Matins, because the sisters who can read are obliged to recite the *Office of the Dead.* When a sister of our monastery shall have passed on, however, let them say the *Our Father* fifty times.

Let the sisters fast at all times. They may eat twice on the Nativity of the Lord, however, no matter on what day it happens to fall. The younger sisters, those who are weak, and those who are serving outside the monastery may be mercifully dispensed as the abbess sees fit. But let the sisters not be bound to corporal fasting in time of manifest necessity.

Let them go to confession, with the permission of the abbess, at least twelve times a year. Let them be careful not to introduce other talk unless it pertains to the confession and the salvation of souls. Let them receive Communion seven times, namely, on the Nativity of the Lord, Thursday of Holy Week, the Resurrection of the Lord, Pentecost, the Assumption of the Blessed Virgin, the Feast of Saint Francis, and the Feast of All Saints. It is lawful for the chaplain to celebrate inside [the enclosure] to give Communion to the sisters, the healthy or the sick.

[Chapter Four]
The Election and Office of the Abbess:
The Chapter, and the Officials and the Discreets

The sisters are bound to observe the canonical form in the election of the abbess. Let them quickly arrange to have the General Minister or the Provincial Minister of the Order of Lesser Brothers present. Through the Word of God, let him dispose them to perfect harmony and the common good in the election to be held. Let no one be elected unless professed. And if a non-professed is elected or otherwise somehow given to them, she may not be obeyed unless she first professes our form of poverty.

At her death let the election of another abbess take place. If at any time it should appear to the entire body of sisters that she is not competent for their service and common good, these sisters are bound as quickly as possible to elect another as abbess and mother according to the form described above.

Let whoever is elected reflect upon the kind of burden she has undertaken on herself and to Whom *she must render an account* of the flock committed to her. Let her also strive to preside over the others more by her virtues and holy behavior than by her office, so that, moved by her example, the sisters may obey her more out of love than out of fear. Let her avoid exclusive loves, lest by loving some more than others she give scandal to all. Let her console the afflicted. Let her also be *the last refuge for those who are troubled*, lest the sickness of despair overcome the weak should they fail to find in her health-giving remedies.

Let her preserve the common life in everything, especially in whatever pertains to the church, the dormitory, refectory, infirmary, and clothing. Her vicaress is bound to preserve it in the same way.

The abbess is bound to call her sisters together at least once a week in the chapter, where both she and her sisters should humbly confess their common and public offenses and negligences. There let her consult with all her sisters concerning whatever concerns the welfare and good of the monastery, for the Lord frequently reveals what is better to the youngest.

No heavy debt may be incurred except with the common consent of the sisters and by reason of manifest necessity, and let this be done through the procurator. Let the abbess and her sisters, however, be careful that nothing be deposited in the monastery; for such practices often give rise to troubles and scandals.

In order to preserve the unity of mutual love and peace, let all who hold offices in the monastery be chosen by the common agreement of all the sisters. In the same way, let at least eight sisters be elected from the more discerning whose counsel the abbess should be always bound to use in those matters which our form of life demands. Moreover, if it seems useful and expedient, the sisters can and should at times remove the officials and discreets and elect others in their place.

[Chapter Five]
Silence, the Parlor, and the Grille

Let the sisters keep silence from the hour of Compline until Terce, except those who are serving outside the monastery. Let them also continually keep silence in the church, the dormitory, and the refectory only while they are eating. At all times, however, they may be permitted to speak with discernment in the infirmary for the recreation and service of the sick. Nevertheless, they may always and everywhere communicate whatever is necessary, briefly and in a quiet voice.

The sisters may not be permitted to speak in the parlor or at the grille without the permission of the abbess or her vicaress. Let those who have permission not dare to speak in the parlor except in the presence and hearing of two sisters. Moreover, let them not presume to go to the grille, unless there are present at least three sisters appointed by the abbess or her vicaress from the eight discreets who were elected by all the sisters for the council of the abbess. Let the abbess and her vicaress be themselves bound to observe this form of speaking. Let this happen very rarely at the grille but never at the door.

Let a curtain be hung inside the grille which may not be removed except when the Word of God is preached or when a sister is speaking with someone. Let the grille have a wooden door which is well provided with two distinct iron locks, bolts, and bars, so that, it can be locked, especially at night, with two keys, one of which the abbess may keep and the other the sacristan. Let it always be locked except when the Divine Office is being heard and for the reasons given above. A sister may not under any circumstance speak to anyone at the grille before sunrise or after sunset. Inside the parlor let there always be a curtain which may not be removed.

No one may speak in the parlor during the Lent of Saint Martin and the Greater Lent, except to a priest for Confession or for some other manifest necessity, which is left to the prudence of the abbess or her vicaress.

[Chapter Six]
Not Having Possessions

After the Most High Heavenly Father saw fit by His grace to enlighten my heart to do penance according to the example and teaching of our most blessed Father Saint Francis, shortly after his own conversion, I, together with my sisters, willingly promised him obedience. When the Blessed Father saw we had no fear of poverty, hard work, trial, shame, or contempt of the world, but, instead, we held them as great delights, moved by piety he wrote a form of life for us as follows:

> Because by divine inspiration you have made yourselves daughters and handmaids of the most High, most Exalted King, the heavenly Father, and have taken the Holy Spirit as your spouse, choosing to live according to the perfection of the holy Gospel, I resolve and promise for myself and for my brothers always to have the same loving care and special solicitude for you as for them.

As long as he lived he diligently fulfilled this and wished that it always be fulfilled by the brothers.

In order that we as well as those who were to come after us would never turn aside from the holy poverty we had embraced, shortly before his death he repeated in writing his last wish for us. He said:

> I, little brother Francis, wish to follow the life and poverty of our most high Lord Jesus Christ and of His most holy Mother and *to persevere* in this *until the end*; and I ask you, my ladies, and I give you my advice that you live always in this most holy life and poverty. And keep careful watch that you never depart from this by reason of the teaching or advice of anyone.

As I, together with my sisters, have ever been solicitous to safeguard the holy poverty which we have promised the Lord God and blessed Francis, so, too, the abbesses who shall succeed me in office and all the sisters are bound inviolably to observe it to the end, that is, by not receiving or having possession or ownership either of themselves or through an intermediary, or even anything that might reasonably be called ownership, except as much land as necessity requires for the integrity and proper seclusion of the monastery, and this land may not be cultivated except as a garden for the needs of the sisters.

[Chapter Seven]
The Manner of Working

Let the sisters to whom the Lord has given the grace of working work faithfully and devotedly after the Hour of Terce at work that pertains to a virtuous life and the common good. [Let them do this] in such a way that, while they banish idleness, the enemy of the soul, they do *not extinguish the Spirit* of holy prayer and devotion to which other temporal things must contribute.

At the Chapter, in the presence of all, the abbess or her vicaress is bound to assign the work that each should perform with her hands. Let the same be done if alms have been sent by anyone for the needs of the sisters, so that an acknowledgement of them be made in common. Let all such things be distributed for the common good by the abbess or her vicaress with the advice of the discreets.

[Chapter Eight]
The Sisters Shall Not Appropriate Anything as Their Own; Begging Alms; The Sick Sisters

Let the sisters not appropriate anything to themselves, neither a house nor a place nor anything at all; instead, *as pilgrims and strangers* in this world who serve the Lord in poverty and humility, let them confidently send for alms. Nor should they be ashamed, since the Lord made Himself poor in this world for us. This is that summit of the highest poverty which has established you, my dearest sisters, heiresses and queens of the kingdom of heaven; it has made you poor in things but exalted you in virtue. Let this be your portion which leads *into the land of the living*. Clinging totally to this, my most beloved sisters, do not wish to have anything else in perpetuity under heaven for the name of our Lord Jesus Christ and His most holy mother.

Let no sister be permitted to send letters or to receive or give away anything outside the monastery without the permission of the abbess. Let it not be permitted to have anything that the abbess has not given or allowed. Should anything be sent to a sister by her relatives or others, let the abbess give it to her. If she needs it, she may use it; otherwise, let her in all charity give it to a sister who does need it. If, however, money is sent to her, let the abbess, with the advice of the discreets, provide for the needs of the sister.

Concerning the sick sisters, let the abbess be strictly bound to inquire with diligence, by herself and through other sisters, what their illness requires both by way of counsel as well as food and other necessities, and let her provide for them charitably and kindly according to the resources of the place. Because all are bound to serve and to provide for their sisters who are ill as they would wish to be served, let them be bound as if they were bound by some illness. Let each confidently make her needs known to another. For if a mother loves and cares for her child according to the flesh, how much more attentively should a sister love and care for her sister according to the Spirit? Those who are ill may lie on sacks filled with straw and may use feather pillows for their head; those who need woolen stockings and quilts may use them.

When these sick sisters are visited by those who enter the monastery, they may briefly respond with some good words to those who speak to them. But the other sisters who have permission may not dare to speak to those who enter the monastery except in the presence and hearing of the two discreets appointed by the abbess or her vicaress. Let the abbess and her vicaress themselves be bound to observe this form of speaking.

[Chapter Nine]
The Penance to be Imposed on the Sisters Who Sin; The Sisters Who Serve outside the Monastery

If any sister, at the instigation of the enemy, has sinned mortally against the form of our profession, and, if after having been admonished two or three times by the abbess or other sisters, she does not amend, let her eat bread and water on the floor before all the sisters in the refectory for as many days as she shall have been obstinate. If it seems advisable to the abbess, let her be subjected to even greater punishment. Meanwhile, as long as she remains obstinate, let the prayer be that the Lord will enlighten her heart to do penance. The abbess and her sisters, however, must beware not to become angry or disturbed on account of another's sin, for anger and disturbance prevent charity in oneself and in others.

If it should happen, may it never be so, that an occasion of trouble or scandal should arise between sister and sister through a word or gesture, let her who was the cause of the trouble, before offering the gift of her prayer to the Lord, not only prostrate herself humbly at once at the feet of the other and ask pardon, but also beg her simply to intercede for her to the Lord that He forgive her. Let the other sister, mindful of that word of the Lord, "If you do not *forgive* from *the heart*, neither will *your* heavenly *Father forgive you*," generously pardon her sister every injury she has done to her.

The sisters who serve outside the monastery may not delay for long unless some manifest necessity requires it. Let them conduct themselves virtuously and say little, so that those who see them may always be edified. Let them strictly beware of having suspicious meetings or dealings with others. They may not be godmothers of men or women lest gossip or trouble arise because of this. Let them not presume to repeat the gossip of the world inside the monastery. Let them be strictly bound not to repeat outside the monastery anything that is said or done within which could cause scandal.

If anyone should innocently offend in these two matters, let it be left to the prudence of the abbess mercifully to impose a penance on her. But if she does this through a vicious habit, the abbess, with the advice of her discreets, may impose a penance on her according to the nature of the fault.

[Chapter Ten]
The Admonition and Correction of the Sisters

Let the abbess admonish and visit her sisters, and humbly and charitably correct them, not commanding them anything that is against their soul and the form of our profession. Let the sisters, however, who are subjects, remember that they have renounced their own wills for the sake of God. Therefore, let them be firmly bound to obey their abbess in all the things they have promised the Lord to observe and which are not against the soul and our profession.

Let the abbess, on her part, be so familiar with them that they can speak and act with her as ladies do with their handmaid. For this is the way it must be: the abbess should be the handmaid of all the sisters.

Moreover, I admonish and exhort the sisters in the Lord Jesus Christ *to beware of all* pride, vainglory, envy, *avarice, care and anxiety about this world*, detraction and murmuring, dissension and division. Let them be always eager, however, to preserve among themselves the unity of mutual love which is *the bond of perfection.*

Let those who do not know how to read not be eager to learn. Let them direct their attention to what they should desire above all else: to have the Spirit of the Lord and His holy activity, to pray always to Him with a pure heart, and to have humility, patience in difficulty and infirmity, and to love those who persecute, blame, and accuse us, for the Lord says: *Blessed are those who suffer persecution for the sake of justice, for theirs is the kingdom of heaven.* But *whoever perseveres to the end will be saved.*

[Chapter Eleven]
The Custody of the Enclosure

Let the portress be mature in her manner of acting, discerning, and of a suitable age. Let her remain in an open cell without a door during the day. A suitable companion may be assigned to her who may take her place in everything whenever necessary.

Let the door be well secured by two different iron locks, with bars and bolts, so that, especially at night, it may be locked with two keys, one of which the portress may have, the other the Abbess. During the day let it never be left without a guard and securely locked with one key.

Let them most diligently take care to see that the door is never left open, except when this cannot be conveniently avoided. Let it never be opened to anyone who wishes to enter, except to those who have been given permission by the Supreme Pontiff or our Lord Cardinal. The sisters may not allow anyone to enter the monastery before sunrise or to remain within after sunset, unless demanded by a manifest, reasonable, and unavoidable cause.

If a bishop has permission to celebrate within the enclosure, either for the blessing of an abbess or for the consecration of one of the sisters as a nun, or for any other reason, let him be satisfied with as few and virtuous companions and assistants as possible.

Whenever it is necessary for other men to enter the monastery to do some work, let the abbess carefully assign a suitable person to the door, who may open it only to those designated for the work and to no one else. Let the sisters be extremely careful at such times not to be seen by those who enter.

[Chapter Twelve]

The Visitator, the Chaplain, and the Cardinal Protector

Let our Visitator always be taken from the Order of the Lesser Brothers according to the will and command of our Cardinal. Let him be the kind of person who is well known for his integrity and good manner of living. His duty shall be to correct any excesses against the form of our profession, whether these be in the head or in the members. Taking his position in an open area that he can be seen by others, let him speak with all and with each concerning what pertains to the duty of the visitation as he sees best.

We ask as a favor of the same Order a chaplain and a clerical companion of good reputation, of prudent discernment, and two lay brothers, lovers of a holy and upright way of life, in support of our poverty, as we have always mercifully had from that Order of Lesser Brothers, in the light of the piety of God and our blessed Francis.

Let the chaplain not be permitted to enter the monastery without a companion. When they enter, let them remain in an open area, in such a way that they can always see one other and be seen by others. They may enter for the confession of the sick who cannot go to the parlor, for their Communion, for the Last Anointing and the Prayers of the Dying.

Moreover, for funeral services, and on the solemnity of Masses for the Dead, for digging or opening a grave, or even for making arrangements, suitable and sufficient outsiders may enter, according to the prudence of the abbess.

Let the sisters be strictly bound always to have as our Governor, Protector, and Corrector that Cardinal of the Holy Roman Church who has been delegated by the Lord Pope for the Lesser Brothers, so that, always submissive and subject at the feet of that same holy Church and steadfast in the Catholic faith, we may observe in perpetuity the poverty and humility of our Lord Jesus Christ and of His most holy Mother and the Holy Gospel we have firmly promised. Amen.

> *Given at Perugia, the sixteenth kalends of October, in the tenth year of the Pontificate of Lord Pope Innocent IV.*
>
> *Therefore, no one is permitted to destroy this document of our confirmation or oppose it recklessly. If anyone shall presume to attempt this, let him know he will incur the wrath of Almighty God and His holy Apostles Peter and Paul.*
>
> *Given at Assisi, the fifth of the Ides of August, in the eleventh year of our Pontificate.*

Clare of Assisi (1194–1253)

Clare of Assisi, born twelve years after Francis to a noble family, made private vows of chastity and poverty before committing herself to the Gospel life. Clare's path to holiness was fostered by her mother. Clare's younger sister, Beatrice, recalled that "after Saint Francis heard of the fame of her holiness, he went many times to preach to her."[1] Beatrice and other eyewitnesses to Clare's youth testified at the time of her canonization that Clare and Francis continued to meet until she "acquiesced to his preaching, renounced the world and all earthly things, and went to serve God as soon as she was able."[2]

This was the beginning of their mutual relationship centered on living the life portrayed by Jesus in the gospel. Clare and Francis were unlikely soul mates. Clare was from the aristocratic society that held the power and controlled the land. Clare's mother Ortulana had the luxury of travel to the great pilgrimage sites of the medieval world. Her father, Favarone Offreduccio, and a band of seven knights from her extended family lived in or nearby the household where Clare was raised. The peasant class raised crops on their properties to feed them and their animals. The men supervised their work, protected their land, and acquired new properties with their swords. They also went to battle against the armies that threatened them and joined the crusades to rescue Jerusalem and the Holy Land from Saracen domination.

Francis's merchant-class family was beginning to overturn the inequities inherent in the feudal system by selling and trading goods enabling them to buy some of the trappings and privileges that the nobility had inherited. Pietro Bernardone, Francis's father, built a successful business in the cloth trade and might well have expected his son to follow his footsteps. After all, he had indulged Francis's desire to become a knight by buying him a horse and a costly suit of armor. Medieval historians estimate that each of them cost as much as a peasant laborer could earn in a year. Francis's experience fighting the nobles in Assisi's civil war and his consequent imprisonment led him to reverse his goals. Upon coming to recognize Jesus in the poor and realizing the evil and injustice of greed, he choose to be like the poor and marginalized. Because his heart was with the poor, Francis identified with society's *minores* and called his followers *fratres minores*.

Clare, too, under the tutelage of her mother Ortulana had witnessed the underside of the societal system and tried to relieve the misery of the poor by sharing from the surplus of her household. Although their families were in opposing camps, Clare and Francis each had a vision to make the world a more equitable place for all by rejecting the social system in which they were raised. The sources claim that Clare was an attractive woman whose inheritance made her a desirable marriage partner in a system where property married property to augment the family's land holdings. Clare chose to make herself ineligible for marriage by divesting herself of her property and taking a vow of virginity. Clare made these moves before Francis entered her story. Their meetings caught fire in her soul. Together with Guido, bishop of Assisi, Francis and Clare appear to have hatched a plot in which Clare was singled out and blessed by the bishop on Palm Sunday 1212. During that night, she escaped from her home and with a companion walked beyond Assisi's walls to be met by some of the brothers and received at the Portiuncula by Francis. Since Francis had been made a deacon, he had the authority to tonsure her hair marking her new way of life as a *conversi*.

Expecting resistance from the Offreduccio household, the brothers went with her to the nearby monastery of San Paolo delle Abbadesse in Bastia where she remained through Holy Week. The Benedictine property of the sisters there had been given the right of asylum protecting it from the constant warfare that characterized the era. When Monaldo, the head of Clare's household, arrived to return Clare to her home, she clung to the altar in the Benedictine chapel as a refuge against their violence. Monaldo and his knights did not dare to use force against her, or they would have been excommunicated from the church.

After Easter because Clare's heart was not at peace in the Benedictine community, Francis, Leo, and her cousin Rufino escorted her to a house of penitential women living at the church of Sant'Angelo in Ponzo. Here Clare experienced living in penance, a popular way of life for women and men in her time. After her sister Catherine, who became known as Agnes, came to join Clare, they relocated to the semi-abandoned church of San Damiano outside the walls of Assisi. At this point, the legendary qualities of Clare's story fade and her challenging work began to establish an enclosed life that did not revolve around property and ownership. Her new way of life is known in the early documents as Clare's privilege of poverty.

At San Damiano, Clare established a community that was not governed by an abbess but by the consent of the members under a leader who was elected to act as their servant. Because no dowry was permitted, women from all the classes were able to join and live with one another in mutual love. They lived on alms collected by Francis's brothers, the work of their hands, and the providence of God. Clare and her sisters wove cloth and used it to make corporals and altar linens used by the neighboring churches. All their goods were held in common, requiring the sisters to ask for special needs. Clare sought Francis's brothers for their spiritual care although this often became a burden for those who had chosen the mendicant lifestyle.

Francis gave Clare a simple form of life soon after she began living at San Damiano and personally guided the path she and her sisters began to follow. But when their juridical status became problematic after the Fourth Lateran Council in 1215, the papal legate and their protector, Cardinal Hugolino, gave Clare and the sisters at San Damiano a Constitutions in 1218. It defined a way of life for them affiliated to the established Order of Saint Benedict. As an ecclesiastical institution, it required enclosure. Hugolino's Constitutions proposed a monastery modeled on a medieval city enclosed by its stone walls. As protector of many new communities of religious women, Hugolino sought to guarantee their security and maintenance through their ownership of large amounts of property. Contrary to Hugolino's intent, Clare envisioned a form of life that would free her sisters for God without excluding them from the suffering and needs of those surrounding them. Her dream for the community to live without corporate ownership was realized on her deathbed in 1253 when Pope Innocent IV approved her Form of Life. With this document, Clare became the first woman to write and receive approbation for a rule of life.

Clare's efforts had been strengthened in 1234 when Agnes of Prague, the princess of Bohemia, chose to live in the manner of the Poor Ladies of San Damiano. Soon after the friars arrived in Prague in 1225, Agnes enlisted the support of her brother Wenceslaus to buy property and build a hospice for the sick poor. In 1232, Agnes obtained land to build a monastery for the Poor Ladies and a nearby *convento* to house the brothers.

With the eyes of the known world upon her, in 1234 Agnes, the most eligible woman in Eastern Europe, refused an arranged marriage with the Emperor Frederick II, the most powerful man of his time. In a public letter that is referred to as the First Letter to Agnes of Prague, Clare praised and blessed Agnes for her decision to become a Poor Lady. Clare framed her letter around the concept of exchange and articulated multiple reasons for Agnes to choose the things of heaven in preference to the goods of the earth.

At the time of Clare's second letter to Agnes in 1235, Cardinal Hugolino, as Pope Gregory IX, was keeping a watchful eye on new houses of women religious. Seemingly eager to guarantee their survival, he suggested that, in order to provide a stable income, Agnes combine the hospice that generated some income with the monastery. Agnes rejected such a plan because holding large properties was incompatible with the vision she shared with Clare to live without common ownership. In desperation, Agnes consulted Clare for advice and received Clare's response, "May you hold what you always hold, what you do may you always do and never abandon."[3] Clare directed Agnes to live according to the counsel of Francis's successor, Brother Elias. Clare reiterated to Agnes, "If anyone would tell you something else or suggest something contrary to your divine vocation, even though you must respect him, do not follow his counsel."[4]

Clare's Third Letter to Agnes in 1238 was precipitated by a crisis surrounding Gregory's directive for them to fast like the Cistercians, who ate very little meat. Gregory proposed to simplify the variety of practices in the new religious houses. He aimed to establish a uniform set of prescriptions patterned on the Benedictine model. One difficulty for Agnes was that it was impossible to raise vegetables and produce to eat the year round because of Prague's northern climate. Finding meat substitutes that were adequately nourishing and could be preserved for the winter months would be extremely difficult and costly. Clare advised that Agnes follow the admonition of Francis, prepare special foods for the feasts, and allow exceptions for those who do not have the strength or health to endure austere fasting. Clare's undemanding way with her sisters is made clear in the closing of her letter: "And I beg you in the Lord to praise the Lord by your very life, to offer to God your reasonable service, and your sacrifice always seasoned with salt."[5]

***

Toward the end of Clare's life in 1253, she sent Agnes a final letter expressing how the crucified Christ had become the center of her spiritual life. Clare's focus on the beatitude of heaven and introductory greeting to Agnes alluding to the lamb of God and the throne of God surrounded by the heavenly host suggest that Clare had pondered the nearness of her own death and resurrection. This letter summarizes her mystical teaching developed through the metaphor of the concave medieval mirror in which the clarity of the reflection is intensified as it moves toward the center. Clare equates the outside edges of the mirror with the poverty of Jesus' incarnation, the middle with the humility of his suffering, and the inner depth with the charity of his death and redemption of humanity.

Clare's four letters are a treasure of her spirituality based on the central mysteries of the Christian religion: incarnation, redemption, and resurrection. In addition to these letters, Clare wrote a *Testament* and *Blessing*. After Pope Innocent IV presented Clare and the Poor Ladies yet another Form of Life in 1247 based on the juridical precepts of the church, she wrote her own Form of Life according to the gospel way of Francis. It included her privilege of poverty and was blessed with the papal approval of Innocent IV in 1253. The following texts taken from Clare's letters to Agnes illustrate the centrality of the life of Jesus in her efforts to imitate and become transformed by the message of the Gospel. They also demonstrate the importance of divine and human relationships in Clare's spirituality beginning with her understanding of the relational God of the Trinity.

The First Letter to Agnes of Prague (1234)

To the esteemed and most holy virgin, Lady Agnes, daughter of the most excellent and illustrious King of Bohemia, Clare, an unworthy servant of Jesus Christ and *useless* handmaid of the enclosed Ladies of the Monastery of San Damiano, her subject and handmaid in all things, commends herself totally with special reverence that *she may attain the glory* of everlasting happiness.

I greatly *rejoice* and exult in the Lord on hearing the fame of Your holy conduct and irreproachable life, [a fame] that has wonderfully reached not only me but almost the whole world, and so not only I, but all who serve and desire to serve Jesus Christ, are able to rejoice. For, though You, more than others, could have enjoyed the magnificence, honor, and dignity of the world and could have been married to the illustrious Emperor with splendor befitting You and His Excellency, You have rejected all these things and have chosen with Your whole heart and soul a life of holy poverty and bodily want. Thus You took a spouse of a more noble stock, Who will keep your virginity ever unspotted and unsullied, the Lord Jesus Christ,

> Whom in loving, You are chaste;
>> in touching, You become more pure;
>>> in embracing, You are a virgin;
> Whose strength is more robust,
>> generosity more lofty,
> Whose appearance is more handsome,
>> love more courteous,
>>> and every kindness more refined.
> Whose embrace already holds you,
>> Who has adorned Your breast with precious stones,
>>> placed priceless pearls on Your ears,
>>> surrounded You completely with blossoms
>>>> of springtime and sparkling gems
>>> and placed on Your head
>>>> *a golden crown as a sign of Your holiness.*

Therefore, most beloved sister, or should I say, Lady worthy of great respect, because You are *the spouse and the mother and the sister* of my Lord Jesus Christ and are beautifully adorned with the banners of an undefiled virginity and a most holy poverty, be strengthened in the holy service of the Poor Crucified undertaken with a passionate desire.

> Who *endured* the suffering of the cross
>> for us all,
>> delivering *us from the power* of the prince
>>> *of darkness*
>> to which we had been enslaved by the disobedience
>>> of our first parent,
>> thus *reconciling* us to God the Father.
> O blessed poverty,
>> who bestows eternal riches
>>> on those who love and embrace her!

O holy poverty,
    God promises the kingdom of heaven
        and, beyond any doubt, reveals eternal glory
            and blessed life to those who have and desire her!
O God-centered poverty,
    whom the Lord Jesus Christ
        Who ruled and still rules heaven and earth,
            Who spoke and things were made,
                came down to embrace before all else!
He says: For the foxes have dens, *and the birds of the air have*
    nests, but the Son of Man, Christ, *has nowhere to lay His head,*
    but bowing His head He gave up His spirit.

If so great and good a Lord, then, on coming into the Virgin's womb, wanted to appear despised, *needy*, and poor in this world, so that people who were very poor and needy, suffering excessive hunger of heavenly nourishment, may become rich in Him by possessing the kingdom of heaven, *be very joyful* and *glad*, filled with a remarkable happiness and a spiritual joy! Because since contempt of the world has pleased You more than its honors, poverty more than earthly riches, You have sought to store up greater treasures not on earth but in heaven, *where* rust does not consume *nor moth destroy nor thieves break in and steal, Your reward is* very *rich in heaven*! And You are virtually worthy to be called *a sister, spouse and mother* of the Son of the Most High Father and of the glorious Virgin.

For I firmly believe that you know *the kingdom of heaven* is promised and given by the Lord only *to the poor* because she who loses what is temporal loses the fruit of love; that *it is not possible to serve God and money*, for *either the one is loved and the other hated*, or *the one* is served and *the other despised*; that one clothed cannot fight another naked, because she who has something to be caught hold of is more quickly thrown to the ground; that one who lives in the glory of earth cannot rule with Christ; and that it is easier for *a camel* to pass *through the eye of a needle than for a rich person* to enter *the kingdom* of heaven. Therefore, You have cast aside Your garments, that is, earthly riches, so that instead of being overcome by the one fighting against You, You will be able to enter the kingdom of heaven through *the straight path and the narrow gate.*

What a great and praiseworthy exchange: *to receive the hundredfold* in place of one, and *to possess* a blessed eternal life. Because of this I have led Your Excellency and holiness, as best I can, to beg with humble prayers *in the heart of Christ*, that You be strengthened in His holy service, progressing from good to better, *from virtue to virtue,* so that He Whom You serve with the total desire of Your soul may bestow on You the reward for which You so long. Therefore, as much as I can, I also implore You in the Lord, to include me in *Your* most holy *prayers,* Your servant, though *useless,* and the other sisters with me in the monastery, who are all devoted to You. With the help [of Your prayers] we are able to merit the mercy of Jesus Christ, so that, equally together with You, we may merit to enjoy the everlasting vision. Farewell in the Lord and *pray for* me.[6]

The Fourth Letter to Agnes of Prague (1253)

To her who is half of her soul and the special shrine of her heart's deepest love, to the illustrious Queen and Bride of the Lamb, the eternal King, to the Lady Agnes her most dear mother, and, of all the others, her favorite daughter, Clare, an unworthy servant of Christ and a *useless* handmaid of His handmaids in the monastery of San Damiano of Assisi: health and may she sing *the new song* with the other most holy virgins before the throne of God and the Lamb and *follow the Lamb wherever He will go.*

O mother and daughter, spouse of the King of all ages, if I have not written to you as often as both your soul and mine desire and long for, do not wonder at all or think that the fire of love for you glows with less delight in your mother's heart. No, this is the difficulty: the lack of messengers and the obvious dangers of the roads.

Now, however, as I write to your love, I rejoice and exult with you *in the joy of the Sprit,* O spouse of Christ, because, since you have totally abandoned the vanities of this world, like the other most holy virgin, Saint Agnes, you have been marvelously espoused to *the spotless Lamb, Who takes away the sins of the world.*

Happy, indeed, is she
to whom it is given to drink at this sacred banquet
so that she might cling with her whole heart
to Him
Whose beauty all the blessed hosts of heaven
unceasingly admire,
Whose tenderness touches,
Whose contemplation refreshes,
Whose kindness overflows,
Whose delight overwhelms,
Whose remembrance delightfully dawns,

Whose fragrance brings the dead to life again,
Whose glorious vision will bring happiness
to all the citizens of the heavenly Jerusalem,
which [vision],
    since He is the radiance of eternal *glory*
        is *the brightness of eternal light and*
        the mirror without blemish.
Gaze upon that mirror each day,
    O Queen and Spouse of Jesus Christ,
        and continually study your face in it,
    that you may adorn yourself completely,
        within and without,
            covered *and arrayed in needlework*
    and similarly adorned
        with the flowers and garments of all the virtues,
            as is becoming, the daughter and dearest bride
            of the Most High King.
Indeed,
    in that mirror,
        blessed poverty,
            holy humility,
                and inexpressible charity shine forth
        as, with the grace of God,
            you will be able to contemplate them throughout
            the entire mirror.
Look, I say, at the border of this mirror, that is, the poverty of
    Him
    Who was placed in a manger and wrapped in swaddling
    clothes.
    O marvelous humility!
    O astonishing poverty!
        The King of angels,
            the Lord of heaven and earth,
                is laid in a manger!
Then reflect upon, at the surface of the mirror,
    the holy humility, at least the blessed poverty,
        the untold labors and punishments
            that He endured for the redemption of the whole human
            race.
Finally contemplate, in the depth of this same mirror,
    the ineffable charity that He chose

to suffer on the tree of the Cross
    and to die there the most shameful kind of death.
Therefore,
that Mirror, suspended on the wood of the Cross,
    warned those passing by that here are things to be
        considering, saying:
        "All you who pass by the way, look and see if there
        is any suffering like my suffering!"
"Let us respond to Him," It says,
    "crying out and lamenting, in one voice, in one spirit:
        'Remembering this over and over
            leaves my soul sinking within me!'"

O Queen of our heavenly King, may you, therefore, be inflamed ever more strongly with the fire of love! As you further contemplate His ineffable delights, riches and perpetual honors, and, sighing, may you cry out from the great desire and love of your heart:

"Draw me after you,
    let us run in the fragrance of your perfumes,
    O heavenly Spouse!
I will run and not tire,
    until *You bring me into the wine-cellar,*
    until Your *left hand is under my head*
        and Your *right hand will embrace me* happily,
    You will kiss me with the happiest *kiss of Your mouth."*

Resting in this contemplation, may you remember your poor little mother, knowing that I *have inscribed* the happy memory of you indelibly *on the tablets of my heart,* holding you dearer than all others.

What more? In your love may the tongue of the flesh be silent; may the tongue of the Spirit speak and say this: "O blessed daughter, because the love that I have for you can never be fully expressed by the tongue of the flesh," it says, "what I have written is inadequate. I beg you to receive my words with kindness and devotion, seeing in them at least the motherly affection that in the fire of charity I daily feel toward you and your daughters to whom I warmly commend myself and my daughters in Christ."

On their part, these daughters of mine, especially the most prudent virgin Agnes, our sister, recommend themselves in the Lord to you and your daughters as much as they can.

Farewell, my dearest daughter, with your daughters until we meet at the throne *of the glory of the great God*, and desire [this] for us.

As much as I can, I recommend to your charity the bearers of this letter, our dearly beloved Brother Amatus, *beloved of God and men*, and Brother Bonaugura. Amen.[7]

Colette of Corbie (1381–1447)

Colette of Corbie lived in the era of the enormous crises of the Hundred Years' War and the Great Schism in the church. She is remembered for restoring the primitive Form of Life written by Clare, which was approved by Pope Innocent IV in 1253 and replaced by the Rule of Saint Clare written by Pope Urban VI in 1263. The privilege of poverty, that is the right to live as enclosed women without owning common property, was lost with Urban's rule, which gave reign to a number of Second Order monasteries acquiring the wealth and affluence that characterized much of monastic life before the poverty movements of Francis and Clare. Colette also worked to reform the friars in Burgundy, for she believed their role as spiritual directors was essential to the renewal of the women's monasteries.

Colette was born in Picardy in northeastern France, but because it was ceded to Burgundy, she carried out most of her renewal work in Burgundy in eastern France. Colette was in her early teens when her parents died. During a seven-year period of restlessness, she distributed her possessions to the poor and, in turn, joined the Beguines, the Benedictines, and the Urbanist Poor Clares. In 1402 she returned to her native Corbie and became a Franciscan tertiary, living as a hermit in a small house attached to the parish church. Still dissatisfied, within four years she went to Nice. During her time as a lay hermit, Colette sensed a call to reform the women and men Franciscans in France. A sympathetic friar, Henry of Baume, assured her of the validity of her new vocation. At the age of twenty-five, she set out to consult the Avignon pope, Benedict XIII, who had two sisters who were Poor Clares in Spain. He received Colette, understood her dream, and made her general abbess over all the monasteries she might found or reform. She came to be called "Mother and abbess of the reform."

Colette founded her first monastery in 1410. She had founded eleven monasteries by the time she had written her Constitutions in 1434. Working tirelessly to simplify the way the Poor Clares were living and filled with years of experience Colette admonished her sisters:

> For love of the great poverty of our Lord, who never had a dwelling place on earth, be content to have those places which are necessary, without superfluity, and which are, as far as you can manage it, humble, lowly and small, made of wood or clay mixed with straw, unless you find constructions already built of stone. Dispose of these in humility and lowliness, in accordance with our poverty. There will be no need to incur any great expense or large debts for such small buildings.[1]

Both Pope Benedict XIII and Pope Martin VI granted Colette generous concessions to promote her reforms. She was given permission to move around on visitations as she judged necessary, to keep four friars to serve each monastery which she could transfer or depose when she located substitutes. William of Casale, the minister general of the Friars Minor in 1434 granted her authority to change both friars and sisters from one house to another. He also gave her permission to have a room annexed to the church in which she could attend Mass and visit with the people at all times without a companion present. James of Bourbon, king of Naples and Sicily, became one of her strongest supporters. Two of his daughters joined Colette's reform. During her travels, she made many contacts with influential persons who opened doors for her work of reform.

Two of Colette's contemporaries left written biographies. Her confessor Peter of Vaux wrote a biography just before her death, and Sister Perrine, one of her sisters and companions, wrote another life of Colette in 1471. Both of them are hagiographies to be used during the process of her canonization, so they embellish the extraordinary aspects of her life. Nevertheless, legends abound concerning Colette's reputation for sanctity, which attracted lagging communities to welcome her reforms throughout France, Germany, Spain, Portugal, and Italy. Even without her direct interventions, Colette's widespread activity created exaggerated reports about the reach of her success, such as the claim by her contemporary, Oliver Marche, that she had reformed 325 monasteries.

Colette was surrounded by stories of miraculous events throughout her lifetime. Her spirituality is distinguished by long periods of solitude and prayer rooted in the theological virtues. Colette's ideals of poverty and prayer were formed early in her life when she was guided by the Friars of the Observance in France. She did not innovate reform but adapted Clare's Form of Life for her time and place in order to protect it, implying in her Constitutions that later there could be other reforms.

Colette's spirituality characterizes the Franciscan movement centered on the suffering Christ of the passion. Experiencing Christ's anguish and pain in long hours of prayer, she wept, groaned, and refused nourishment. In her vivid meditations, Colette visualized graphic details about Christ's passion and crucifixion. Typical of the phenomenon of the mystics during this eschatological age pointing to the end of the world, Colette felt the pains of Christ in her hands, feet, and side during Holy Week and on Good Friday. Many of her devotions were also linked to the Eucharist. Her extraordinary physical suffering is the result of a prevailing image of a God of justice judging a sinful people.

Peter of Vaux, an eyewitness and one of Colette's biographers said she entered death as if she were entering a hermitage, closing her eyes, and plunging into silence. Her canonization was initially delayed through the heat of the division between the Observant and Conventual Franciscans. She was declared a saint 360 years after her death in Gant.

***

> Surviving written works include Colette's letters, her reflections on the rule of Clare entitled *Sentiments*, and her 1438 *Constitutions*, which accents poverty and austerity. A summary of her spiritual teaching, duplicated by Henry of Baume, has been accepted by the Colettine sisters as Colette's *Testament*. It was translated into English and circulated by the Poor Clare Colettines of Roswell, New Mexico. Excerpts from that document, which concern the three evangelical vows—obedience, poverty, and virginity —exemplify Colette's spirit of reform.

From *The Testament of St. Colette*

On Obedience

> Take note, my beloved daughters, that you have been called by grace to perfect obedience, so as to obey in all things all the time so long as there is no sin. Jesus Christ did just that right up to his death.
>
> For it does not suffice to obey sometimes and in certain things only, but until death and in all things that are not at odds with God nor opposed to one's own soul nor the holy Rule, and this after the

example of our merciful Redeemer who made himself obedient for us right up to his death. And in the same way, we ought to obey unto death.

And let us not prefer our judgment to that of our superiors. For Jesus Christ who is true wisdom itself, submitted himself to Joseph and to his sweet Virgin Mother.

The truly obedient person ought to take into account only the work of true obedience performed purely for God and (do it) with as much reverence as if the obedience had been received from the sweet lips of Jesus. And the more lowly the command by human standards, the more precious before God is reverent obedience to it.

And the truly obedient person ought to dread losing out on obedience more than some physical dying, after the example of our blessed Savior Jesus Christ of whom St. Bernard used to say: "Remember, my Brothers, that Jesus Christ held it a dearer thing to lose his life in his bitter Passion than to lose obedience to God his Father."

Nothing but evil comes of disobedience. About that, a saint has said again: "The prayer of an obedient person is worth more than one hundred thousand prayers of a disobedient one." If we obey God, and our superiors for God's sake, God himself will obey us in all our good desires.

So throw off your own will, then, for it is the only fuel for the fire of hell.

Among all the virtues, I commend holy obedience to you first of all, for in it is found the fullness of charity when one renders obedience to a creature in all things for the love of the Creator.

Oh, may we be able to die with Jesus on the cross in this virtue and to obtain life eternal! Amen![2]

On Poverty

After the renunciation of self in full obedience, our Savior wills that we carry the cross every day. This is our vow of holy poverty, the demanding cross of desiring nothing under heaven save him alone who carried the cross upon his shoulders and deigned by his love to die on that cross after having been pierced with nails, crowned with thorns, defiled with spittle and crushed with blows, and his side laid open.

O holy poverty! The clothing of our Redemption! Precious jewel! Sure sign of salvation! It is to poverty that the King gives full possession of the kingdom of heaven which lasts forever. O you children of Adam and Eve, why do you not love this precious stone, this noble pearl whose price equals in worth and dignity the (very) kingdom of heaven and is greater than worlds without end.

Alas! And more than one hundred thousand times, alas!—you could have this poverty more easily and doubtless at a better price than the paltry world full of sins, snares, traps, treachery and uncleanness for which often enough people forfeit the kingdom of heaven, winning only eternal pains and torments.

O my dearly loved Sisters,—love, love, love very perfectly this noble and precious and most excellent virtue. Gospel poverty loved by God and loathed by the world.

And after the example of Jesus Christ who did not have here below anywhere to rest his precious head, and after the example of our glorious Father St. Francis and our Mother Madame St. Clare, be grandly content with the form of your poor habit given you by your Rule and hold all the rest suspect, such as books, chaplets, thread, needles, pins, jewels of any kind, kerchiefs, veils and other things (given) for your particular use to which your special affection might cling.

But have only what is really necessary, and all things held in common. In this present life be content with just what is necessary, the more lightsomely to arrive at the true goods of the heavenly kingdom of which you already have possession under the title of holy poverty freely promised and vowed for the love of God.

The kingdom of God cannot be wanting to us if we are not wanting to the Lady holy Poverty.

By this cross of poverty, I mean this: to live in continual abstinence, never eating meat; to fast every day; to have bare and cold feet; to sleep on a hard bed. I mean poverty of garments; and to be content with limited amounts of plain foods; and finally, your manual and spiritual work.

Whoever is found at the hour of death to be a proprietor whether in actual fact or by the will to be so, will be excluded from the kingdom of heaven.

Live and die truly poor, my well-beloved daughters, as did our sweet Savior upon the cross for us. And if, nonetheless, few people esteem poverty, that is for you the occasion to love it the more.

After Madame holy Obedience in the Order, I commend to you above all, poverty, the straight ladder by which one mounts lightly, without counterbalance or difficulty, into God's own proper kingdom thanks to the complete renunciation of all transitory things for the love of our so-good God who promises the kingdom and does not deceive us.[3]

On Virginity

Then our Lord said "And follow Me." By this I understand that we ought to follow Jesus Christ, the Lamb without spot, a Virgin and Son of a virgin, by full purity of heart and body until death. By this true vow of angelic chastity, one is the loyal spouse of Jesus Christ in virtue of the faith promised and even now given in the pact made in the hands of superiors, the lieutenants of God on earth—a pact made in the presence of witnesses: the blessed Virgin Mary, St. Francis, St. Clare, and all the saints, and the witnesses present who hear the promise of holy Profession made by which one obtains the remission of all sins and the full assurance of life eternal.

O noble and very precious virtue of chastity!—loved by God as his loyal spouse, honored by the angels as the bride of their Lord and King, highly praised by all the saints, and grandly approved in holy Scripture! You will bear this noble crown to the kingdom of heaven for the true nuptials with your true Spouse, Jesus.

O most excellent garden full of truly good plants! You never allow thorns to grow there, or nettles or poisonous herbs, and you do not admit there any ill-smelling rubbish. Oh! How good is your firm cloister!

How loyal and good the Gate-keeper who faithfully guards you and allows no one to enter your enclosure save only the true messengers of your true Spouse and King!

One well understands (in this) the symbolic expression of holy Scripture: O very beautiful flowering trees bearing this noble fruit by which the King of true love is worthily served in his kingdom!

O worthy and excellent virtue! It is impossible to understand very well your price and your value and the excellence of your victory and to write about them. God alone is your reward in the vision and divine enjoyment (of himself!) This virtue, after the others (of obedience and poverty), I recommend to you in its order and merit before God, O lover of holy chastity, so that you will have honor and merit at the great judgment through her.

But the souls who violate this truth which they have pledged before God and do not make proper reparation will undergo terrible tortures in eternal damnation.

Let happy penance be done before the end of this present life, for this alone, my dearly loved daughters, can bring about full reconciliation with the well-beloved Father of those for whom our merciful Redeemer lived in most high obedience, poverty and virginity, himself the only Fountain of all virtues.[4]

Catherine of Bologna (1413–1463)

In Italy the fourteenth-century renewal of the life of the Second Order took place without changing the Rule of Urban IV. In 1418 when the monastery of Ursula in Milan adapted the Rule of Saint Clare, it sparked a number of other monasteries in Northern Italy to abandon the Urbanist Rule in favor of Clare's Form of Life. One of the monasteries adopting Clare's primitive rule was in Ferrara where Catherine Vigri went to be educated in the court of the Este family. Born in Bologna in 1413 to an influential and wealthy family, Catherine grew up in the new Renaissance culture. Accordingly, she became popularized as Catherine of Bologna. In 1431, she entered a Third Order Regular community in Ferrara that had taken Clare's Form of Life.

While in Ferrara, Catherine began writing descriptions of the memories of her visions. Her paintings, miniatures, and an illuminated breviary are still preserved. She also could play several instruments and compose music. In 1434, during a skirmish over jurisdiction, Catherine and thirteen other sisters left the monastery in Ferrara for Corpus Christi monastery in Bologna. Some of the external problems of the time stemmed from the responses to Franciscan preaching that sometimes took place outside the boundaries of accepted ecclesiastic institutions. Because the intention was to establish an order that did not follow the Ferrara reform, the first abbess of Corpus Christi was not supposed to come from Ferrara. Nonetheless, Catherine was elected as abbess. Soon the new Poor Clare foundation of Corpus Christi developed internal divisions between Catherine's defense of poverty without common property and the sisters who wanted to own farms for economic security.

Catherine's spiritual autobiography, *The Seven Spiritual Weapons*, is a short text, only sixty-four pages in the English version translated by Hugh Feiss, o.s.b., and Daniela Re. Intended for the novices of Corpus

Domini, it is both didactic and visionary, stemming from her spiritual experience. Catherine describes what she considers as seven spiritual weapons: (1) diligence or solicitude in doing good, (2) mistrust of self, (3) trust in God, (4) memory of the pilgrimage of Christ, (5) *memento mori*, (6) memory of the good works of paradise, and (7) memory of Holy Scripture. Sarita Tamayo's unpublished dissertation, *Hiddenness and the Imitation of Christ in Caterina Vigri's "Le Sette Armi Spirituali,"* is the only in-depth study of this work in the English-speaking world. The following comments flow from Tamayo's textual analysis of Catherine's work.

Religious writing in the vernacular began to circulate at the turn of the fourteenth century, especially by women of means. Catherine combines elements of the monastic tradition of spiritual combat with the Franciscan concentration on the imitation of Christ. Because Catherine experienced God as veiled, she may have come to understand God as veiled or hidden in the passion. She changed Francis's teaching that Christ reveals God to emphasize instead how Christ's passion conceals who God is. For this reason, hiddenness becomes a central component of her mysticism. The beginning part of her book treats the first six weapons while the remainder discusses the seventh weapon and concludes with Catherine's account of her own spiritual struggles.

Catherine's experience of temptations, obedience, and the breakdown of her will shapes her view of spiritual combat and the imitation of Christ as an ascetic process. These experiences lead her to a deeper understanding of the hiddenness of God. Thus her own spiritual path influences how she teaches others about the path to God through the spiritual weapons. Both the second and third weapons address trust, which is necessary in persevering through the tribulations of the spiritual life. Self-trust is one type and trust in God is another. She perceived doubt to be the opposite side of trust. To illustrate this precept, Catherine relates a story indicating that the more responsibility a person has, the more they need God. Those in doubt ask for the judgment of others because they mistrust their own self-perceptions.

The most important weapon is the fourth, for without remembering Christ's life and passion through contemplation, none of the other weapons has value. The passion is at the heart of Catherine's spiritual path. Employing the "eyes of the intellect," the sisters will come to understand and to know God. The passion of Christ is an object of contemplation as well as a model for action. Seeing the world through the passion leads to living the passion. This is how contemplation and action fuse as a single activity. The passion functions for Catherine as a mother, lover, spouse, and guide nurturing and protecting her. She teaches her novices that the passion of Christ is the path of love.

Catherine's second spiritual weapon has a modern ring to it, for she cautions her sisters to turn to God rather than to claim their accomplishments for themselves, echoing St. Francis's cry, "My God and my all." In the fourth weapon, Catherine's reflection on Jesus' passion touches her soul deeply and results in an affective outpouring of love. The passage illustrates the importance of the incarnation in Franciscan prayer and the movement from the exterior senses to the interior mind culminating in the heart.

* * *

From *The Seven Spiritual Weapons*

The Second Spiritual Weapon

> The second weapon is mistrust of self, that is, to believe firmly and without doubt that one could never do anything good by oneself, as Christ Jesus said: "Without me you can do nothing" (Jo 15.5). Nor could one resist successfully the fury of the infernal enemies for their cunning wickedness. And if someone does confide in her own wisdom and will not do this, let her know for certain that by just judgment she will fall into great ruin and let her be aware that just as this enemy is more malicious than we, so is this wickedness. And therefore, the second weapon for fighting against this enemy tells one not to trust in oneself, and blessed is she who has this noble quality in herself. And the more that person is in a greater state of virtue or exercises the office of prelate, the more she has need for it.
>
> I received this example from an old and very proven religious who said that when he was a prelate, whenever he was about to begin some task pertaining to his office of governing the monastery, if he did it according to his inclination, God most often allowed some anxiety or tribulation and if on the contrary, he did it according to the counsel and inclination of the majority of his subjects, it always turned out well and often he found himself consoled. Now, then, how could the subject, especially one newly entered into religion, have such presumption that she would want to live by her own lights and her foolish fervour and not rather by the counsel and will of her superior and mistress so that the virtue of holy humility might shine in her and the weapon of self diffidence might be wielded by her? To the praise of Christ. Amen.[1]

The Fourth Spiritual Weapon

The fourth is the memory of the glorious pilgrimage of that immaculate lamb, Christ Jesus, and especially his most holy death and passion, keeping always before the eyes of our minds the presence of his most chaste and virginal humanity. This is the best means for winning each battle, and without it, we will not achieve victory over our enemies. Every other weapon will achieve little without this one which surpasses all the rest.

O most glorious passion and cure for all our wounds, O mother most faithful, who lead your children to the heavenly Father. O true and gentle refuge in all adversities. O supportive nurse who guide child-like minds to the heights of perfection. O refulgent mirror, who illumine those who look at you and recognise their deformities. O impenetrable shield who most smartly defend those who hide behind you. O manna suffused with every fulsome sweetness, you are the one who guards those who love you from every deadly poison. O ladder most high who raise up to infinite goods those who fly upward upon you. O true and restorative hospice for pilgrim souls. O ever flowing font who provide drink for the thirsty who are inflamed for you. O abundant sea for those who row on you in their derelict boat. O sweet olive tree who stretch your branches through all the universe. O spouse, gentle to the soul which is always in love with you and does not look toward others.

And so exercise yourselves untiringly in this, dearest and kindest sisters, and gaze upon yourselves in his radiant splendour that, in this way, you can conserve the beauty of your souls. Truly this passion is that wise mistress who will lead you, most beloved novices to the beauty of all the virtues, and in this way, you will attain the mantle of victory. To the praise of Christ. Amen.[2]

Veronica Giuliani (1660–1727)

Although Veronica Giuliani describes her experience of God without theological definitions and structures, the clear mystical teaching of her *Diaries* has led her to be considered as a Doctor of the Church. Veronica was born in Mercatello, Italy, the seventh daughter of Francesco and Benedetta, and manifests the precocious spirituality of many of the great saints. Veronica's mother died after the death of two of her daughters. Before she died Veronica's mother gathered her five living daughters to her, dedicating each of them to one of the five wounds of Jesus. Veronica, about seven years old at the time, was dedicated to the wound in Jesus' side. Throughout her life, she experienced a flame of love in her heart. Her writings trace the progression of her spiritual experience, which culminated in what she describes in "The Purgatory of Love" as the "three fires" in her soul.

In 1678 Veronica made her religious profession in the Capuchin branch of the Poor Clare community of Cittá di Costello in Umbria. She continued to feel exceptional moments of God's love. One year on the feast of Pentecost, she felt as if she had been consumed and could only repeat, "O Love, O Love, O Love." On Good Friday in 1681, she experienced the imposition of the crown of thorns upon her head, which stimulated her desire to suffer and expiate her sins through penance. Her life of extraordinary mystical phenomena related to the passion of Christ culminated in 1697 when she received the stigmata of the five wounds in her flesh. In order to authenticate her experience, in the years following Veronica was obliged to undergo tedious examinations, trials, and humiliations. She was isolated in the infirmary for fifty days, deprived of active and passive voice in the community for seventeen years, deposed as mistress of novices for a time, and isolated from outside visitors and correspondence. Veronica endured years of inner purification and darkness. When the ban was lifted from her in 1716, she was elected abbess.

Eighteen years after Veronica's death, her cause for canonization was introduced and she was canonized in 1839. Far from the mystics of the medieval period, Veronica's spirituality is characteristic of the extravagance of the baroque era. Her writings reflect mortification, self-punishment, constant temptations, and terrifying visions of hell. What appears to be her intense desire to appease a wrathful God seems to counter the joy, freedom of spirit, and positive regard for the gifts of life that characterize the Franciscan spirit. To appreciate Veronica is to understand that this image is shaped by her day-to-day experience of internal struggles, temptations, and doubts. At the heart of redemptive suffering and pain is the joy of resurrection. Upon the request of her confessors and superiors, Veronica recorded her inner experiences in the form of a diary that comprises about twenty thousand manuscript pages, accessible as five and one-half volumes of the *Acta Sanctorum*. Only a few of her texts have been translated into English.

Franciscan friars had served in the town of Mercatello since the thirteenth century. During Veronica's youth three of her sisters entered the foundation of Urbanist Poor Clares in Mercatello. These local and personal connections made Veronica at home with both Francis and Clare. Because Città di Costello was an Urbanist foundation, the monastery had a source of revenue and goods including a substantial stock of books written by Franciscans before 1726. They provided readings for common prayers. The penitential framework of Francis and Clare formed her spirituality and they became central figures in Veronica's spirituality. She made constant references to their lives and writings and their image of God became her own. Veronica adopted Clare as her "holy Mother" who became a subject of her visionary experience. Extensive scholarship continues to be written in Italy about Veronica. The following selections from Veronica's *Diaries* illustrate how the lives of Francis and Clare became significant features of her spirituality as they continue to be throughout the Franciscan Tradition.

***

From *Diaries*

January 1694 during a spiritual exercise called
"thirty-three days of suffering"

> The Lord seemed to tell me that *He was entrusting me to the care of our mother St. Clare. She seemed to embrace me and make me understand that she would consider me one of her dearest daughters.* When she had said this, everything vanished. I came back to myself feeling both happy and sad. I could find nothing more to console me. . . . I've been here seventeen years and can't seem to see the slightest sign of what I saw there. I'm referring to the strictness of life and all that. I am probably the worst of all. . . . *As for the consolation I received when God entrusted me to our mother St. Clare, it was so satisfying that I can't explain it in writing.*[1]

August 1696 while reading in the refectory after doing
an act of kindness for her sisters

> As I was reading, I began to feel the ardent love of our holy mother Clare. When I came to the word *love*, I repeated it over and over, although it appeared only once in the book. I added some words of praise, even though nothing was written there. They kept telling me this, but I wasn't aware of doing it! When I read the words *spouse of Jesus*, I began to speak of our holy mother's great desire to be united and alone with her spouse Jesus. I repeated the word *spouse* many times. I kept saying it over and over, even though it wasn't in the book. I felt such sweetness and delight that I wanted to keep reading forever. My heart rejoiced, and when I said the word *spouse* it leapt for joy.[2]

May 1697 on the feast of the Ascension upon hoping for
the spiritual renewal of her sisters

> The Blessed Virgin led me first to our mother St. Clare, who told me that now she acknowledged me as her daughter. I commended our entire community and all the sisters to her care. She told me to remain calm, that everything would be renewed through the wounds of Jesus, and that I must be a guide to all. Then she kissed me tenderly . . . and went around with me to all the saints present. All of them gave me the kiss of peace.[3]

January 1698 when she feared being elected as
the chapter of elections approached

> The Supreme Pontiff with a golden pen which he kept dipping into
> the side of Jesus. He was writing in a book. . . . When he finished,
> the pope made a sign to the bishop to take a cross and book and
> give them to me. . . . The Lord showed me that the cross represents
> the burden of being superior of the community and the book stands
> for the holy Rule. He showed me *that I must restore the primitive ob-*
> *servance of St. Clare, and I should put away all doubts because He would*
> *help me.*[4]

August 1705 upon mystically renewing her vows on the feast of Saint Clare

> It seemed to me that the Blessed Virgin and our mother St. Clare
> were holding in their hands a habit like the one we wear. Suddenly
> it turned white as snow. But at the same time I seemed to be wearing
> an old rag. I couldn't imagine what this meant. Then I understood
> the reason, I had never been a true daughter of St. Clare. I had worn
> the habit, but that's all. I had been a religious only in name and
> habit. Such great confusion, my God! . . . At that point I realized
> that the Blessed Virgin was praying to St. Clare for me. . . . Sud-
> denly *the Blessed Virgin and our mother St. Clare clothed me in that*
> *bright habit.* . . . I was struck by the obligations of those who profess
> this Rule and the life of perfection they must lead. . . .
>
> It seemed to me that the Blessed Virgin wanted me to renew my
> profession. . . . *And as she entrusted me to St. Clare as daughter, she*
> *once again proved herself a true mother.*[5]

August 1714 on the feast of Saint Clare

> Our holy mother St. Clare was standing next to Mary and calling
> me. . . . The Blessed Virgin told my guardian angels *to take me by*
> *the hand and lead me to the feet of our holy mother St. Clare, so that she*
> *might receive me once again as her daughter.* The angels received the
> message. As they brought me to St. Clare, *I saw a ray of light coming*
> *from the heart of Mary. It came to rest in the heart of St. Clare, who was*
> *looking at me with love in her eyes. At first she seemed not to recognize*
> *me as her true daughter. But then, obedient to Mary's command, she gave*
> *me the kiss of peace and lovingly acknowledged me as her daughter.*
>
> I begged her to accept all the sisters as her daughters, especially
> those whom I didn't know how to guide in the true way of religious

life. I asked her to supply for me in the sight of the Most High. *I asked her blessing on the entire order, that we might all be one heart and one soul in God.*

As I was making these requests, *the ray of light came to me. Then it returned to the heart of St. Clare, who brought me back to the feet of the Blessed Virgin and seemed to be awaiting orders from her.* . . . Our holy mother St. Clare received the command to take me as her daughter. At once I committed myself to a new life. . . .

From the hearts of Jesus and Mary came a ray of light that went directly to the heart of St. Clare. Once again she gave me a warm embrace and the kiss of peace. *Then those rays came to this heart. All at once they returned to the heart of St. Clare, then immediately to the hearts of Jesus and Mary.*[6]

August 1717 while preparing for the feast of Saint Clare with a novena

I understood that *the Blessed Virgin Mary was about to give me our holy mother St. Clare as a guide. She would be the one to teach me true and perfect observance of our holy Rule.*[7]

August 1717 at the time of communion when her premonition was fulfilled on the feast of Saint Clare

It seems to me that Mary entrusted me to our holy mother St. Clare. She turned to me and said she was giving me the holy mother *as guide and teacher, that I might learn the true path of perfect and exact observance of our holy Rule.* Then she confirmed me in the office of superior.[8]

The Third Order of
the Brothers and Sisters
of Penance

An Exhortation of St. Francis
to the Brothers and Sisters of Penance

In the Name of the Lord!

[Chapter One]
Those Who Do Penance

All those who love the Lord *with their whole heart, with their whole soul and mind, with their whole strength* and love their neighbors as themselves, who hate their bodies with their vices and sins, who receive the Body and Blood of our Lord Jesus Christ, and who produce worthy fruits of penance.

O how happy and blessed are these men and women while they do such things and persevere in doing them, because *the Spirit of the Lord will rest upon them* and *make* Its home and *dwelling place* among them, and they are children of the heavenly Father Whose works they do, and they are spouses, brothers, and mothers of our Lord Jesus Christ. We are spouses when the faithful soul is joined by the Holy Spirit to our Lord Jesus Christ. We are brothers to Him when we do *the will of the Father who is in heaven.* We are mothers when we carry Him in our heart and body through a divine love and a pure and sincere conscience and give birth to Him through a holy activity which must shine as an example before others.

O how glorious it is to have a holy and great Father in heaven! O how holy, consoling to have such a beautiful and wonderful Spouse! O how holy and how loving, gratifying, humbling, peace-giving, sweet, worthy of love, and, above all things, desirable: to have such a Brother and such a Son, our Lord Jesus Christ, Who laid down His life for His sheep and prayed to His Father, saying: *Holy Father, in your name, save those whom you have given me in the world; they were yours and you gave them to me. The words that you gave to me I have given to them, and they accepted them and* have believed *in truth that I have come from you and* they have known *that you have sent me. I pray for them and not for the world.* Bless and *sanctify them; I sanctify myself for them. I pray not only for them, but for those who will believe in me through their word that they might be* sanctified *in being one as we are. I wish, Father, that where I am, they also may be with me that they may see my glory in your kingdom.* Amen.

[Chapter Two]

Those Who Do Not Do Penance

All those men and women who are not living in penance, who do not receive the Body and Blood of our Lord Jesus Christ, who practice vice and sin and walk after the evil concupiscence and the evil desires of their flesh, who do not observe what they have promised to the Lord, and who in their body serve the world through the desires of the flesh, the concerns of the world and the cares of this life:

They are held captive by the devil, whose children they are, and whose works they do. They are blind because they do not see the true light, our Lord Jesus Christ. They do not possess spiritual wisdom because they do not have the Son of God, the true wisdom of the Father. It is said of them: *Their wisdom has been swallowed up* and *Cursed are those who turn away from your commands.* They see and acknowledge, know and do evil, and knowingly lose their souls.

See, you blind ones, deceived by your enemies: the flesh, the world, and the devil, because it is sweet for the body to sin and it is bitter to serve God, for every vice and sin flow and *proceed from the human heart* as the Lord says in the Gospel. And you have nothing in this world or in that to come. And you think that you will possess this world's vanities for a long time, but you are deceived because a day and an hour will come of which you give no thought, which you do not know, and of which you are unaware when the body becomes weak, death approaches, and it dies a bitter death. And no matter where, when, or how a person dies in the guilt of sin without penance and satisfaction, if he can perform an act of satisfaction and does not do so, the devil snatches his soul from its body with such anguish and distress that no one can know [what it is like] except the one receiving it.

And every talent, ability, *knowledge, and wisdom* they think they have will be taken away from them. And they leave their wealth to their relatives and friends who take and divide it and afterwards say: "May his soul be cursed because he could have given us more and acquired more than what he distributed to us." Worms eat his body and so body and soul perish in this brief world and they will go to hell where they will be tortured forever.

In the love which is God we beg all those whom these words reach to receive those fragrant words of our Lord Jesus Christ written above with divine love and kindness. And let whoever does not know how to read have them read to them frequently. Because *they are spirit and life,* they should preserve them together with a holy activity to the end. And whoever has not done these things will be held accountable *before the tribunal of* our Lord Jesus *Christ on the day of judgment.*

Angela of Foligno (1248–1309)

During Francis's lifetime, many laywomen and laymen wished to follow his gospel way of poverty and penance. Angela of Foligno led a contemplative life as an active woman affiliated with the penitential movement. Her writings reveal the intensity of her mystical life, centered around the "God-Man" who suffered on the cross. Through prayer, Angela came to have visionary experiences of Jesus' life, suffering, and death on the cross. She does not describe a method of prayer, but rather identifies the virtues that God loves and, therefore, that Jesus chose to embrace—poverty, suffering, and contempt. These are the virtues she experienced while in God, and the virtues she passed on to followers whom she called her spiritual sons. As one of the most remarkable mystics in the Franciscan Tradition, Angela is known as the "nightingale of the ineffable," for she describes what cannot be described of her life in God.

Angela represents the spirituality of the first century of the Franciscan movement following Francis. In his history of Western Christian mysticism, Bernard McGinn describes this time as introducing a form of mysticism that reinterprets traditional mysticism in light of Francis's bodily revelation of the crucified Christ. The new mysticism of the thirteenth century emphasizes meditation on the mysteries of Christ's life as a distinct means to access God. The affections begin to take on a key role in prayer both within and beyond the Franciscan movement. Angela's experience presents another new characteristic of prayer in which excessive states of rapture became common, especially among female mystics. Angela became one of the early mystics from this period who demonstrated the new forms of ecstasy that distinguish late medieval mysticism from traditional monastic experience.

Angela was born in 1248 to a prosperous family, married in 1270, and had several children. According to her writings, her conversion began about fifteen years later when she became aware of her sinfulness. In 1288, the death of her husband, sons, and mother freed her to devote her life entirely to God. Around 1290, she made a pilgrimage to Assisi, began to wear the simple dress of the penitents of Assisi, made private vows of chastity and poverty, sold her goods, and used the money to help Umbria's poor and destitute. While traveling on pilgrimage to the Basilica of Saint Francis in Assisi with her companion Masazuola, Angela had a transforming spiritual experience. She heard the Holy Spirit speak to her in intimate and endearing terms:

> My daughter, my dear and sweet daughter, my delight, my temple, my beloved daughter, love me, because you are very much loved by me; much more than you could love me.
> . . . I love you so much more than any other woman in the valley of Spoleto. I have found a place to rest in you; now you in turn place yourself and find your own rest in me.[1]

Later when she stood in the lower level of the basilica before the stained glass window with the stained glass panel depicting Jesus in the womb of Mary paired with a panel of Francis in the womb of Jesus, Angela had another overpowering experience of God. In her ecstasy, Angela shrieked and began to take off her clothing in imitation of Jesus who came into the world and died without possessions. Brother Arnaldo, a relative of hers and a friar serving in the basilica, escorted her out because of the spectacle she was creating and forbade her to return.

In 1292 shortly after the beginning of Brother Arnaldo's ministry in Foligno, he began to wonder about the passion within this stormy woman and started to question Angela about the nature of her spiritual experiences. This began his composition of the *Memorial*, a record of how God worked in her soul. Between 1292 and 1296, Angela recounted for Arnaldo her experiences of God since the time of her conversion. The *Memorial* is a collection of her memories, dictated in Angela's Umbrian dialect and recorded by "Brother A." in Latin to give it ecclesiastical authority. Between 1297 and 1303, he finished recording his version of the progress of Angela's mystical path, including her culminating experiences of both the absence and presence of God. Brother A. completed Angela's *Memorial* by arranging it into thirty steps and seven supplementary steps, perhaps in imitation of the spiritual tracts organized into seven steps, such as Saint Bonaventure's *Soul's Journey into God*.

Angela did not dictate any new experiences after 1303. About that time, Ubertino of Casale, one of the prominent leaders of the Franciscan

Spiritual movement, became increasingly outspoken as a reformer. Although Angela's *Instructions* are versions of her teachings on the spiritual life, perhaps to a group of penitential tertiaries in Foligno, Angela's message echoes the concerns of Ubertino and the Spirituals for a return to the Gospel life practiced by Francis and his primitive followers. Angela died in 1309 and was declared blessed in 1701. Her burial place, the church of Sant'Anna in Foligno, is a popular pilgrimage site to this day. This church also houses the shrine of Angelina of Montegiove, a fourteenth-century tertiary.

***

The *Memorial* is an exceptional mystical text in that it provides much more evidence of Angela's interior life than of her external activities. Her writing is filled with visual and often erotic images to convey the intimate story of God's work in her soul. On the other hand, the *Instructions* are didactic and intended to move her followers to take up the Gospel life in the footprints of Jesus. They demonstrate Angela's way of holiness amid the activity of the world. The first excerpt from the *Memorial* tells how, like Francis, Angela found God in a world of lepers. It takes place on Maundy Thursday and echoes Saint John's account of Eucharist as service. The revelations of Angela's experience are graphic and may be offensive to modern readers who do not accommodate her radical behavior to her passionate pursuit of God.

While the *Memorial* indicates Angela's effort to be faithful to her experience through the hand of a male scribe, contemporary scholars view the *Instructions* as a compilation composed by more than one scribe. Nonetheless, Angela's message through both texts continues to be relevant for our time. They represent the earthy quality of her spirituality, her acute awareness of the presence of God, and her desire to share her thirst for God with her followers. Angela's writings illustrate how the message of Francis of Assisi stirred the laity of the thirteenth century to spiritual depth.

From the *Memorial*:

Finding Christ among the Lepers

This is what she told me: On Maundy Thursday, I suggested to my companion that we go out to find Christ: "Let's go," I told her, "to the hospital and perhaps we will be able to find Christ there among the poor, the suffering, and the afflicted." We brought with us all the head veils that we could carry, for we had nothing else. We told Giliola, the servant at that hospital, to sell them and from the sale to buy some food for those in the hospital to eat. And, although initially she strongly resisted our request, and said we were trying to shame her, nonetheless, because of our repeated insistence, she went ahead and sold our small head veils and from the sale bought some fish. We had also brought with us all the bread which had been given to us to live on.

And after we had distributed all that we had, we washed the feet of the women and the hands of the men, and especially those of one of the lepers which were festering and in an advanced stage of decomposition. Then we drank the very water with which we had washed him. And the drink was so sweet that, all the way home, we tasted its sweetness and it was as if we had received Holy Communion. As a small scale of the leper's sores was stuck in my throat, I tried to swallow it. My conscience would not let me spit it out, just as if I received Holy Communion. I really did not want to spit it out but simply to detach it from my throat.[2]

The World Is Pregnant with God

Afterward [God] added: "I want to show you something of my power." And immediately the eyes of my soul were opened, and in a vision I beheld the fullness of God in which I beheld and comprehended the whole of creation, that is, what is on this side and what is beyond the sea, the abyss, the sea itself, and everything else. And in everything that I saw, I could perceive nothing except the presence of the power of God, and in a manner totally indescribable. And my soul in an excess of wonder cried out: "This world is pregnant with God!" Wherefore I understood how small is the whole of creation—that is, what is on this side and what is beyond the sea, the abyss, the sea itself, and everything else—but the power of God fills it all to overflowing.[3]

Standing or Lying in the Midst of the Trinity

On the other hand, God draws me to himself. But if I say that he draws me to himself with gentleness or love or anything which can be named, conceived, or imagined, that is completely false; for he does not draw me by anything which can be named or conceived by even the wisest in the world. Even if I say that it is the All Good which draws me, I destroy it. For in this state, it seems to me that I am standing or lying in the midst of the Trinity, and that is what I see with such darkness. This draws me more than anything else I have experienced so far, more than any good ever spoken of before. So much more so that there is nothing to compare to it. Everything I say now about it seems to say nothing or to be badly said.[4]

The Bed to Rest On

At this moment, my desire is to sing and praise:

> I praise you God my beloved;
> I have made your cross my bed.
> For a pillow or cushion,
> I have found poverty,
> and for other parts of the bed,
> suffering and contempt to rest on.

When I, brother scribe, asked her for a better explanation of what she had said, Christ's faithful one added: This bed is my bed to rest on because on it Christ was born, lived, and died. Even before man sinned, God the Father loved this bed and its company (poverty, suffering, and contempt) so much that he granted it to his Son. And, in concord with the Father, the Son wanted to lie in this bed and continued to love it. This is why this bed is my bed, namely, the cross where Christ suffered in his body and much more in his soul, and on it I have placed myself and I have found my rest. On this bed I believe I die and through this bed I believe I am saved. I cannot describe the joy which I expect from those hands and feet and the marks from the nails which pierced them on that bed. Humming, I say to the Son of the Blessed Mary: "What I feel there are no words for; what I see I never want to depart from. Because for me to live is to die. Oh, draw me then to yourself!"[5]

The Vision of "The One Who Is"

. . . Furthermore, I saw the One who is and how he is the being of all creatures. I also saw how he made me capable of understanding those realities I have just spoken about better than when I saw them in that darkness which used to delight me so. Moreover, in that state I see myself as alone with God, totally cleansed, totally sanctified, totally true, totally upright, totally certain, totally celestial in him. And when I am in that state, I do not remember anything else.

On one occasion, while I was in that state, God told me: "Daughter of divine wisdom, temple of the beloved, beloved of the beloved, daughter of peace, in you rests the entire Trinity; indeed the complete truth rests in you, so that you hold me and I hold you."[6]

* * *

From the *Instructions*:

The Highest Form of Love

The perfect and highest form of love, one without defects, is the one in which the soul is drawn out of itself and led into the vision of the being of God. For when the soul is so drawn out of itself and led into this vision, it perceives how every creature has its being from the one who is the supreme Being; how all things and all that exists come to be through the supreme Being; how God is indeed the only one who has being, and that nothing has being unless it comes from him. The soul drawn out of itself and led into this vision derives from it an ineffable wisdom, one that is deep and mature. In this vision, the soul discovers that only what is best comes from the supreme Being and it cannot deny this, for it sees in truth that all things that are from him are excellently made; things are done badly when we have destroyed those things he made. This vision of the supreme Being also stirs up in the soul a love corresponding and proportionate to its object, for it teaches us to love everything which receives existence from the supreme Being. It likewise teaches us to love everything which has being, that is, every creature, rational and nonrational, with the supreme Being's own love. It teaches us to love rational creatures, especially those we know are loved and cherished by him. When the soul sees the supreme Being stoop down lovingly toward creatures, it does likewise.[7]

Blessed Francis, Example of True Poverty

What a perfect example is given to us by our glorious father, blessed Francis, who possessed the ineffable light of the truest poverty! He was so filled, and more than filled, with this light, that he opened up a very special way and showed it to us all. I cannot think of any saint who demonstrated to me more remarkably than he did the way found in the Book of Life, the model being the life of the God-man, Jesus Christ. I know no other saint who more remarkably set himself to follow this way. He set himself with such determination along that path that his eyes never left it, and the effects could plainly be seen in his body. And because he set himself with such total determination to follow this path, he was filled to overflowing with the highest wisdom, a wisdom which he filled and continues to fill the whole world.[8]

The Cross of Christ and the Book of Life

O dearest son, if you wish to have the light of divine grace, and a heart free from all care, if you wish to curb all harmful temptations, and to be made perfect in the ways of God, do not tarry in running to the cross of Christ. Truly there is no other way for the sons of Christ to manage to find God, and having found him, to hold on to him, but in the life and the way of the suffering God and man which, as I have been in the habit of saying and which I reaffirm here, is the Book of Life, the reading of which no one can have access to except through continual prayer. Continual prayer elevates, illumines, and transforms the soul. Illumined by the light perceived in prayer, the soul sees clearly the way of Christ prepared and trodden by the feet of the Crucified; running along this way with an expanded heart, it not only distances itself from the weighty cares of the world but rises above itself to taste divine sweetness. Then it is set ablaze by divine fire. Thus illumined, elevated, and set ablaze, it is transformed into the God-man. All this is achieved by gazing on the cross in continual prayer.[9]

The Birth of Christ in the Soul

O dearest one, part of my soul, I desire with my whole self that I might hear tell of you, that in your soul you desire, as the saints did, and do now, the Child who is soon to come and be born; and that he be born in your soul according to my desire.

O dearest one to my soul, strive to know yourself, because, in truth, I do not believe that there is a greater virtue on earth. Try to rid yourself of every thought, every imagination harmful to your soul. Prepare yourself, as is my desire, to receive this Son about to be born, because, in truth, he is the one who will grant you knowledge of yourself. He will be the salvation of your soul, which I desire from the depths of my soul. And now may the Consoler console you, my soul![10]

The Three Schools of Prayer

It is in prayer that one finds God. There are three schools, that is, three types of prayer, without which one does not find God. These are bodily, mental, and supernatural.

Bodily prayer takes place with the sound of words and bodily movements such as genuflections. I never abandon this type of prayer. For sometimes when I want to devote myself to mental prayer, I am impeded by my laziness or by sleepiness. So I turn to bodily prayer, which leads to mental prayer. It should be done with attention. For instance, when you say the Our Father, you should weigh carefully what you are saying. Do not run through it, trying to complete a certain number of them, like little ladies doing piece work.

Prayer is mental when meditating on God so occupies the soul that one thinks of nothing but God. If some other thought comes to mind I no longer call such prayers mental. Such prayer curbs the tongue and renders one speechless. The mind is so totally filled with God's presence that it cannot think or speak about anything except about God and in God. From mental prayer, then, we move on to supernatural prayer.

I call prayer supernatural when God, bestowing this gift upon the soul and filling it with his presence, so elevates the soul that it is stretched, as it were, beyond its natural capacities. In this type of prayer, the soul understands more of God than would seem naturally possible. It knows that it cannot understand, and what it knows it cannot explain, because all that it sees and feels is beyond its own nature.

In these three schools of prayer you come to know who you are and who God is. From the fact that you know, you love. Loving, you desire to possess what you love. And this is the sign of true love: that the one who loves is transformed, not partially, but totally, into the Beloved. But because this transformation does not go on without interruption, the soul is seized by the desire to seek all the ways by which it can be transformed into the will of the Beloved, so it can return again to that vision. It seeks what was loved by the Beloved. God the Father provided a way for us to attain this transformation and this way is through the Beloved, that is, through God's own Son, who he made the Son of poverty, suffering, contempt, and true obedience.[11]

The Third Order Regular

Mary of the Passion (1839–1904)

Helene de Chappotin was born and spent her childhood in Nantes, the youngest of ten children in a faith-filled family. She demonstrated an innate love for the poor and a sense to move quickly to implement what she considered the "great causes." A number of family deaths including that of her mother necessitated her family to move to Brittany. Her grief and anguish brought her to reexamine the direction of her own life. Later she reflected upon this uncertainty as the time of her "infidelities." In 1860, she joined the Poor Clares in Nantes who had just opened a monastery. Although poor health caused her stay with them to be brief, there she became certain of her call to religious life. She came under the guidance of Fr. Petit who had recently helped to found the new Congregation of Mary Reparatrix. She entered at the age of twenty-four and received the name Mary of the Passion. The nineteenth century was dedicated to Mary, the Mother of God.

Although it was not a missionary congregation, Mary of the Passion was sent as a novice to Madurai in India. Within a few years, she became the provincial. Throughout her travels in southern India, she met the problems of mission life: the challenge of bridging relations in a world with diverse religious beliefs, unfamiliar cultures and languages, as well as coping with the disparities and rivalries of local populations. Painful internal difficulties in Madurai where the Congregation of Mary Reparatrix had worked for the betterment of the people for nearly six years eventually resulted in the separation of Mary of the Passion and nineteen other sisters from the Reparatrix community.

At the age of thirty-seven, Mother Mary of the Passion and three companions traveled to Rome to obtain permission from Pope Pius IX to found a new congregation of Missionaries of Mary. The congregation was authorized in 1877, and Monsignor David, bishop of Brieu, France, welcomed them to open a novitiate in France. Mary of the Passion returned to Brittany and began to receive new candidates. She went back to Rome and, desiring to affiliate with a religious order, turned to the minister general of the Order of Saint Francis. In 1882 in the midst of the celebration of the seventh centenary of St. Francis, she was received into the Third Order Regular. After enduring another trial during which she was investigated, deposed, and later reinstated as superior general, her institute officially became a Third Order Regular congregation. The new name of Franciscan Missionaries of Mary was approved by Pope Leo XIII in 1885.

Affiliated with the Franciscan Order and with her Constitutions revised and juridically approved, Mary of the Passion returned to St. Briene in Brittany. Upon seeing the good that had been accomplished in her absence, she is said to have exclaimed, "Oh Lord, while I prayed and wept, you have made the desert bloom." And Mary of the Passion's desert continued to bloom during the twenty remaining years of her life. Large numbers of young women sought admission and requests for the ministry of her sisters came from across the globe. By the time of her death, she had established foundations in Asia, Europe, Africa, and both Latin and North America. The congregation swelled to three thousand members.

Mary of the Passion's vision of mission was rooted in eucharistic contemplation. She taught that mission took place in the heart long before any activity was undertaken. She felt that her congregation was shaped for service, not of just one type, but any service that women could do that would be a means of evangelization. Once when asked what her apostolate was, Mary of the Passion answered, "What you as a woman can undertake is your limit." Community life was also of utmost importance to Mary of the Passion, and she wanted each community to make their home a Nazareth in which the sisters could support each other. Imitation of Mary as a way within the way to God was central to her missionary spirituality.

Before her death, Mary of the Passion knew "the grace of martyrdom" experienced by seven of her sisters who were massacred in the Boxer uprising of 1900. She spoke of them as "my seven joys and seven sorrows." In 1898, she was asked to send missionaries to China to administer and serve in an orphanage, a hospital, and a dispensary. Seven women were sent: Marie Hermine of Jesus, age 33, French; Marie della Pace, 24, Italian; Marie Chiara, 27, Italian; Marie de Nathalie, 35, French; Marie de St. Just, 33, French; Marie Adolphine, 33, Dutch; and Marie

Armandine, 27, Belgian. Within a year after their arrival, the Boxer Rebellion broke out and the governor issued a manifesto to kill all Christians. Two bishops, two priests, and the seven Franciscan Missionaries of Mary were imprisoned. On July 9, 1900, soldiers invaded the prison, dragged them to a tribunal for a mock trial, and the governor ordered their massacre. Their bodies were mutilated and their severed heads were displayed on pikes at the North gate of the city of Shansi. The thirty-three who were massacred there were beatified by Pope Pius XII in 1946 and were among those who were canonized on October 1, 2000, by Pope John Paul II.

The Franciscan Missionaries of Mary came to Quebec in 1892 to establish their first North American house. In 1903 a group of them came to the United States to serve the immigrants from Canada. Where they saw need they tried to supply what was deficient and established an orphanage in Woonsocket, Rhode Island. By 1912 they had spread through southern New England to staff schools, care for orphans, and serve the Canadian, Italian, and Portuguese immigrants. Later they worked among populations of African Americans, Hispanics, and Native Americans. In 1917 they built a house in Providence, Rhode Island, and in 1929 added a novitiate. They continued to grow throughout the remainder of the twentieth century. Today the Franciscan Missionaries of Mary comprise the largest group of Third Order Franciscan sisters in the world. Currently, they have around seven thousand members who are present in seventy-eight countries on six continents. Mother Mary of the Passion was beatified October 20, 2002.

Mary of the Passion wrote legislative documents, liturgical meditations, reflections on the sisters' way of life, prayer, and the apostolate as well as biographies of saints and numerous letters to the sisters. Recently her spiritual writings, which often are notes or letters to her spiritual director, the Franciscan friar Raphael Delarbe, have been made accessible in book form. Her writings mirror her vision of the beauty and mystery of God, her understanding that love is the center of everything that exists, and that the trinitarian God personifies this love. She understands the Scripture to reveal the same process of love. Mary of the Passion describes love as the starting point from which flow the great mysteries of the Incarnation, Crucifixion, Eucharist, and mission. She portrays Eucharist as the sacrament of mission because here the Christ who has emptied himself appears powerless but upholds the world as its Savior. Mission becomes the permanent radiation of the presence of Jesus. The following excerpt and the commentary by a community member,

Marie-Thérèse de Maleissye, is a reflection on universal mission, the identifying character of the Franciscan Missionaries of Mary.

* * *

From *Fifteen Days of Prayer with Mary of the Passion*

Mission: Total Commitment for the Salvation of the World

Mary of the Passion's first experience of a call to the missions had occurred during her childhood. It was when one of her father's fellow-students, now a bishop of the Amerindians, had paid the family a visit.

"One day," she tells us, "the good bishop began to arouse my interest in the pagans. 'They know nothing about Jesus or Mary. Isn't that sad, little Helen?' [. . .] I replied, 'I don't want to leave Mummy!' My mother objected vigorously. However the bishop continued, 'The pagans don't know either Jesus or Mary.' [. . .] At last, heavy-hearted at the sacrifice I was making, I knelt down and said, 'Very well, my Lord, I will be a missionary.' I think this was a genuine promise on my part, but later on, I did not think of honouring my commitment. It was God's doing rather than mine; He was at work within me urging me on."

It was indeed at God's urging that she would follow her path, learning gradually, through a succession of discoveries, what God wanted to accomplish in her and through her. First came the sudden, overwhelming revelation of God's beauty and the beginning of the dialogue with Him, which was the basis of her whole life: *"I will always love you more than you will ever love Me."* Then there was the conferring of her new name like a consecration, which drew her to follow Christ in his Paschal Mystery.

For her part, at that juncture she could only foresee her offering taking place in the silence of the cloister; but God continued to urge her forward. "Passion, I am sending you off," she was suddenly told by the superior of the Reparatrix Sisters shortly before her departure for India. Her response was equally terse: *"I will go wherever you send me."* So all that she had experienced so far was to find its fulfillment in the distant mission field! She had been sent in Jesus' wake "to bring the Good News to the poor," "to seek and to save that which was lost." Her whole life, even its most concrete details, was to be a sharing in the mission of Him whom the Father had sent: "As the Father has sent Me, even so I send you" (Jn 20:21). In exemplary fashion she would have to tread the path leading from Nazareth to Calvary before emerging into the light of Easter. She would live its material poverty, its moral isolation, its contradictions and opposition, the setback of the Cross. In this way she would bestow life, like the grain of wheat which, if it consents to die, brings forth much fruit.

In the work which she was led to initiate, Mary of the Passion would never forget the platform on which this enterprise was constructed: her union with the sacrificial Lamb, "Who bore our afflictions and offered his life as a ransom for many" (Is 53). For her, mission would always be seen, not as a primary objective, but rather as a consequence of her unreserved commitment to Christ, in the mystery of His Incarnation and Passion. For her, as for Francis of Assisi, mission revealed itself as the outcome of their vocation to love.

One fundamental article of the first Constitutions of her Institute expresses this clearly in the language of her time:

As our Lord Jesus Christ became man and immolated Himself on the Cross for the salvation of souls, the Franciscan Missionaries of Mary will dedicate themselves to expiation and the apostolate, offering themselves as victims to God for the Church and for souls. They will establish themselves according to the desire of the Holy See in even the most distant and dangerous foreign missions (Const. No. 3).

There, expressed in a few lines, we have the chief characteristics of mission as envisioned by Mary of the Passion: the vital self-offering is inseparable from the apostolate; mission has no geographical limits, it depends on the requests from the Church; dangers and risk are all part of mission. And since it means total availability and a response to the appeals made to the Church and in the Church, mission, according to Mary of the Passion, cannot choose its field of apostolate in advance. She herself had been a missionary in a specific region, Madurai, in the south of the subcontinent. But as soon as God had moved her on to a new path and then on to Rome, her outlook expanded to include the uttermost limits of the Church. In the first Plan that she drew up for the Missionaries of Mary in 1877 she did not hesitate to write: . . . *the objectives of the Institute making it universal.*

In 1882 she was even more specific. Writing to the Sisters who were still in India she said she wanted them to be: . . . *true missionaries, ready, for the love of our Lord, to go from Jerusalem to Rome like the Apostles. I believe that your Sisters in Europe are prepared to go anywhere, just as they are ready to remain in the most wretched little corner: there you have the only true missionary spirit. Any other, like one that clings to such and such a place or loyalty, to Africa rather than to*

Europe, to America rather than to Asia, is really only self-love hiding under so-called apostolic zeal. The true apostle does not concern himself with places; he goes from north to south and from south to north wherever he is called for the glory of the Name of his God.

The vision of universal mission was linked to her self-offering for the Church, which gave her the Church's horizons to be her own. Many years later, Vatican II's Constitution on the Church (*Lumen Gentium*) would describe them thus: "All persons are called to belong to the new People of God. This People, therefore, remaining one and only one, is to be spread throughout the whole world, and to all ages, in order that the design of God's Will may be fulfilled: He made human nature one in the beginning and had decreed that all His children who were scattered should be finally gathered together as one" (cf. Jn 11:52) (*Lumen Gentium*, No.13). . . .

There was one conviction in particular that the foundress often expressed: *Our native land is the whole earth!* And on this earth there would always be risks to be run and unknown dangers to be confronted. Risk-taking is an integral part of mission and so missionaries must not be afraid of facing up to them. On the contrary, they must always be ready and willing to take them on with good will. . . .

From the contrasts of unity found in Mary of the Passion's life, which was both mystical and apostolic, a message of universal relevance stands out: mission is indivisible. It is life, the ready availability of all baptized persons to allow themselves to be sent forth by God to wherever their individual vocation was calling them. Far beyond all specifically apostolic activity, it is the very expression of the Christian identity of those baptized and confirmed, taking love out to the world.

In today's society, characterised by globalisation—which is not without its perils—this Christian vocation must be able to blossom and to find an appropriate field of ministry.

John Paul II, in his encyclical, *"Redemptoris Missio"* (1990), emphasises the scope of the new fields opening up to the presence and witness of Christians. Work, as well as tourism, would take members of the Church "towards regions where Christianity is unknown and occasionally banished and persecuted. The startling developing of the mass media, the globalisation of culture and of finance—everything is calling for new ways of expressing one's faith in Christ. The many situations of injustice and disregard for human rights summon us all to share in the struggle for justice and peace.

In circumstances such as these, mission, as envisaged by Mary of the Passion in its universal dimension, takes on a prophetic role. It means unreserved involvement in the life of the Church and in the mission of Christ, the Redeemer. It calls the Christian to be united with Christ, "rooted and built up in Him, supported by faith and overflowing with thanksgiving" (Col 2:6).

It is a call that banishes fear and opens the door to hope.[1]

Marianne Cope of Molokai (1838–1918)

Mother Marianne Cope worked with the Belgian priest Damien de Veuster for five months in Molokai before he died of leprosy. Damien had spent sixteen years among those afflicted with leprosy before the Board of Health selected her to continue the work he had begun. With her sisters, she devoted herself to care for and to improve the lives of those suffering from Hansen's disease, or leprosy as it was known in Mother Marianne's time. She was fifty years old when she came to Molokai and remained there for thirty years. Mother Marianne was beatified in Rome in May 2005.

She was born in Germany in 1838 as Barbara Koob; her family name was changed to Cope upon their immigration to the United States. She grew up in Utica, New York, where she met the Sisters of Saint Francis. In 1862 at the age of twenty-four, she joined the Sisters of the Third Franciscan Order of Saint Francis of Syracuse, New York, one of six congregations who trace their origins to Philadelphia's Bishop John Neumann. Given the name Marianne, she served as a teacher and principal in the state of New York and later helped to establish two of the first hospitals in central New York: St. Elizabeth's in Utica and St. Joseph's in Syracuse. In 1870, she became the nurse-administrator of Saint Joseph Hospital in Syracuse, a former saloon and dance hall the sisters had converted into a fifteen-bed hospital in 1869. Because Sister Marianne insisted that cleanliness would prevent the spread of infections, Saint Joseph's stood apart from other hospitals for its order and cleanliness.

As administrator of St. Joseph Hospital for six years, Mother Marianne was able to stabilize it as the first hospital to survive in Syracuse. She employed innovative management techniques to provide better service to patients. Under her leadership, the College of Medicine in Geneva, New York, relocated as the College of Physicians and Surgeons at the newly established Syracuse University. Mother Marianne accepted its medical students for clinical instruction at St. Joseph's. She insisted, however, that it was the right of patients to decide if they were willing to be brought before the students. Although many in the medical profession at this time were hesitant to treat patients who were "outcasts," such as alcoholics, Mother Marianne refused to permit discrimination in the hospital's admission policies. Before nursing schools were established in the United States, Mother Marianne worked with the doctors from one of the nation's most progressive medical colleges. Here she learned practical information about hospital systems, nursing techniques, and pharmacy. This experience coupled with her innate intelligence, energy, and winning ways account in part for her success in Hawaii.

In 1877 Mother Marianne was elected to follow Mother Bernardina, the congregational foundress, as general minister. She was reelected to a second three-year term in 1881. Her term marked a turning point in the life of the congregation by beginning a mission to the Hawaiian people, especially for those afflicted with leprosy. In 1883 at the request of the Hawaiian King Kalakaua and Queen Kapiolani, Father Leonor Fouesnel sent letters to the United States in search of a community of women religious who would care for patients with leprosy. On receiving his letter, Mother Marianne recalled that her "interest awakened" and she felt "an irresistible force driving me to follow this call."[1] When the priest stopped in Syracuse on a canvassing trip for missionaries from the United States, he described Hawaii's medical needs to the entire community. When Mother Marianne asked for volunteers, thirty-five professed sisters and all of the novices volunteered. Mother Marianne and the council selected six sisters to establish a mission in Hawaii. She intended to help them get established and then return to Syracuse to complete her term. In the interim, she prepared Sister Antonia Eulenstein to fill the office in her absence.

When the long journey by train and then across the ocean by steamer was completed and the ship docked, the sisters, later referred to as "angels of mercy," were warmly welcomed by Father Leonor, many dignitaries of state, and the minister of foreign affairs, Walter Gibson, who became Mother Marianne's valuable advocate in the years ahead. Contrary to the extravagant promises given to them, upon their arrival nothing was ready. Construction of the convent had just begun, but Walter Gibson located a house for them.

Mother Marianne learned that the sisters were to care for two hundred patients in the Branch Hospital at Kakaako in the Honolulu harbor. The compound that was built to house one hundred served as a large receiving station for persons suspected of having Hansen's disease. The conditions they found were lamentable. The resident steward was cruel to the patients and antagonistic toward the sisters. The sisters reported finding unsanitary conditions, neglect of the patients, and immorality, for when the sisters returned to their residence in the evenings, the hospital became a kind of brothel. In 1884 the sisters were given full charge of the hospital. That same year they founded Malulani Hospital, the first general hospital on Maui. The next year, they established Kapiolani Home on Oahu as a place to care for the children born to mothers with leprosy and to keep them from becoming infected. Two years after her arrival on the islands, Mother Marianne was decorated with the medal of the Royal Order of Kapiolani for all she had accomplished to help Hawaii's suffering outcasts.

In 1886 when Father Damien came to Honolulu for medical treatment, Mother Marianne and her sisters began to care for him. She promised to continue his work in Kaluapapa on Molokai, the island where more than one thousand persons with leprosy had been exiled. Although Mother Marianne served in Kakaako from 1844 to 1888, she left to open the C. R. Bishop Home on Molokai for homeless women and girls with leprosy. While the government officials continued to oppose spending money uselessly on the poor victims on Molokai, Mother Marianne worked tirelessly to improve their conditions. She and her sisters "purified" the buildings with hot water, disinfectants, and hard scrubbing. The residences of the patients were painted to make their living quarters look clean and pleasant. The areas around their drab dwelling places were landscaped with a variety of trees and flowering plants transforming its prison-like atmosphere to a home for a family of outcasts. The trees also provided recreational areas for the people and served as protection from the storms on Molokai.

Mother Marianne took charge of Boys Home from 1889 to 1895 and rebuilt it. Later the Boys Home was renamed Baldwin Home in honor of its chief benefactor. She did not perform miraculous physical cures for the sick and disfigured victims of leprosy, but she restored their human dignity, made their lives more comfortable, and loved them like a mother. Two sisters who were coming to work in Molokai happened to be on a boat with Robert Louis Stevenson who stayed there with them for a week and donated a piano "so there will always be music."[2] Mother Marianne remained there until her death in 1918.

The legacy of Mother Marianne continues in Hawaii as well as in other states. Mother Marianne's sisters are now known as the Sisters of

St. Francis of the Neumann Communities following the union and merger of four of the original congregations formed by Bishop Neumann. They have committed themselves to continue the spirit and vision of Mother Marianne in Hawaii as they focus on the care of people at the end of their lives through two inpatient hospices, adult services, and educational services. Although the number of patients with Hansen's disease today are few, Mother Marianne's sisters continue their presence in Kalaupapa still caring for former patients who have chosen to remain in their familiar surroundings for the remainder of their lives. Far ahead of current medical knowledge and practices about infectious diseases, Mother Marianne's stringent procedures regarding hand-washing and sanitation, safeguarded her sisters. No sister working with her has ever contracted leprosy.

The harvest of Mother Marianne's work continues in other ways, touching lives of people on all the islands of Hawaii and elsewhere. Although no longer owned or operated by the sisters, Malulani Hospital, known today as Maui Medical Center, is the oldest and second largest state-operated medical facility. St. Francis Hospital in Honolulu and St. Francis West, opened in 1927 by the sisters, operate now as Hawaii Medical Center and Hawaii Medical Center West to serve Hawaii's healthcare needs. In New York state, the sisters continue to operate medical centers in Utica, Syracuse, and Poughkeepsie.

The Sisters of Saint Francis continue to be enriched by the legacy of their diverse ethnic cultures. Sister Marion Kikukawa, general minister during their 140th anniversary in 1999 wrote, "Our commitment is no different from that of Mother Marianne. In the spirits of Saints Francis and Clare of Assisi, she embraced with great affection her own family and her sisters in community even under most trying circumstances. Whether she was laboring in a factory, administering a hospital, serving in congregational leadership, dealing with royalty or bureaucracy, or gently tending to the broken lives of outcasts in Hawaii, Mother Marianne was on fire with the God who loved her and whom she loved."[3] At the time of their anniversary, the congregation issued this directional statement: "With the same spirit that breathed through Francis and Clare, we proclaim ourselves on fire with a passion for building community wherever we live and minister."

* * *

Sister Mary Laurence Hanley of the Syracuse Franciscans and O. A. Bushnell, have written a biography, *Pilgrimage and Exile: Mother Marianne of Molokai* (Honolulu: University of Hawaii Press, 1991), which is placed in the context of the Franciscan mission to the islands of Hawaii. Sister Mary Laurence is director of Mother Marianne's cause for canonization at the headquarters in Syracuse. Dr. Bushnell was a member of the Historical Commission for the Cause of Mother Marianne and a former professor of microbiology at the University of Hawaii. The following article, "A Spiritual View of Mother Marianne Cope," written by Sr. Grace Anne Dillenschneider appeared in translation by Gilda Sisera in the Vatican newspaper *L'Osservatore Romano* on May 14, 2005, at the time of her beatification. It articulates some of Mother Marianne's virtuous qualities.

From "A Spiritual View of Mother Marianne Cope"

The church has recently recognized Mother Marianne Cope, OSF, as a woman of exceptional holiness and faith as witnessed by her dedication to the most afflicted of God's people. Mother Marianne would never have dreamed in her life that such an honor would be hers.

"Should I live a thousand years I could not in ever so small a degree thank God for His gifts and blessings. . . . I do not expect a high place in heaven—I shall be thankful for a little corner where I may truly love God for all eternity." This quote from Mother Marianne Cope's letter to her nephew epitomizes Mother Marianne's spirit and life. She was a woman who placed God and God's holy will at the center of her life, and who always spoke of Him in terms of gratitude. Her words are also an expression of her humility and her self-effacing love that was expressed in courageous, compassionate service.

Mother Marianne did not see herself as a special person. All of the work she undertook in her life was done with great reverence for people, with faith in God and a desire to fulfill God's will in her life. Whether she was teaching, serving as an administrator of a school or hospital, serving in leadership positions in her Religious Community or cleansing the wounds of those suffering the effects of leprosy (Hansen's disease) her attitude was that she was simply doing the will of God and caring for His people.

She did not look upon her service to the most afflicted of God's people as heroic. She considered herself a sister to all in her Franciscan tradition. In a 1905 letter written to Jean Sabate, a traveling writer, Mother Marianne wrote, "God giveth life; He will take it away in His own good time. In the meantime, it is our duty to make life as pleasant and as comfortable as possible for those of our fellow creatures . . . afflicted with this terrible disease." Her remarks to this writer were in reference to her work among the people of Hawaii who were stricken with Hansen's disease (or leprosy as it was called in Mother Marianne's time) but applied to her work in New York State as well.

Her faith in God was extraordinary and sustained her as she encountered many difficulties in her life. In a letter written to Mother Bernardina Dorn, the foundress of the Sisters of St. Francis of Syracuse and Mother Marianne's spiritual guide she wrote, "We all came with a will to do good and to work for God's honor and glory, which is sometimes hard." She accepted with love and gratitude the call of Jesus to "take up thy cross and come follow me." Recognizing the dark side of life, she chose how to carry her cross, with love, gratitude and a cheerful heart. In this same letter to Mother Bernardina she wrote, ". . . I think life is all too short to spend any part of it in worry or anxiety."

Her cheerful heart and peaceful spirit were evident to all who encountered her. This cheerful spirit inspired, encouraged and calmed the spirits of all whom she met. In an article which appeared in the *Honolulu Advertiser* shortly after Mother Marianne's death Mrs. John Bowler wrote: "Seldom has the opportunity come to a woman to devote every hour of 30 years to the mothering of people isolated by law from the rest of the world.

She risked her own life in that time, faced everything with unflinching courage and smiled sweetly through it all."

Her great faith and dependence on God in her life, gave her great courage. She was not afraid to confront health officials or others in positions of authority when she was advocating for improved conditions for the suffering or justice for the people in her care. Her understanding of God's love and His will for her gave her the strength and patience to calm others, to take great risks in the service of God's people, to strengthen those around her, to confront evil and injustice, to inspire others in their faith development and to be a "Mother" to society's outcasts.

Her life is a call to others to reflect on their own relationship with God and how each one follows God's will and reverences other people. This was dramatically clear in the poem written by Robert Louis Stevenson on the occasion of his visit in 1899 to the people of Kalaupapa, Molokai. While there he saw the work of Mother Marianne and the sisters and wrote of his experience.

> *To see the infinite pity of this place,*
> *The mangled limb, the devastated face,*
> *The innocent sufferers smiling at the rod,*
> *A fool were tempted to deny his God.*
>
> *He sees, and shrinks; but if he look again,*
> *Lo, beauty springing from the breast of pain!*
> *He marks the sisters on the painful shores,*
> *And even a fool is silent and adores.*[4]

The Third Order Secular

The Martyrs of Nagasaki (1597)

Japan's first contact with Christianity took place when Portuguese traders visited the islands in 1543. Three Japanese accompanied them to Goa, where they were baptized, met St. Francis Xavier, and persuaded him to return home with them. Until 1587 the faith flourished, undoubtedly because many daimyos had become Christian. When the Jesuits began to be a threat to the bonzes, however, they were exiled by a decree of Taiko Hideyoshi, the regent and actual ruler at the time, and their churches were destroyed. Four years later, however, the Jesuit visitor general, Alessandro Valignano, was able to convince Hideyoshi to abrogate his decree permitting ten Jesuits to reside in Nagasaki and to move about freely.

When Japan threatened to invade the Philippines in 1592, the governor of Manila sent an embassy that was shipwrecked and lost. The following year, he sent another headed by the Franciscan Custos, Father Pedro Bautista Blazques, and accompanied by three of his confreres. Taiko Hideyoshi not only signed a treaty with the Filipinos but granted the Franciscans permission to stay in Japan, telling them, "Not only will I allow you to open a house in my country but I shall also contribute to your maintenance."[1] Within two years, he gave the friars property in the imperial city of Kyoto and encouraged their efforts in developing what became known as "Los Angelos Machi," a small community of Christians committed to living an intense Christian life.

Pedro Bautista encouraged his Spanish confreres—Francisco Blanco, a priest; Francisco de San Miguel and Gonzalvó Garcia, who were lay brothers from Spain and Baçaim, India—with these words: "In Japan we are the first Franciscans and, therefore, we must not only portray a true image of St. Francis, but by our way of living we must also make better known Jesus Christ and His perfectly holy life. Our faith is based on poverty, humility, and the cross. In propagating the faith, therefore, the true disciple of the poor, humble, and crucified Christ must use means in accordance with the crucified God he preaches."[2] Although much of their time was spent struggling to learn the difficult Japanese language, which Francis Xavier had called "the language of the devil," their lives communicated their belief in the Gospel, brought many converts to the faith, and established a vibrant fraternity of Third Order lay Franciscans whose influence grew stronger and more widespread.

After three years, in the summer of 1596, however, a series of natural disasters in which thousands were killed was blamed on the Japanese neglect of their gods. More incendiary was the October shipwreck of a Spanish ship, the San Filipe, bound for Mexico during a typhoon. It was forced to take refuge in the Japanese port of Urado where it was discovered that there was a valuable cargo on board. The Japanese ruling class had sufficient evidence to poison the daimyo's attitude toward the Franciscans and maliciously accused them of being agents of the Spanish government that they described as preparing for the conquest of Japan. "I will kill all missionaries," Hideyoshi exclaimed at the beginning of December, "the Franciscans as well as the Christians. Ten years ago I forbade them to preach the Christian religion, but neither the friars nor the Jesuits obey my orders. Here in Kyoto in my very presence . . . they make converts not only among the poor but among the lords. They must be punished immediately, put under arrest, and a list of their followers made."[3] The following day, December 8, the friars were placed under house arrest. By this time their number had grown: a young twenty-four-year-old Mexican brother, Felipe de Jesús de las Casas, was traveling from the Philippines to Mexico to be ordained and had had to take temporary refuge with his confreres when the San Felipe was shipwrecked.

On December 30, the soldiers arrested another Franciscan, thirty-year old Martín de la Ascención Aguirre, and his four lay companions: Michael Kosaki, the porter at the friary in Osaka; his fourteen year old son, Thomas; Joachim Sakakabara, the cook; and thirteen-year-old Anthony, Dōjoku of the Franciscans. The soldiers marched them to Kyoto there they imprisoned them together with a thirty-two-year-old Jesuit, Paul Miki, and two Jesuit aspirants: a nineteen-year-old, John Soan de Gotō, and another, Diego Kisai, who was sixty-four. On January 4 the five friars of Kyoto were led with a group of their parishioners to join those from Osaka and, the following day, by an explicit order of Hideyoshi, each of them had part of his left ear cut off. The group of twenty-four then began the long march from Kyoto to Osaka on public display as a warning to all of the consequences of embracing "a forbidden religion." Four days later they were condemned to death and began the long journey to Nagasaki. As they marched, two others followed them: Francis Kichi, a carpenter with something of a drinking problem, and Peter Sukejiro, a young man sent with some money to provide for their needs. The newly baptized Francis was initially brushed aside as someone not closely connected with the friars; he used his alcohol to bribe his way into the group. Peter, on the other hand, was forced into the group after the soldiers confiscated his money. When someone tried to have him excused, he refused.

After a grueling march of thirty days the group of twenty-six arrived on February 5 at a hill now called Nishizaka, the place of execution facing the city of Nagasaki and its bay: six Franciscans—four Spanish, one Mexican, one Portuguese Indian; three Japanese Jesuits—the two associated had been received into the Society a few days before; fourteen laymen—members of the Third Order or associates of the Franciscans, three young boys who were fourteen, thirteen, and twelve years old. Upon their arrival, they found this sentence of death posted for all to see:

> As these men came from the Philippines under the guise of being ambassadors, and chose to stay in Miyako preaching the Christian law, which I had severely forbidden all these years, I come to decree that they be put to death together with the Japanese who have accepted that law.[4]

This description of how criminals were executed by crucifixion can be found in the annals of Japanese history:

> The criminals are not nailed to the cross but attached to it with iron rings and with ropes. The cross is composed of four pieces: an upper cross beam to which the wrists and the upper arms are fastened; a lower cross beam on which the victim stands with his legs apart and to which the legs are likewise bound; in the middle of the vertical beam there is a protruding piece of wood upon which the victim can support himself; ropes are also placed around the waist and the neck. After the victim is thus thoroughly fastened to the cross, the cross is erected and lowered into a deep pit and fixed there with earth and stones.[5]

The twenty-six men were fastened with cords and iron rings to crosses that had been made according to their size—the three small ones standing in tragic contrast to the others—and were lifted into place almost simultaneously. One eyewitness later testified: "the martyrs were cheerful, calm, and devout, not showing any sign of fear. I testify that they sang hymns and psalms and, after the erection of their crosses, some of them thanked the Lord for the great mercy shown them, while others prayed for the soldiers."[6] Two other witnesses recounted how the twelve-year-old, Luis, asked which of the crosses was his. When it was pointed out to him, the boy ran to it and embraced it. From his cross Pedro Bautista led the others in singing the *Te Deum*.

The first to die was the Mexican Felipe de Jesús. The weight of his body forced the ring around his neck to choke him prompting his executioners to stab him with their lances. With his death, the executioners went from one to another killing each one in the same manner. The last was Pedro Bautista who echoed the words of Jesus as the lance pierced his side: "Father, into your hands I commend my spirit."

The bodies of all the martyrs were left on their crosses from February to October during which time guards were posted to prevent Christians from tending to them or from taking relics. Miraculously their bodies were preserved from corruption and birds of prey never touched them.

* * *

Pedro Bautista was able to send two letters during the march from Kyoto to Nagasaki. The first was written to his Franciscan provincial in Manila on two different days. On January 13, 1597, Pedro wrote asking for repayment of a specific amount of money that he had requested as a loan for the safe departure of the galleon "San Felipe." The following day he provided his provincial with more details of the circumstances in which he and his companions found themselves.

From a Letter to His Provincial

May Jesus dwell in our souls. Amen.

We are en route—being taken to be crucified—because we have taught and preached the Word of God—and, having only the time secretly afforded me by the good man who accompanies us, I will write a few brief lines. As it happened, when the ship of Don Mathias arrived in Japan, he sent me to negotiate for everything necessary for the ship; and [he authorized me] to say and do whatever I thought best for the ship's benefit; and he gave me this authority both in writing and in words.

I cannot tell you much more, except that they are transporting us by land—to date, almost one hundred leagues—without being in communication with anyone; I do not know what [more] to say but ask you to commend us to God. . . .

Today, 14 January 1597. The General sent Brother Juan in a ship, so that he could translate some petitions into the Japanese language, so that these petitions could be given to the King. [The expense of] this ship was paid from the remaining part of the alms sent there by the Governor for the works of our house—the total amount given was 8 *taes*. "Your Charity" should also see what should be done in this matter, since, with the approval of those who were there who gave [the gift], I responded to this need.

We, six brothers among those who are here, have been prisoners for many days; and they have taken us through the public streets of Macao with three Japanese of the Society [of Jesus]—one of whom was already a professed Brother and the other two [are] Christians; all told, we [prisoners] number 24. And they cut off a piece of one ear of each of us; and afterwards, they paraded us through two very large cities, named Usaca and Sacay. And afterwards, we were sentenced to be crucified in Nangasaqui, where we are now heading by the overland route—the distance is more than one hundred Castillian leagues; the weather is very cold, because it is this month [January]; they are taking us on horseback and [we are] very well guarded—some days there are more than two hundred men in our guard. Nevertheless, we journey with great consolation and joy in the Lord, for the sentence imposed on us stated that the reason for our crucifixion is that we preached the law of God contrary to the command of the King, while the others [received the same sentence of death] for being Christians. Although we still do not have any news about what sentence will be passed on the brothers who are in Nangasaque—namely, Brother Agustín, Brother Bartolomé, and Brother Marcelo—we understand that they will receive the same sentence as we [have received].

Before he arrived, I advised Brother Herónimo, who was about to go to Meaco when we were prisoners, that he should hide in order to comfort the Christians who remained—such [assistance] would be very great. Although he would have liked to join us in our sufferings, I told him that, if necessary, he should put aside his religious habit, in order to minister more effectively to the needs of the Christians, who well deserve it because they have shown themselves very eager to die for Christ; and we understand that many of them will die, as stated in the sentence [of death].

Those who now have the courage to die for Christ now have a good opportunity to do so. I feel that the [Japanese] Christians would be very inspired, if they could see religious of our Order here; although they can be certain that while this King rules, our habits will not remain in Japan for too many more days, because soon they will soon take us to the other life—*may He lead us to it.*

Farewell, dearest brother, Brother Provincial, *until the vision of God.* Since Brother Herónimo remains alone, and the work is so holy, may "Your Charity" favor him, *for love of God.* All the brothers send many greetings to "Your Charity" and we ask *humbly,* for Masses. Brother Pedro Bautista.[7]

A few hours before he was crucified, Pedro Bautista was able to write the following farewell letter to three of his confreres who were interned in the Portuguese ship in the harbor:

From a Letter to His Confreres

Jesus be always with you!
Dear Brothers

This small letter is my last farewell. It has pleased the Lord to show us His mercy immediately; therefore with this letter I send you my heart and my will. . . .

We ask you to recommend to the Lord, with all your heart, our passage to the coming life. You want to participate in our happiness; if it is possible and the Lord inspires you, the door remains open because I think we all should have been together this day; but the Lord says through Isaiah: "My will is not your will."

If the Lord sends you back to Manila, please greet all our confreres. I humbly beg everyone to recommend me to God so that I might, with God's grace, please Him in heaven, where I hope to go.

Be one in the Lord and, once more, greetings to everyone. Brother Pedro Bautista.[8]

Jean-Marie Vianney (1786–1859)

Jean-Marie Vianney, born in Dardilly, northwest of Lyons, France, on May 8, 1786, was a diocesan priest. He grew up in the wake of the French Revolution when frequenting the sacraments was forbidden and priests were forced to minister to the people secretly with the threat of death over them should they be discovered. The revolution even affected the French education system so that young people such as Jean-Marie had to learn how to read and write at home. In 1802 the government promulgated a concordat that guaranteed free worship to the church and permitted young men to enter seminaries.

When he was sixteen, Jean-Marie made a pilgrimage to the shrine of Saint John Francis Regis in LaLouvesc and decided to approach Monsigneur Balley, the curé of nearby Ecully, who had established a school for young men discerning a call to the priesthood. Monsigneur Balley and his colleagues never seemed to doubt the young man's vocation but came to realize that his education was deficient and undoubtedly set back by the revolution. In 1809, however, Jean-Marie was erroneously conscripted by Napoleon's army to fight in Spain. On the morning of his scheduled departure, he went to church, became lost in prayer, was threatened with imprisonment for dereliction of duty, but was released and sent to the barracks in Lyons. A young man he met on the way volunteered to lead him back but instead led him to a mountain village, Les Noes, where deserters were protected from the gendarmes by the deep snows of winter. Persuaded by the village's mayor to remain there under an assumed name, he fell out of contact with his family for fourteen months until the imperial decree of 1810 granted exemption to all deserters. When his younger brother offered to serve out his military commitment, Jean-Marie returned to Ecully and, two years later, to the seminary at Verrieres, where, in 1815, he was ordained.

Jean-Marie's first assignment was as an assistant to his former mentor, Monsigneur Balley, in Ecully. When his old friend and patron died in 1818, he was sent to a small village of only 280 inhabitants, Ars-en-Dombres, not far from Lyons. The young priest quickly learned that the lasting effects of the revolution could be seen in the ignorance and indifference of the people of Ars and so he threw himself into catechizing them, visiting their homes, and embarking on a life of prayer and penance to win them back to God. In 1821 he founded a home for destitute girls that he called La Providence. He organized guilds for women and men hoping that through their activities they would raise the religious fervor of Ars. Above all, he spent hours hearing confessions. By 1827 thousands came from Ars to confess their sins and to be absolved by the saintly curé. By this time, his every day unfolded in this way: He rose shortly after midnight, walked from his residence to the church, rang the bell announcing his availability for confessions, and remained there until he celebrated Mass at seven. After his thanksgiving he returned to the confessional until eleven when he gave a catechesis on the faith to whoever was in the church. At noon, he went back to the rectory for some nourishment; a quarter of an hour later, he visited the sick, and then returned to be available in the church. After long hours there, he retired to his residence where he shut himself up in his room for about three hours before beginning another day.

While his embrace of penance for the conversion of sinners and his dedication to their salvation grew with each day, at the same time he suffered strange, extraordinary phenomena that he attributed to the devil: weird noises during the night, unexplainable beatings, even awakening to finding his bed in flames. The last thirty years of his life were repeatedly characterized by these happenings as they were also by the harsh, unjustified criticism of the clergy.

Nevertheless, a more contemplative life continued to call him. He tried a number of times to embrace a simpler, more reclusive way of life. A rumor circulated that the beloved curé wanted to be a Capuchin. The people, who were now coming in droves for his reconciling ministry, would not permit it and petitioned his bishop to keep him in Ars. Indeed, in 1848, he had spoken of his desire to a Capuchin of the Les Broteaux Friary in Lyons and had expressed his desire to join them. Assuring the curé that he would achieve more good by remaining in his parish, the Capuchin encouraged him to join the Third Order of St. Francis. Some have suggested that living such a lifestyle was the greatest miracle of Ars.

Worn out by his unimaginably long hours of prayer, ministry, and penance, Jean-Marie Vianney collapsed on May 31, 1859, lingered for the next two months, and died peacefully on August 4. He was beatified in 1905, canonized twenty years later, and proclaimed the patron of diocesan and, particularly, parish priests.

* * *

John Vianney's *Little Catechism* is a collection of the daily instructions the Curé d'Ars gave to the children. It found a much larger audience who found every basic aspect of our spiritual struggle and the means to overcome our spiritual problems stated in a profound yet simple and direct way. Two of the most memorable are the following.

From *The Little Catechism*

An Instruction on Prayer

Consider, children, a Christian's treasure is not on earth, it is in heaven. Well then, our thoughts should turn to where our treasure is. Man has a noble task: that of prayer and love. To pray and to love, that is the happiness of man on earth. Prayer is nothing else than union with God. When the heart is pure and united with God it is consoled and filled with sweetness; it is dazzled by a marvelous light. In this intimate union, God and the soul are like two pieces of wax molded into one; they cannot any more be separated. It is a very wonderful thing, this union of God with his insignificant creature; happiness passing all understanding.

We had deserved to be left incapable of praying; but God in his goodness has permitted us to speak to him. Our prayer is incense that is delightful to God. My children, your hearts are small, but prayer enlarges them and renders them capable of loving God. Prayer is a foretaste of heaven, an overflowing of heaven. It never leaves us without sweetness; it is like honey, it descends into the soul and sweetens everything. In a prayer well made, troubles vanish like snow under the rays of the sun.

Prayer makes time seem to pass quickly, and so pleasantly that one fails to notice how long it is. When I was parish priest of Bresse, once, almost all my colleagues were ill, and as I made the long journeys I used to pray to God, and, I assure you, the time did not seem long to me. There are those who lose themselves in prayer, like fish in water, because they are absorbed in God. There is no division in their hearts. How I love those noble souls. Saint Francis of Assisi and Saint Colette saw Our Lord and spoke to him as we speak to one another.

As for ourselves, how often do we come to church without thinking what we are doing or for what we are going to ask. And yet, when we go to call on someone, we have no difficulty in remembering why it was we came. Some appear as if they were about to say to God: "*I am just going to say a couple of words, so I can get away quickly.*" I often think that when we come to adore our Lord we should get all we ask if we asked for it with a lively faith and a pure heart.

Private prayer is like straw scattered here and there: If you set it on fire it makes a lot of little flames. But gather these straws into a bundle and light them, and you get a mighty fire, rising like a column into the sky; public prayer is like that.[1]

Catechism on the Priesthood

My children, we have come to the Sacrament of Orders. It is a Sacrament which seems to relate to no one among you, and which yet relates to everyone. This Sacrament raises man up to God. What is a priest? A man who holds the place of God—a man who is invested with all the powers of God! "Go," said Our Lord to the priest; "as My Father sent Me, I send you. All power has been given Me in Heaven and on earth. Go then, teach all nations. . . . He who listens to you, listens to Me; he who despises you despises Me." When the priest remits *sins*, he does not say, "God pardons you"; he says, "I absolve you." At the Consecration, he does not say, "This is the Body of Our Lord;" he says, "This is My Body."

St. Bernard tells us that everything has come to us through Mary; and we may also say that everything has come to us through the priest; yes, all happiness, all graces, all heavenly gifts. If we had not the Sacrament of Orders, we should not have Our Lord. Who placed Him there, in that tabernacle? It was the priest! Who was it that received your soul, on its entrance into life? The priest! Who nourishes it, to give it strength to make its pilgrimage? The priest! Who will prepare it to appear before God, by washing that soul, for the last time, in the blood of Jesus Christ? The priest—always the priest! And if that soul comes to the point of death, who will raise it up, who will restore it to calmness and peace? Again the priest! You cannot recall one single blessing from God without finding, side by side with this recollection, the image of the priest.

Go to confession to the Blessed Virgin, or to an angel; will they absolve you? No. Will they give you the Body and Blood of Our Lord? No. The Holy Virgin cannot make her Divine Son descend into the Host. You might have two hundred angels there, but they could not absolve you. A priest, however simple he may be, can do it; he can say to you, "Go in peace; I pardon you." Oh, how great is a priest! The priest will not understand the greatness of his office till he is in Heaven. If he understood it on earth, he would die, not of fear, but of love. The other benefits of God would be of no avail to us without the priest. What would be the use of a house full of gold, if you had nobody to open you the door! The priest has the key of the heavenly treasures; it is he who opens the door; he is the steward of the good God, the distributor of His wealth. Without the priest, the Death and Passion of Our Lord would be of no avail. Look at the heathens: what has it availed them that Our Lord has died? Alas! they can have no share in the blessings of Redemption, while they have no priests to apply His Blood to their souls!

The priest is not a priest for himself; he does not give himself absolution; he does not administer the Sacraments to himself. He is not for himself, he is for you. After God, the priest is everything. Leave a parish twenty years without priests; they will worship beasts. If the missionary Father and I were to go away, you would say, "What can we do in this church? There is no Mass; Our Lord is no longer there: we may as well pray at home." When people wish to destroy religion, they begin by attacking the priest, because where there is no longer any priest there is no sacrifice, and where there is no longer any sacrifice there is no religion.

When the bell calls you to church, if you were asked, "Where are you going?" you might answer, "I am going to feed my soul." If someone were to ask you, pointing to the tabernacle, "What is that golden door?" "That is our storehouse, where the true Food of our souls is kept." "Who has the key? Who lays in the provisions? Who makes ready the feast, and who serves the table?" "The priest." "And what is the Food?" "The precious Body and Blood of Our Lord!" O God! O God! how Thou hast loved us! See the power of the priest; out of a piece of bread the word of a priest makes a God. It is more than creating the world. . . . Someone said, "Does St. Philomena, then, obey the Cure of Ars?" Indeed, she may well obey him, since God obeys him.

If I were to meet a priest and an angel, I should salute the priest before I saluted the angel. The latter is the friend of God; but the priest holds His place. St. Teresa kissed the ground where a priest had passed. When you see a priest, you should say, "There is he who made me a child of God, and opened Heaven to me by holy Baptism; he who purified me after I had sinned; who gives nourishment to my soul." At the sight of a church tower, you may say, "What is there in that place?" "The Body of Our Lord." "Why is He there?" "Because a priest has been there, and has said holy Mass."

What joy did the Apostles feel after the Resurrection of Our Lord, at seeing the Master whom they had loved so much! The priest must feel the same joy, at seeing Our Lord whom he holds in his hands. Great value is attached to objects which have been laid in the drinking cup of the Blessed Virgin and of the Child Jesus, at Loretto. But the fingers of the priest, that have touched the adorable Flesh of Jesus Christ, that have been plunged into the chalice which contained His Blood, into the pyx where His Body has lain, are they not still more precious? The priesthood is the love of the Heart of Jesus. When you see the priest, think of Our Lord Jesus Christ.[2]

Matt Talbot (1856–1925)

Matt Talbot was about twelve years old when he began to drink alcohol. It was in his genes: his father was an alcoholic before him. The day after his death at the age of sixty-eight, the Irish Independent notes:

> An elderly man collapsed in Granby Lane yesterday, and on being taken to Jervis Street Hospital he was found to be dead. He was wearing a tweed suit, but there was nothing to identify who he was.[1]

As word of his death began to spread, so too did his reputation for holiness. Six years later the first of two official tribunals were held that initiated the process for his canonization as men and women struggling with alcoholism began to recognize in him a model and to pray for his intercession in their battle for sobriety.

Matthew Talbot was born on May 2, 1856, in Dublin, Ireland. The second born, he had three sisters and nine brothers, three of whom died young. His father, Charles, was a dockworker; his mother, Elizabeth, was a housewife who struggled with an alcoholic husband who spent much of what little money he earned on satisfying his addiction. The world that surrounded the Talbot family was harsh. The British government was siphoning the profits coming from the Irish crops and livestock, which intensified *An Gorta Mór* (The Great Hunger) caused by a blight on the people's staple food, the potato. From 1845 to 1852, approximately one million people died while a million more emigrated. Many of those who were not delivered from such poverty, depression, desperation by death or by immigration found refuge in alcohol. Whisky, even of the best quality, was cheap, so inexpensive that it was within the means of the poorest.

Sadly, it was the youth who frequently suffered the most in these circumstances and Matt Talbot was one of them. There was no compulsory education in Ireland at the time, giving the young boy plenty of opportunity to enjoy himself and providing him little to broaden his horizons through the written page. On May 6, 1867, Matt and his older brother, John were enrolled in the Dublin school of the Christian Brothers. His teacher, Brother Otteran Ryan, somehow managed to get the eleven-year-old Matt through at least some of his first year of classes. The following May, however, Brother Ryan registered a simple comment next to his name: "A Mitcher," informing whatever teacher would succeed him that Matthew Talbot was a frequent truant.

At twelve Matt got his first job as a messenger boy for E & J Burke, the firm that bottled Guinness Stout. As he delivered the stout to pubs throughout the city, Matt soon learned to drink the dregs of the returned bottles. Before a year had expired, he came home drunk. His father gave him a severe beating but did him no favor when he secured him a job with his own employer, the Port and Docks Board, this time delivering bottles of whiskey to the pubs. In Burke's he drank stout, at the Port and Docks it was whiskey. Three years later, Matt left the Port and Docks Board and became a bricklayers' hodman with Pembertons, the building contractors, fetching mortar and bricks at their beck and call. The oldest of his three sisters, Mary, later testified that, even as his alcoholism intensified, he had the desire to be a good man and was known to be an excellent workman who never neglected his work and would set the pace for others. At the end of the day, however, he went with his friends to a local pub and set the pace in another way: drinking until closing time or until the money ran out. "Though he always worked very hard," Mary continued, "all his wages went to drink."[2] He would not listen to his mother's pleas to stop drinking, would not give her any of his wages, and repeatedly gave her a deaf ear when she would speak about his faith. "I broke her heart," he later confessed.[3] He had stopped going to church and his prayers consisted of blessing himself when he got out of bed in the morning. Slowly he lost respect for those around him and, eventually, for himself.

At a young age he became addicted. His friends claimed: "[Matt] wanted only one thing—the drink; he wouldn't go with us to a dance or a party or a school function. But for the drink he'd do anything."[4] By the time he was in his twenties, he spent all his spare time in O'Meara's, the pub closest to his home. His employer would deposit his week's wages there, as he did those of his coworkers at their own local pubs. Matt would pick up his check on Saturday noon at O'Meara's and begin drinking. Each evening he returned so that, by Tuesday, his wages were usually gone and he would be forced to drink on credit. He pawned his shoes, his coat, whatever he could; he begged from his friends, went deep into debt, and even became a thief, once stealing a fiddle from a blind man. His drinking companions had several hobbies: swimming, playing cards, and girlfriends. Matt had only one: alcohol. His life had become unmanageable.

By the time he was twenty-eight, he was well on the road to self-destruction, when, on a Saturday morning in 1884, he waited outside O'Meara's without a penny hoping to mooch money from his friends. One by one, they passed him by. Some greeted him; others ignored him. Perhaps he had scrounged money from them too often, but they left him standing on the corner. Matt Talbot was "cut to the heart," as he admitted years later. Nonetheless, it was the jolt he needed to realize how totally addicted to alcohol he had become.

One of the most prominent problems in the second half of nine-teenth-century Ireland was excessive drinking. "Intemperance," an 1875 pastoral letter of the Irish bishops maintained, "has wrecked more homes than ever fell beneath the crowbar in the worst days of eviction."[5] This was a warning the bishops had to repeat in 1900 and, in a more positive way, addressed in 1905 when they approached the Capuchins to under-take a national crusade. It then became common for someone who wished to stop drinking to take a solemn pledge before a priest to abstain for a period of time. "I promise," it stated, "to abstain from all intoxicating drinks except used medicinally and by order of a medical man and to discountenance the cause and practice of intemperance."[6] Four years before that turning point Saturday morning, Capuchin Father Theobald Mathew who had spearheaded Ireland's temperance movement had visited Dublin three times and, according to some records, witnessed as many as 173,000 persons take the pledge. Dublin's Archbishop Daniel Murray wrote to him in November 1840:

> . . . while vast benefits had been produced by the pledge, the publicans sustained little injury. They re-opened their shops for the sale of clothes, Irish manufacturers and other such articles, and one business supplied the place of the other. The largest prison in Dublin was closed for want of prisoners.[7]

That the desperate Matt Talbot would return home to announce to his mother his intention to take the pledge may not have been a surprise, nor would have been her seemingly cynical reaction. How many similar Irishmen had been momentarily caught up in Theobald's fervor and, once on their feet, simply fallen over and again! Years later Mary testified that her mother "smiled and said, 'Go, in God's name, but don't take it unless you are going to keep it.'"[8] The words of his long-suffering mother must have hit home for he responded: "Then I'll go in the name of God." Immediately he set off for Dublin's diocesan seminary, Holy Cross College, Clonliffe, where he asked to see a priest for confession and to ask him to accept his pledge of sobriety for three months. The next day he went back to church and received communion for the first time in years. Another of Matt's sisters, Susan, testified:

> He was a changed man immediately after taking the pledge. We never heard him swear again. He put two pins in the cuff of his coat to check any temptation to swear. . . . His workmates were astonished when they heard of Matt taking the pledge; and they were still more astonished when he kept it.[9]

The terrifying withdrawal symptoms of alcoholism were not understood in those days, so how Matt battled the nausea, hallucination, and depression that accompanied must have been terrifying. How he did so without the supports we now recognize as essential for overcoming addictive behavior is extraordinary and form part of his legacy.

To fill in the time he used to spend in O'Meara's, Matt would walk the streets of Dublin every evening after work. One of those evenings he passed Bushe's Pub, about a mile from his home, caught a whiff of the ale, and saw the comradeship of many of his friends. He walked in but was ignored by the busy bartender, humiliated for the second time within a few weeks. He left, continued his lonely walk, and entered the Jesuit church near his home. That evening he resolved never to carry money with him, a resolution he also kept for the rest of his life. More important, however, was the practice of stopping in churches that began to characterize his daily life. At the time of his first pledge, Matt was neither physically nor religiously fit. Walking the Dublin streets would quickly tire him. Previously he would comfortably find rest, companionship, and something to quench his thirst in one of the many pubs he would pass. Now it was in one of the churches he would pass where he found respite and, in the process, grappled with his unmanageable life and his own powerlessness.

In one church after another he would stop and in each would come in contact with a divine power that perhaps he didn't understand but gradually discovered was providing him the self-control he needed: the Jesuit church of Saint Francis Xavier; the Franciscan church of the

Immaculate Conception, popularly called Adam and Eve after a popular pub with that name; the Capuchin church of Saint Mary of the Angels; the Dominican church of Saint Saviour; and the diocesan church of Saint Joseph. In addition to what became long hours before the Blessed Sacrament, Matt began attending daily Mass before work. When his parish church changed its first Mass from five o'clock in the morning to six thirty, he quit his job at Pemberton's and found a new one in T. & C. Martin's timber yard where he took on the meanest and hardest jobs. It made little difference since he could still start his day with Mass.

Slowly but surely Matt also came to grips with his sinfulness and began to frequent the sacrament of reconciliation on a regular basis. Although there is little evidence that at this time he had a spiritual director, he frequently sought out for the sacrament and for advice Father Michael Hickey, professor of philosophy at Holy Cross; he may have also spoken with Father O'Donnell, professor of theology at the seminary, and a chaplain at Mountjoy Prison where he undoubtedly encountered many alcoholics like Matt. It may well have been this priest's patience that helped this struggling, searching young man to take stock of his moral life and, on a regular basis, to wrestle with his own humanity.

Matt's sister, Mary, once again provides insights into how much both of these practices—his daily routine of spending time in churches and his frequent confessions—influenced his life. She stated:

> For a long time after his conversion, he was repaying money which he owed for drink. He had had drink on credit and used to go into public-houses, hand over in an envelope the money which he thought was due, and hastily depart. . . . He also made a careful search through all the Poorhouses in Dublin for [the fiddler whose violin he had stolen] in order to repay [its] value; but he was unable find him.[10]

Susan, Matt's other sister, also noticed that he embraced a harsh life of penance that included fasting, getting little sleep and that on a board and wooden pillow, and early each morning going to Mass, all of which he attempted to keep secret. Despite all his austerities, however, Matt was a small tough man whom his fellow workers at T. & C. Martin's and on Dublin's waterfront described as "strong as a little horse."[11] He had an iron will and a constitution to match. None of them had any idea that he was leading a life modeled on the asceticism of the early Irish saints. He soon developed a reputation for being "a happy little man, more silent than others . . . who smiled at everything except a dirty joke."[12] As time went on, many did come to know firsthand of his generosity as he quietly lent them money to buy clothes or shoes for their children or to pay overdue rent. At the end of three months, Matt found the inner strength to renew his pledge for six months and, finally, for life.

Throughout these first years of sobriety, Matt's mother passed on a story that her granddaughter, Annie Johnson, eventually shared:

> While working on a building job at the residence of a Protestant clergyman, Matt attracted the attention of a cook by his holiness. The cook, who was a pious Catholic girl, seeing that Matt did not speak to the maids as the other men did, decided to speak to him, and finally suggested marriage. She informed him that she had considerable savings and was in a position to furnish a home. Matt said that he would let her know his answer after he had done a novena asking for enlightenment. This he did, and at the conclusion of the novena he told the girl that he had got an answer in prayer that he was to remain single. He was very firm in his resolution, as when some of his fellow-workmen in later years spoke of marriage he always said he would never marry, as it would interfere with the manner of life he had decided to live. To a confidant he said that "the Blessed Virgin told him not to marry."[13]

Hearing the story now, it becomes clear that Matt had made a decision to surrender his life to the care of God. To discern what was God's will, his hours before the Blessed Sacrament intensified as he sought not only to discover knowledge and understanding of God and himself but also to receive whatever power he needed to carry out the divine plan.

That search also led Matt to another dimension of these early years of his recovery: his hunger to learn about the spiritual life. As a result of his "mitching," he may well have been initially at a loss: his reading skills were minimal. Many of the books found in his possession at his death contained leaflets, memorial cards, or scraps of paper with ideas or passages that struck him. Some of these have dates from this early period, that is, from the 1880s. Two of those books were bibles, one of which contained both Testaments, the other was a pocket-sized New Testament; both were well used, heavily annotated, and indicative of the spiritual struggles Matt was enduring. In addition to this biblical spirituality, however, there were a number of easy-to-read primers on the spiritual life, such as Cardinal Bona's *The Principles of a Christian Life*, the Benedictine writer Blosius's *The Book of Instruction*, Butler's *Lives of the Saints*, and the lives of various saints such as Augustine of Hippo and Francis Xavier. One book, in particular, points to another dimension of Matt's life at this time: *The Franciscan Manual* published in 1884.

Six years after that turning-point Saturday morning in 1884, Matt became a novice in the Third Order of Saint Francis of Assisi, which we now call "The Secular Franciscans." While his investiture and profession were not extraordinary—he later joined other church-related associations, confraternities, or sodalities—his attendance at the monthly fraternity meetings was. In 1948 Cormac Daly, O.F.M., testified:

> Matt Talbot was received into the Third Order at the Franciscan Church, Merchants' Quay, Dublin, on October 12, 1890, by Rev. P. J. Cleary, O.F.M., and was admitted to profession by the same Father on October 18, 1891. He was therefore, thirty-five years a member of the Third Order of St. Francis.
>
> His attendance was remarkable. In the first twenty years of his membership he was—according to the Register—absent only on *two* occasions from the monthly meetings—once in 1899 and once in 1909; he never seems to have been absent from the monthly Communion.

The friar continued in some detail to review the years between 1910 and 1917 when he seems to have missed a total of four meetings and noted that, in 1918, there was a change in the manner of recording attendances making it impossible to determine "the exact number of his attendances for the seven years preceding his death." Then he adds: "Still it is pretty clear that he attended with usual regularity during those years, for he was a well-known member at the meetings. This attendance is all the more remarkable seeing that during his thirty-five years of membership he changed his address on six occasions, and at no period of his life was he in the immediate vicinity of Merchant's Quay."[14]

The American Franciscan Mark Hegener maintains that "In the Third Order of Saint Francis and its ideal of penitential love [Matt] found the training ground for holiness."[15] Was it simply that or was it something more? A close friend and drinking companion of the Talbot brothers, Pat Doyle, later testified that two years after taking the pledge Matt came looking for him and led him to Clonliffe College where he persuaded him to take the pledge. Years later, Doyle's telling of the story reveals that Matt was not only eager to free his friend of his addiction but also to introduce him to a life of virtue, neither of which he was ready to embrace. From his perspective, however, the incident may well reveal how two years after he had taken the pledge Matt Talbot discovered how he needed support or companionship in his struggles and in the pursuit of his ideals. His remarkable fidelity to the monthly Third Order Fraternity meetings—as well as the other associations and societies which he joined—may well prove how effective they were in providing the support and encouragement needed in his battle for sobriety.

While his places of residence changed frequently over the next ten years, whatever furnishings he had in them did not. Each one had only the bare necessities: a bed, a chair, a crucifix, and perhaps a holy picture. His diet too was equally unchanging: his sister Mary testified that he "lived practically on dry bread, and shell-cocoa without milk or sugar."[16] By 1890, Matt's austere daily program seems also to have been in place. By ten thirty each night, he was in bed. He allowed himself just four or five hours sleep after which he got up to pray, left his room at five o'clock for church and preparation for Mass at a quarter after six. After a quick breakfast he set off for work where he maintained his reputation as being a conscientious worker even, according to one of his foremen, "the best worker in Dublin" who was often chosen to set the pace for others.[17] Whenever there was a break, however, he found a quiet place to pray. At six o'clock, when he left work, he stopped in church. If he had a meeting to attend—which was almost every evening—he would then have a light supper, head back to church for the meeting or for devotions, and return home in time for his spiritual reading. He did not go to work on Sunday but went to one of Dublin's many churches where he would kneel in an obscure corner from the first mass at six o'clock until midday. In the afternoons and evening, he would visit the sick or shut-ins. Years later men began coming to him eager to learn the secrets of his success in battling his addiction. To one he said: "What I can do, you surely can!" To another: "It's constancy God wants!" On a scrap of paper in one of his books, however, he wrote: "There is only a step between me and death."[18] That may well sum up his approach to sobriety: one step at a time.[19]

In March 1899, Matt's father, Charles Talbot, died prompting Matt to move back to live with his mother. Shortly thereafter, he received permanent employment with T. & C. Martin's. His work habits were such that they earned him above-average wages, wages that he generally gave away to his poor neighbors, to the Poor Clares in Keady, Armagh, to other needy religious, and to charities as far away as Father Drumgoole's Catholic Orphanage in New York. He kept only 50 pence a week, for his needs were few.

In order to understand the next twenty-five years of Matt Talbot's life, however, it is important to recognize the forces that were shaping the Irish world in which he was living. It was a time of national awakening as the labor movements, the Gaelic Athletic Association, and the resurgence of Irish literature coalesced in the struggle for Irish independence.

At the turn of the century, the Dublin slums had a population of roughly eighty-seven thousand as people suffered from unemployment and low wages. In 1911 Matt joined the Builders Labourer's branch of the Irish Transport and General Workers Union of which James Connelly and James Larkin were prominent figures. "The cause of labour is the cause of Ireland," Connelly had argued. "The cause of Ireland is the cause of labour. They cannot be dissevered."[20] A number of Matt's coworkers testified that, during these years, they never heard him speak about his employers but they did know that the laborers were frequently paid insufficiently. In Dublin's Great Lock-Out of 1913 Larkin roused workers to strike in demand of fair wages. "Some 100,000 workers and their families faced starvation or submission," Mark Tierney notes, "as month after month dragged by."[21] Among them was Matt Talbot who, according to one of his coworkers, "did not take any active part in picketing."[22] At first Talbot refused his strike pay, saying that he had not earned it. Later he asked that it be shared with the families of the men on strike. One of the Jesuit lay brothers who testified on his behalf said: "[Matt] was on the side of the workmen whom he wanted to see fairly treated. One morning I asked him if the strike had been settled yet. He said that it had not and added: 'I hope they will get what they are looking for: a fair wage.'"[23]

James Tallon, a tailor, provided this piece of testimony that provides insight into Matt's approach to those turbulent disputes:

> The big strike of 1913 troubled me. I asked Matt what were the rights of it. He said that it had troubled him also and that he spoke to a priest in Gardiner Street who gave him a book to read. On the third or fourth page he read that no one had the right to starve the poor into submission; he told me that that was enough for him and settled his conscience.[24]

Among the books Matt had been reading at the time were Leo XIII's *Rerum Novarum*, Leon Garriguet's *The Social Value of the Gospel*, and Hillaire Belloc's *An Examination of Socialism* and *The Church and Socialism*. At another time the men in T. & C. Martin's asked his opinion on some labor-related question, were disappointed that he had none, and were later surprised when he returned to them a few months later. In the meanwhile he had been reading Joseph Husslein's *Democratic Industry* and other works on the living and family wage. For someone with rudimentary reading skills, he became quite literate in the church's social teachings.

Events transpired rapidly during the next three years: the founding of the Irish Citizen Army at the end of August 1913, a sort of home guard founded by James Larkin to counteract the police; the establishment of the Irish Volunteers during the last week of November 1913 whose motto was "Defense not Defiance," which characterized them as anything but serious; the Howth gun-running incident in July 1914 in which Volunteers carrying arms smuggled from Germany were attacked by British troops resulting in three deaths and thirty-two wounded; the beginning of World War I nine days after the Howth Incident; the funeral of O'Donovan Rossa, an émigré to America espousing Irish independence from Britain; and, finally, the agreement of the Supreme Council of the Irish Republican Brotherhood that an uprising take place during the Easter holidays in 1916. Matt seemingly kept out of the political fray and could not be drawn into it. Nonetheless, there are a number of those scraps of paper found in his books that indicate that he kept abreast of these events and kept in his prayers many of their victims. The same may be said of Matt's reactions to the attempts lead by the Siin Féin between 1917 and 1921 to obtain complete independence from Britain and the Civil War of the newly formed Republic that lasted from 1921 to 1923. Matt's daily life of prayer, penance, and work maintained its pulse. His faith enabled him to transcend all that held him back from God. Witnesses even saw him dodging bullets to make sure he made it to Mass on that fateful Easter Sunday, 1916.

If faith is what enables sailors to put their trust in the few planks of a boat, that of Matt Talbot's was tested by the storms of the sickness of his last years. In June 1923 he had to stop working and was admitted to Dublin's Mater Hospital where he was diagnosed with cardiac and kidney problems. "I got the impression," Doctor Henry Moore stated, "that he was quite indifferent to his ailment and was prepared to accept whatever it pleased God to send him."[25] After a month he was discharged but readmitted two months later. He was never the same, as during the next year and a half he suffered especially from pain in his heart and from shortness of breath. Although he was sustained by the National Health Insurance provided by Builders Labourer's section of the Irish Transport and General Workers' Union, his benefits decreased after twenty-six weeks, at which point the Saint Vincent de Paul Society assisted him. By March 1925, he was penniless and asked to return to his old job at T. & C. Martin's. His excuse was that he was "tired of being idle and knocking around."[26] On June 7, 1925, Trinity Sunday, he went to the six o'clock Mass, returned to his flat for a light breakfast, and set out again for the ten o'clock Mass at the Dominican Church of St. Saviour. He suffered a massive cardiac arrest on the way.

* * *

From *Matt Talbot and His Times*

> Paddy Laird and his father were employees of T. & C. Martin's during the same years as Matt. He testified that the three of them would frequently walk home from work together, a prospect that Paddy confessed he did not always relish because Matt would invite them to pay a visit to the Blessed Sacrament or would say nothing at all but simply lead the way into the church.

He took an interest in whatever we'd be talking about coming up from work. In those days it was either politics, or the strikes, but sometimes the talk would be about football matches. Matt never went to matches, but he'd listen when you were describing the play, and he'd remember the names of the players and their teams and whenever the next game came in which those players figured he'd ask how they had played. Not, I believe now, that he had any interest himself in sport, but just to be affable and good company. And, though he would never allow bad language to go unchecked, he used plenty of harmless slang. I don't remember well now what exactly were the slang expressions used then, but I do remember Matt having picked up one of them and he used it long after it had gone out of date. It was—'Ah, go and get your hair cut'—when anyone was trying to rush him at the loading or unloading of the timber he'd say that—in a jolly sort of way. If you asked him to buy a ticket for anything, he always would, but he'd ask a day's grace to bring the money, because he never carried money.[27]

* * *

> Raphael O'Callaghan became a close friend of Matt during the last thirteen years of his life. Theirs became a friendship that centered on spiritual literature with the result that O'Callaghan provided unknown insights into Matt's reading habits.

There was nothing striking or impressive in Matt Talbot's appearance. To meet him on his daily rounds he was a very commonplace type of workingman, poorly clad, but clean. He was somewhat below middle height, of slight and wiry build, he walked rapidly, with long strides and loose, swinging gait. His bearing indicated recollection rather than preoccupation.

Meeting him at close quarters, one was at once struck by the high forehead and rounded temples. His eyes were large, with drooping lids which gave his face a serious, thoughtful expression. . . . His topics of conversation were nearly always of a religious nature, and on the rare occasions when he referred to social or political questions, he simply stated the views of others as he had heard them at his daily work. . . . He had a retentive memory and could quote appropriate passages and incidents bearing on matters discussed. His strong points seemed to be a certain native wit which enabled him to get hold of his subject with a personal grip which made him sure of his ground.[28]

* * *

Daniel Manning and his wife lived in a house in a portion of the T. & C. Martin yards and came to know Matt during his daily working hours from 1904 to 1923 and during the months prior to his death. Their testimony provides interesting insights from two different points of view—his work habits and his dress habits.

He was a most conscientious workman, who would not waste a moment of his time. When he had time free, e.g., during lunch hour, I several times saw him reading or praying. My belief is that he had his own method of praying and did not merely recite prayers which he had off by heart. It was common knowledge that he went to daily Mass (6 o'clock) in Gardiner Street after which he might take something to eat and then went to the 7 a.m. Mass in St Laurence O'Toole's Church—on his way to work. Sometimes I think he received Holy Communion in the Church of St Laurence O'Toole and had a light meal prepared for him by [my wife] before beginning work. He used to make a visit to the Blessed Sacrament in the same church on his way home from work. He was very abstemious with regard to food. My wife told me that at his mid-day meal she used to make at his request a mixture of tea and cocoa. She remonstrated with him and he said he was doing that as a "little penance."

In spite of his penance he was able to do his work. He took particular care of doing what he was told to do regarding his work. He was a good, conscientious workman. He tried to avoid notice; he carefully avoided all ostentation, especially as regards his pen-

ances. He was a very silent man; he was retiring, with no interest
in worldly things; but he would answer politely when spoken to.
He went about with his eyes cast down. Once I asked him had he
seen some item of news on the placards; he replied that he never
looked at the placards, that he was not interested in such matters. . . . I never met anybody like him. He was totally wrapt up
in God. He was always in good humour, yet he led a holy life per-
severingly; he was very popular with his fellow-workers, who respected him as a holy man.

He was very punctual; he used to open the yard, presumably by
arrangement with Mr. Carew, and was always there before the hour.
He was very nice and obliging always. His work was more or less
routine; he never made difficulties about doing it; he was always
anxious to do his work, even extra work if occasion arose. He was
always mild and agreeable and gentle. He was not a storeman in the
yard, just an ordinary worker; he would be handed written orders
from Head Office for sale or distribution of timber; his job was to
see that the timber was loaded according to order. If any special
difficulty arose he might have to refer to Mr. Carew. He impressed
me as a man of calm, even temperament, though inclined to get a
bit fussy at times—if people were rushing him with work. But generally he was quiet and genial, good humoured and easy to get on
with. He could not say anything harsh under any circumstances,
though I can easily believe that in his earlier life he may have had a
struggle with himself to overcome his strong temperament.[29]

I do not think he ever bought new clothes. In the morning, coming to work, he wore a long tail-coat—"swallow-tail"—and a hard
bowler hat. When he came to the yard, he took off his good coat
and put on working clothes. I think he wore clothes some friends
gave him and never bought a suit. I never saw him wear an over-
coat. He was always very clean and tidy in his dress. In between
loading the cars, my children often saw him on his knees praying
in a little shed in the yard. Sometimes they saw him there praying
with arms outstretched; he was not praying aloud.

When he finished his work in the evenings he always washed
his face and hands with cold water at a pipe in the yard. He did not
dry his face and hands and would not accept the use of a towel I
offered him. Then he took off his old clothes and a sack he used to
wear over his shoulders carrying the timber, and put on his good
coat and hat and went to St. Laurence O'Toole's Church. I saw him
going there and Canon Flood, now dead, told me Matt used to visit

there in the evenings. He always told me which Saint's Feast it was; his normal conversation was about the feast of the day; his only interest was heavenly things.

The men usually left the yards at 5.30 p.m., but Matt left at 5 p.m. because he worked during the lunch Interval—or portion of it. One evening I was in the house about 6 p.m.; the yard had been closed and everyone, as I thought, had gone home. There was a knock at the back door of my house which led on to the yard. I was rather frightened, wondering who it could be—and it was dark. I asked who it was and Matt replied. He said he had been "saying a few prayers" and did not notice the dark coming on; the yard door being locked he had come to ask me to let him out through the house.

I regarded him as a holy man, as did the men who worked with him. . . . I cannot think of any particular reason why I thought of him as holy—there was something about the man which I cannot explain. To all outward appearances he was just an ordinary work-man. The other men restrained themselves in his presence. They respected him and did not regard him as being in any way odd or peculiar. He was the most extraordinary man I ever met; he impelled respect. Matt was always happy; he was cheerful and good-humoured. I could not imagine him angry.[30]

New Rules

The Secular Franciscan Order

In 1221 Cardinal Hugolino drew up a text that was officially approved by Pope Honorius III titled *Memoriale Propositi* (The Remembrance of the Proposal . . .), which spelled out the penitential life in greater detail than the Exhortation left them by Francis. While remaining in the world and centering their lives on God, the document offered guidelines for a simple way of life, fraternal gatherings, religious instruction, practices of penance, prayer, almsgiving, and promoting peace. By about 1247 the movement had grown so large that Pope Innocent IV placed it under the direction of the Franciscan friars.

In 1289, Pope Nicholas IV approved a new Rule, *Supra Montem*, which, in turn, was replaced in 1883 by *Misericors Dei Filius* approved by Pope Leo XIII, and then that approved by Pope Paul VI in 1978. Its foundation is The Exhortation of St. Francis to the Brothers and Sisters of Penance, which began this treatment of the Third Order. As such it follows the mandate of the Second Vatican Council to return to the spirit of the founder.

The Rule of the Secular Franciscan Order
Approved by Pope Paul VI

(1978)

[Chapter One]
The Secular Franciscan Order

1. The Franciscan family, as one among many spiritual families raised up by the Holy Spirit in the Church, unites all members of the people of God—laity, religious, and priests—who recognize that they are called to follow Christ in the footsteps of Saint Francis of Assisi.

   In various ways and forms but in life-giving union with each other, they intend to make present the charism of their common Seraphic Father in the life and mission of the Church.

2. The Secular Franciscan Order holds a special place in this family circle. It is an organic union of all Catholic fraternities scattered throughout the world and open to every group of the faithful. In these fraternities the brothers and sisters, led by the Spirit, strive for perfect charity in their own secular state. By their profession they pledge themselves to live the gospel in the manner of Saint Francis by means of this rule approved by the Church.

3. The present rule, succeeding "Memoriale Propositi" (1221) and the rules approved by the Supreme Pontiffs Nicholas IV and Leo XIII, adapts the Secular Franciscan Order to the needs and expectations of the Holy Church in the conditions of changing times. Its interpretation belongs to the Holy See and its application will be made by the General Constitutions and particular statutes.

[Chapter Two]
The Way Of Life

4. The rule and life of the Secular Franciscans is this: to observe the gospel of our Lord Jesus Christ by following the example of St. Francis of Assisi who made Christ the inspiration and the center of his life with God and people. Christ, the gift of the Father's love, is the way to him, the truth into which the Holy Spirit leads us, and the

167

life which he has come to give abundantly. Secular Franciscans should devote themselves especially to careful reading of the gospel, going from gospel to life and life to gospel.

5. Secular Franciscans, therefore, should seek to encounter the living and active person of Christ in their brothers and sisters, in Sacred Scripture, in the Church, and in liturgical activity. The faith of St. Francis, who often said, "I see nothing bodily of the Most High Son of God in this world except His most holy body and blood," should be the inspiration and pattern of their Eucharistic life.

6. They have been made living members of the Church by being buried and raised with Christ in baptism; they have been united more intimately with the Church by profession. Therefore, they should go forth as witnesses and instruments of her mission among all people, proclaiming Christ by their life and words. Called like Saint Francis to rebuild the Church and inspired by his example, let them devote themselves energetically to living in full communion with the pope, bishops, and priests, fostering an open and trusting dialog of apostolic effectiveness and creativity.

7. United by their vocation as "brothers and sisters of penance" and motivated by the dynamic power of the gospel, let them conform their thoughts and deeds to those of Christ by means of that radical interior change which the gospel calls "conversion." Human frailty makes it necessary that this conversion be carried out daily. On this road to renewal the sacrament of reconciliation is the privileged sign of the Father's mercy and the source of grace.

8. As Jesus was the true worshipper of the Father, so let prayer and contemplation be the soul of all they are and do.

   Let them participate in the sacramental life of the Church, above all the Eucharist. Let them join in liturgical prayer in one of the forms proposed by the Church, reliving the mysteries of the life of Christ.

9. The Virgin Mary, humble servant of the Lord, was open to His every word and call. She was embraced by Francis with indescribable love and declared the protectress and advocate of his family. The Secular Franciscans should express their ardent love for her by imitating her complete self-giving and by praying earnestly and confidently.

10. United themselves to the redemptive obedience of Jesus, who placed His will into the Father's hands, let them faithfully fulfill the duties

proper to their various circumstances of life. Let them also follow the poor and crucified Christ, witness to Him even in difficulties and persecutions.

11. Trusting the Father, Christ chose for Himself and His mother a poor and humble life, even though He valued created things attentively and lovingly. Let the Secular Franciscans seek a proper spirit of detachment from temporal goods by simplifying their own material needs. Let them be mindful that according to the gospel they are stewards of the goods received for the benefit of God's children.

    Thus, in the spirit of the Beatitudes, and as pilgrims and strangers on their way to the home of the Father, they should strive to purify their hearts from every tendency and yearning for possession and power.

12. Witnessing to the good yet to come and obligated to acquire purity of heart because of the vocation they have embraced, they should set themselves free to love God and their brothers and sisters.

13. As the Father sees in every person the features of his Son, the first-born of many brothers and sisters, so the Secular Franciscans with a gentle and courteous spirit accept all people as a gift of the Lord and an image of Christ.

    A sense of community will make them joyful and ready to place themselves on an equal basis with all people, especially with the lowly for whom they shall strive to create conditions of life worthy of people redeemed by Christ.

14. Secular Franciscans, together with all people of good will, are called to build a more fraternal and evangelical world so that the kingdom of God may be brought about more effectively. Mindful that anyone "who follows Christ, the perfect man, becomes more of a man himself," let them exercise their responsibilities competently in the Christian spirit of service.

15. Let them individually and collectively be in the forefront in promoting justice by the testimony of their human lives and their courageous initiatives. Especially in the field of public life, they should make definite choices in harmony with their faith.

16. Let them esteem work both as a gift and as a sharing in the creation, redemption, and service of the human community.

17. In their family they should cultivate the Franciscan spirit of peace, fidelity, and respect for life, striving to make of it a sign of a world

already renewed in Christ. By living the grace of matrimony, husbands and wives in particular should bear witness in the world to the love of Christ for His Church. They should joyfully accompany their children on their human and spiritual journey by providing a simple and open Christian education and being attentive to the vocation of each child.

18. Moreover they should respect all creatures, animate and inanimate, which "bear the imprint of the Most High," and they should strive to move from the temptation of exploiting creation to the Franciscan concept of universal kinship.

19. Mindful that they are bearers of peace which must be built up unceasingly, they should seek out ways of unity and fraternal harmony through dialogue, trusting in the presence of the divine seed in everyone and in the transforming power of love and pardon. Messengers of perfect joy in every circumstance, they should strive to bring joy and hope to others. Since they are immersed in the resurrection of Christ, which gives true meaning to Sister Death, let them serenely tend toward the ultimate encounter with the Father.

[Chapter Three]
Life In Fraternity

20. The Secular Franciscan Order is divided into fraternities of various levels—local, regional, national, and international. Each one has its own moral personality in the Church. These various fraternities are coordinated and united according to the norm of this rule and of the constitutions.

21. On various levels, each fraternity is animated and guided by a council and minister who are elected by the professed according to the constitutions. Their service, which lasts for a definite period, is marked by a ready and willing spirit and is a duty of responsibility to each member and to the community. Within themselves the fraternities are structured in different ways according to the norm of the constitutions, according to the various needs of their members and their regions, and under the guidance of their respective council.

22. The local fraternity is to be established canonically. It becomes the basic unit of the whole Order and a visible sign of the Church, the community of love. This should be the privileged place for develop-

ing a sense of Church and the Franciscan vocation and for enlivening the apostolic life of its members.

23. Requests for admission to the Secular Franciscan Order must be presented to the local fraternity, whose council decides upon the acceptance of new brothers and sisters. Admission into the Order is gradually attained through a time of initiation, a period of formation of at least one year, and profession of the rule. The entire community is engaged in the process of growth by its own manner of living. The age for profession and the distinctive Franciscan sign are regulated by the statutes.

    Profession by its nature is a permanent commitment.

    Members who find themselves in particular difficulties should discuss their problems with the council in fraternal dialogue. Withdrawal or permanent dismissal from the Order, if necessary, is an act of the fraternity council according to the norm of the constitutions.

24. To foster communion among members, the council should organize regular and frequent meetings of the community as well as meeting with other Franciscan groups, especially with youth groups. It should adopt appropriate means for growth in Franciscan and ecclesial life and encourage everyone to a life of fraternity. The communion continues with deceased brothers and sisters through prayer for them.

25. Regarding expenses necessary for the life of the fraternity and the needs of worship, of the apostolate, and of charity, all the brothers and sisters should offer a contribution according to their means. Local fraternities should contribute toward the expenses of the higher fraternity councils.

26. As a concrete sign of communion and co-responsibility, the councils on various levels, in keeping with the constitutions, shall ask for suitable and well prepared religious for spiritual assistance. They should make this request to the superiors of the four religious Franciscan families, to whom the Secular Fraternity has been united for centuries.

    To promote fidelity to the charism as well as observance of the rule and to receive greater support in the life of the fraternity, the minister or president, with the consent of the council, should take care to ask for a regular pastoral visit by the competent religious superiors as well as for a fraternal visit from those of the higher fraternities, according to the norm of the constitutions.

"May whoever observes all this be filled
in heaven with the blessing of the most high Father,
and on earth with that of his beloved Son,
together with the Holy Spirit, the Comforter."
(Blessing of St. Francis from the *Testament*)

The Third Order Regular of St. Francis

Following World War II and the changes it produced in society, religious throughout the world desired adaptation in their ways of life. The Second Vatican Council deepened this desire. In 1965 twenty-five congregations of Franciscan Sisters of France and Belgium began discussing possible adaptation, as did nineteen Dutch and ten German congregations. The IV Inter-Obediential Congress of the Third Order Regular in 1974 initiated a project called "An Understanding of Franciscan Penitential Life" or simply "The Madrid Document." Two years later an International Congress of Franciscan Sisters took place in Assisi in which the French, Dutch, German, and Madrid documents were discussed. An international Franciscan meeting was held in Assisi in 1979 in which two international organizations were also established: the International Franciscan Bureau and the International Franciscan Commission. These two bodies met the following year and decided that a projected text should be the same for men and women Franciscan groups, that this text should take into account the basic principles of Franciscan spirituality and the fundamental values that had inspired the various congregations, and that a group would be set up to work on the project.

A general assembly took place in 1982, the most important to that date, in which representatives from 285 Third Order Regular congregations from thirty-seven countries and the five continents were present. In spite of a variety of origins, apostolates, and styles of life, a text was prepared that expressed common fundamental values and, at the same time, a rich and precious diversity. This text was presented to the Sacred Congregation of Religious and later confirmed by Pope John Paul II with the brief *Franciscanum Vitae Propositum* on December 8, 1982.

The Rule and Life
of the Brothers and Sisters
of the Third Order Regular of St. Francis
Approved by Pope John Paul II

(1982)

In the name of the Lord!
Here begins the Rule and Life of the Brothers and
Sisters of the Third Order Regular of St. Francis

[Chapter I]
Our Identity

1. The form of life of the Brothers and Sisters of the Third Order Regular of Saint Francis is this: to observe the Holy Gospel of Our Lord Jesus Christ by living in obedience, in poverty and in chastity. Following Jesus Christ after the example of St. Francis, let them recognize that they are called to make greater efforts in their observance of the precepts and counsels of Our Lord Jesus Christ. Let them deny themselves (cf. Mt 16:24) as each has promised the Lord.

2. With all in the holy Catholic and apostolic Church who wish to serve the Lord, the brothers and sisters of this order are to persevere in true faith and penance. They wish to live this evangelical conversion of life in a spirit of prayer, of poverty, and of humility. Therefore, let them abstain from all evil and persevere to the end in doing good because God the Son Himself will come again in glory and will say to all who acknowledge, adore and serve Him in sincere repentance: "Come blessed of my Father, take possession of the kingdom prepared for you from the beginning of the world" (Mt 25:34).

3. The sisters and brothers promise obedience and reverence to the Pope and the Holy Catholic Church. In this same spirit they are to obey those called to be ministers and servants of their own fraternity. And wherever they are, or in whatever situation they are in, they should diligently and fervently show reverence and honor to one

another. They should also foster unity and communion with all the members of the Franciscan family.

[Chapter II]
Acceptance into this Life

4. Those who through the Lord's inspiration come to us desiring to accept this way of life are to be received kindly. At the appropriate time, they are to be presented to the ministers of the fraternity who hold responsibility to admit them.

5. The ministers shall ascertain that the aspirants truly adhere to the catholic faith and to the Church's sacramental life. If they are found to have a vocation, they are to be initiated into the life of the fraternity. Let everything pertaining to this gospel way of life be explained to them, especially these words of the Lord: "If you wish to be perfect (Mt 19:21) go and sell all your possessions and give to the poor. You will have treasure in heaven. Then come, follow me." And, "if anyone wishes to follow me, let him deny himself, take up his cross, and follow me" (Mt 16:24).

6. Led by the Lord, let them begin a life of penance, conscious that all of us must be continuously and totally converted to the Lord. As a sign of their conversion and consecration to gospel life, they are to clothe themselves plainly and to live in simplicity.

7. When their initial formation is completed, they are to be received into obedience promising to observe this life and rule always. Let them put aside all attachment as well as every care and worry. Let them only be concerned to serve, love, adore, and honour the Lord God, as best they can, with single-heartedness and purity of intention.

8. Within themselves, let them always make a dwelling place and home for the Lord God Almighty, Father, Son, and Holy Spirit, so that, with undivided hearts, they may increase in universal love by continually turning to God and to neighbor (Jn 14:23).

[Chapter III]
The Spirit of Prayer

9. Everywhere and in each place, and in every season and each day, the brothers and sisters are to have a true and humble faith. From

the depths of their inner life let them love, honour, adore, serve, praise, bless, and glorify our most high and eternal God who is Father, Son, and Holy Spirit. With all that they are, let them adore Him "because we should pray always and not lose heart" (Lk 18:1); this is what the Father desires. In this same spirit let them also celebrate the Liturgy of the Hours in union with the whole Church.

The sisters and brothers whom the Lord has called to the life of contemplation (Mk 6:31), with a daily renewed joy, should manifest their special dedication to God and celebrate the Father's love for the world. It was He who created and redeemed us, and by His mercy alone shall save us.

10. The brothers and sisters are to praise the Lord, the King of heaven and earth (cf. Mt 11:25), with all His creatures and to give Him thanks because, by His own holy will and through His only Son with the Holy Spirit, He has created all things spiritual and material and made us in His own image and likeness.

11. Since the sisters and brothers are to be totally conformed to the Gospel, they should reflect and keep in their hearts the words of Our Lord Jesus Christ who is the word of the Father, as well as the words of the Holy Spirit which "are spirit and life" (Jn 6:63).

12. Let them participate in the sacrifice of Our Lord Jesus Christ and receive His Body and Blood with great humility and reverence remembering the words of the Lord: "He who eats My Flesh and drinks My Blood has eternal life" (Jn 6:54). Moreover, they are to show the greatest possible reverence and honour for the most sacred name, written words, and most holy Body and Blood of Our Lord Jesus Christ through whom all things in heaven and on earth have been brought to peace and reconciliation with Almighty God (Jn 6:63).

13. Whenever they commit sin the brothers and sisters, without delay, are to do penance interiorly by sincere sorrow and exteriorly by confessing their sins to a priest. They should also do worthy deeds that manifest their repentance. They should fast and always strive to be simple and humble, especially before God. They should desire nothing else but our Savior, who offered Himself in His own Blood as a sacrifice on the altar of the Cross for our sins, giving us example so that we might follow in His footsteps.

[Chapter IV]

The Life of Chastity for the Sake of the Kingdom

14. Let the brothers and sisters keep in mind how great a dignity the Lord God has given them "because He created them and formed them in the image of His beloved Son according to the flesh and in His own likeness according to the Spirit" (Col 1:16). Since they are created through Christ and in Christ, they have chosen this form of life which is founded on the words and deeds of our Redeemer.

15. Professing chastity "for the sake of the kingdom of heaven" (Mt 19:12), they are to care for the things of the Lord and "they have nothing else to do except to follow the will of the Lord and to please Him" (1 Cor 7:32). In all of their works the love of God and all people should shine forth.

16. They are to remember that they have been called by a special gift of grace to manifest in their lives that wonderful mystery by which the Church is joined to Christ her spouse (cf. Eph 5:23-26).

17. Let the brothers and sisters keep the example of the Blessed Virgin Mary, the Mother of God and of our Lord Jesus Christ, ever before their eyes. Let them do this according to the exhortation of St. Francis who held Holy Mary, Lady and Queen, in highest veneration, since she is "the virgin made church." Let them also remember that the Immaculate Virgin Mary, whose example they are to follow, called herself "the handmaid of the Lord" (Lk 1:38).

[Chapter V]

The Way to Serve and Work

18. As poor people, the brothers and sisters to whom the Lord has given the grace of serving or working with their hands, should do so faithfully and conscientiously. Let them avoid that idleness which is the enemy of the soul. But they should not be so busy that the spirit of holy prayer and devotion, which all earthly goods should foster, is extinguished.

19. In exchange for their service or work, they may accept anything necessary for their own temporal needs and for that of their sisters or brothers. Let them accept it humbly as is expected of those who are servants of God and seekers of most holy poverty. Whatever they may have over and above their needs, they are to give to the poor.

And let them never want to be over others. Instead they should be servants and subjects to every human creature for the Lord's sake.

20. Let the sisters and brothers be gentle, peaceful and unassuming, mild and humble, speaking respectfully to all in accord with their vocation. Wherever they are, or wherever they go throughout the world they should not be quarrelsome, contentious, or judgmental towards others. Rather, it should be obvious that they are "joyful, good-humored," and happy "in the Lord" as they ought to be (cf. Phil 4:4). And in greeting others, let them say, "The Lord give you peace."

[Chapter VI]
The Life of Poverty

21. All the sisters and brothers zealously follow the poverty and humility of Our Lord Jesus Christ. "Though rich" beyond measure (2 Cor 8:9), He emptied Himself for our sake (Phil 2:7) and with the holy virgin, His mother, Mary, He chose poverty in this world. Let them be mindful that they should have only those goods of this world which, as the apostle says, "having something to eat and something to wear, with these we are content" (1 Tim 6:8). Let them particularly beware of money. And let them be happy to live among the outcast and despised, among the poor, the weak, the sick, the unwanted, the oppressed, and the destitute.

22. The truly poor in spirit, following the example of the Lord, live in this world as pilgrims and strangers (cf. 1 Pet 2:1). They neither appropriate nor defend anything as their own. So excellent is this most high poverty that it makes us heirs and rulers of the kingdom of heaven. It makes us materially poor, but rich in virtue (cf. Jn 2:5). Let this poverty alone be our portion because it leads to the land of the living (Ps 141:6). Clinging completely to it let us, for the sake of Our Lord Jesus Christ, never want anything else under heaven.

[Chapter VII]
Fraternal Love

23. Because God loves us, the brothers and sisters should love each other, for the Lord says, "This is my commandment, that you love one another as I have loved you" (Jn 15:12). Let them manifest their love in deeds (cf. 1 Jn 3:18). Also whenever they meet each other, they should show that they are members of the same family. Let them

make known their needs to one another. Blessed are they who love another who is sick and seemingly useless, as much as when that brother or sister is well and of service to them. Whether in sickness or in health, they should only want what God wishes for them. For all that happens to them let them give thanks to our Creator.

24. If discord caused by word or deed should occur among them, they should immediately (Mt 18:35) and humbly ask forgiveness of one another even before offering their gift of prayer before the Lord (cf. Mt 5:24). And if anyone seriously neglects the form of life all profess, the minister, or others who may know of it, are to admonish that person. Those giving the admonition should neither embarrass nor speak evil of the other, but show great kindness. Let all be careful of self righteousness, which causes anger and annoyance because of another's sin. These in oneself or in another hinder living lovingly.

[Chapter VIII]
The Obedience of Love

25. Following the example of the Lord Jesus Christ who made his own will one with the Father's, the sisters and brothers are to remember that, for God, they should give up their own wills. Therefore, in every kind of chapter they have let them "seek first the kingdom of God and His justice" (Mt 6:33), and exhort one another to observe with greater dedication the rule they have professed and to follow faithfully in the footprints of Our Lord Jesus Christ. Let them neither dominate nor seek power over one another, but let them willingly serve and obey "one another with that genuine love which comes from each one's heart" (cf. Gal 5:13). This is the true and holy obedience of Our Lord Jesus Christ.

26 They are always to have one of their number as minister and servant of the fraternity whom they are strictly obliged to obey in all that they have promised the Lord to observe, and which is not contrary to conscience or this rule.

27. Those who are ministers and servants of the others should visit, admonish, and encourage them with humility and love. Should there be brothers or sisters anywhere who know and acknowledge that they cannot observe the rule according to its spirit, it is their right and duty to have recourse to their ministers. The ministers are to

receive them with such love, kindness, and sympathy that the sisters or brothers can speak and act toward them just as an employer would with a worker. This is how it should be. The ministers are to be servants of all.

28. No one is to appropriate any office or ministry whatsoever as if it were a personal right; rather each should willingly relinquish it when the time comes.

[Chapter IX]

Apostolic Life

29. The brothers and sisters are to love the Lord "with their whole heart, with their whole soul and mind, and with all their strength," and to love their neighbour as themselves. Let them glorify the Lord in all they do. For He has sent them into the world so that they might give witness by word and work to His voice and to make known to all that the Lord alone is God (cf. Mk 12:30, Mt 22:30).

30. As they announce peace with their lips, let them be careful to have it even more within their own hearts. No one should be roused to wrath or insult on their account, rather all should be moved to peace, goodwill and mercy because of their gentleness. The sisters and brothers are called to heal the wounded, to bind up those who are bruised, and to reclaim the erring. Wherever they are, they should recall that they have given themselves up completely and handed themselves over totally to Our Lord Jesus Christ. Therefore, they should be prepared to expose themselves to every enemy, visible and invisible, for the love of Him because the Lord says: "Blessed are they who suffer persecution for the sake of justice, theirs is the kingdom of heaven" (Mt 5:10).

31. In that love which is God (1 Jn 4:16) all the brothers and sisters, whether they are engaged in prayer, or in announcing the word of God, or in serving, or in doing manual labour, should strive to be humble in everything. They should not seek glory, or be self-satisfied, or interiorly proud because of a good work or word God does or speaks in or through them. Rather in every place and circumstance, let them acknowledge that all good belongs to the most high Lord and Ruler of all things. Let them always give thanks to Him from Whom we receive all good.

Exhortation and Blessing

32. Let the sisters and brothers always be mindful that they should desire one thing alone, namely, the Spirit of God at work within them. Always obedient to the Church and firmly established in the Catholic faith, let them live according to the poverty, the humility, and the holy Gospel of Our Lord Jesus Christ which they have solemnly promised to observe.

    "Whoever will observe these, things shall be filled with the blessings of the Most High Father in Heaven, and on earth with the blessing of His beloved Son, with the Holy Spirit, and with all virtues and with all the saints.

    "And I, Brother Francis, your little one and servant, in so far as I am able, confirm to you within and without this most Holy Blessing."

Notes

Introduction, pages xi–xv

1. Francis, The Legend of Three Companions (L3C) 24, FA:ED II 83. Citations of Francis's works come from *Francis of Assisi: Early Documents*, 3 vols., ed. Regis J. Armstrong, J. A. Wayne Hellmann, and William J. Short (New York: New City Press, 1999–2001).

2. Thomas of Celano, The First Life of Saint Francis (1C) 36, 37, FA:ED I 214–17.

The Franciscan Tradition pages xvii–xxvii

1. Francis, The Testament, FA:ED I 124.

2. Francis, The Admonitions 1–5, FA:ED I 129.

3. Francis, The Testament 6, FA:ED I 125.

4. Francis, The Testament 14, ibid.

5. Clare, Form of Life VI 3, CA:ED. See Regis J. Armstrong, *The Lady: Clare of Assisi: Early Documents*, rev. ed. (New York: New City Press, 2006).

6. Clare, Form of Life VI 8–9, CA:ED.

7. Francis, Later Rule X 8, FA:ED I 105.

8. Francis, Later Rule V 2, FA:ED I 102.

9. Thomas of Celano, The Remembrance of the Desire of a Soul (2C) 95, FA:ED II 310.

10. The Assisi Compilation 83, FA:ED II 185.

11. Francis, Canticle, FA:ED I 113–14.

12. Francis, Canticle, FA:ED I 114.

13. Ibid.

14. Francis, Earlier Rule XXII 9, FA:ED I 79.

15. Francis, Canticle, FA:ED I 114.

Francis of Assisi (c. 1182–1226), pages 1–8

1. Francis, The Testament 34, FA:ED I 127.

2. Francis, The Testament 2, FA:ED I 124.

3. Francis, The Testament 14, FA:ED I 125.

4. Bonaventure, Major Legend IX 9, FA:ED II 603–4.

5. The Assisi Compilation 18, FA:ED II 132–33.

6. Francis, Later Rule I 1, FA:ED I 100.
7. Francis, Later Rule X 8, FA:ED I 105.
8. Francis, Earlier Rule XXII 9–55, FA:ED I 79–81.
9. Francis, A Letter to a Minister, FA:ED I 97–98.

The Rule of the Friars Minor, pages 11–16

1. Francis, Later Rule, FA:ED I 99–106.

Anthony of Padua (1195–1231), pages 17–22

1. Francis, Later Rule X 7, FA:ED I 105.
2. Francis, Letter to Brother Anthony of Padua, FA:ED I 107.
3. St. Anthony of Padua, *Seek First His Kingdom*, ed. Livio Poloniato (Padova: Edizioni Messaggero Padova, 1988), 71–75.

Bonaventure of Bagnoregio (c. 1217–1274), pages 23–29

1. Bonaventure, *A Letter in Response to an Unknown Master* 13, in *Writings Concerning the Franciscan Order*, Works of Saint Bonaventure, vol. 5, trans. and ed. Dominic Monti (St. Bonaventure, NY: Franciscan Institute Publications, 1993), 54.
2. Bonaventure, I Sent., pro., q. 3 (1, 131-b).
3. Bonaventure, *The Mind's Journey into God*, Prol. 2.
4. Bernard McGinn, *The Flowering of Mysticism*, The Presence of God Series (New York: Crossroad, 1998), 88.
5. Bonaventure, *Itinerarium mentis in Deum* IV 2.

Felix of Cantalice (1515–1587), pages 30–36

1. Thomas of Celano, The Remembrance of the Desire of a Soul (2C) 189, FA:ED II 367.
2. These references are taken from the *Process of Canonization* as translated or paraphrased by Ignatius McCormick in Mariano D'Alatri, *The Capuchin Way: Lives of Capuchins* (Pittsburgh, PA: North American Capuchin Conference, 1986), 27–48. In this instance Statement of Sanctes a Priverno, October 1618, *Testimonia ex Processo Apostolico*.
3. Statement of Alexius a Sezze, August 1621, *Testimonia ex Processo Apostolico*, cf. Mariano D'Alatri, ed., *Processus sistinus Fratris Felicis a Cantalice cum selectis de eiusdem vita vetustissimus testimoniis* (Rome: Istituto Storico dei Cappuccini, 1964), 338.
4. D'Alatri, *The Capuchin Way*, 34.
5. Ibid.
6. Augustinus a Bergamo, Angelus a Penne, *Processus Sixtinus*, 280, 283.
7. Dominicus a Carbognano, *Processus Sixtinus*, 45.
8. Matthias a Salò, *Processus Sixtinus*, 30.
9. Domenico a Carbognano, *Processus Sixtinus*, 45.
10. Pietro a Bergamo, *Processus Sixtinus*, 84.
11. D'Alatri, *The Capuchin Way*, 44–45.
12. Ibid., 46–47.
13. Original Italian texts found in "Fratris Felicis Carmina," in *Processus Sixtinus*, 386–89. Unpublished translation by William J. Short.

14. "Varia Quaedam Fragmenta," in *Processus Sixtinus*, 408. Cf. D'Alatri, *The Capuchin Way*, 43.

15. "Varia Quaedam Fragmenta," in *Processus Sixtinus*, 409–10. Cf. Cuthbert, *The Capuchins*, vol. 1 (Pt. Washington, NY: Kennikat Press, 1926; reissued 1971), 176.

Junipero Serra (1713–1784), pages 37–49

1. The words—which became his motto—are found in the letter he wrote to a confrere, Francisco Serra. It was first translated and published in *The Los Angeles Tidings*, August 8, 1913, 3–4.

2. Maynard Geiger, ed., *Palóu's Life of Fray Junípero Serra* (Washington: Academy of American Franciscan History, 1955), 5.

3. Ibid.

4. Ibid., 9.

5. John Paul II, Meeting with Native American Indians, Phoenix, Arizona, September 14, 1987.

6. Ibid.

7. John Paul II, Homily, Beatification of Junípero Serra, September 25, 1988.

8. *The Tidings*, August 8, 1913, 3–4.

Maximilian Mary Kolbe (1894–1941), pages 50–56

1. Patricia Treece, *A Man for Others* (San Francisco: Harper & Row, 1982), 1.

2. Quoted by Jerzy Domanski, "St. Maximilian Kolbe and the Eucharist," in *Mother of All Peoples Magazine* III 30.

3. Treece, *Man for Others*, 43.

4. Diana Dewar, *The Saint of Auschwitz* (San Francisco: Harper & Row, 1982), 94.

5. Ibid., 84.

6. Treece, *Man for Others*, 175.

7. Ibid., 171.

8. Dewar, *Saint of Auschwitz*, 98.

9. Treece, *Man for Others*, 178.

10. Pope Paul VI, Homily for the Beatification of Maximilian Mary Kolbe, October 17, 1971.

11. Pope John Paul II, Homily at the Canonization of Bl. Maximilian Mary Kolbe, October 10, 1982.

12. Excerpted from *The Kolbe Reader: The Writings of St. Maximilian M. Kolbe, OFM Conv.*, ed. Anselm W. Romb (Libertyville, IL: Franciscan Marytown Press, 987), 198–99.

Solanus Casey (1870–1957), pages 57–63

1. *Solanus Casey: The Official Account of a Virtuous American Life*, ed. Michael Crosby (New York: Crossroad, 2000), 47.

2. Ibid., 47.

3. Ibid.

Clare of Assisi (1194–1253), pages 78–88

1. Process of Canonization XII 2, CA:ED 183.

2. Process of Canonization III 2; IV 5; VI 3; XVI 9, 18; XVII 7–9, CA:ED.
3. Second Letter to Agnes of Prague 11, CA:ED 48.
4. Second Letter to Agnes of Prague 17, ibid.
5. Third Letter to Agnes of Prague 42, CA:ED 53.
6. CA:ED 43–46.
7. Ibid., 54–58.

Colette of Corbie (1381–1447), pages 89–94

1. Celsus O'Brien, "Some Fifteenth Century Poor Clares: St. Colette," *The Story of the Poor Clares* (Limerick: Franciscan Friary, 1992), 23–24.
2. Mother Mary Francis, *The Testament of St. Colette* (Chicago: Franciscan Herald Press, 1987), 2–4.
3. Ibid., 4–6.
4. Ibid., 6–8.

Catherine of Bologna (1413–1463), pages 95–98

1. Catherine of Bologna, *The Seven Spiritual Weapons*, trans. Hugh Feiss and Daniela Re (Toronto: Peregrina Translation Series, 1998), 35–36.
2. Ibid., 37–38.

Veronica Giuliani (1660–1727), pages 99–103

1. Lazaro Iriarte, "The Franciscan Spirit of St. Veronica Giuliani," trans. Edward Hagman, *Greyfriars Review* 7, no. 2 (1993): 205.
2. Ibid., 205–6.
3. Ibid., 206.
4. Ibid.
5. Ibid., 206–7.
6. Ibid., 207.
7. Ibid.
8. Ibid., 207–8.

Angela of Foligno (1248–1309), pages 110–117

1. Paul Lachance, *Angela of Foligno*, CWS #77 (Mahwah, NJ: Paulist Press, 1993), 139–40.
2. Ibid., 162–63.
3. Ibid., 169–70.
4. Ibid., 204–5.
5. Ibid., 205–6.
6. Ibid., 215.
7. Ibid., 227–28.
8. Ibid., 240.
9. Ibid., 268.
10. Ibid., 269–70.
11. Ibid., 286–87.

Mary of the Passion (1839–1904), pages 121–127

1. Marie-Thérèse de Maleissye, *Fifteen Days of Prayer with Mary of the Passion* (Bandra, Mumbai: St. Pauls, 2000), 96–104.

Marianne Cope of Molokai (1838–1918), pages 128–134

1. Mary Laurence Hanley and O. A. Bushnell, *Pilgrimage and Exile: Mother Marianne of Molokai* (Chicago: Franciscan Herald Press, 1980; rev. ed. University of Hawaii Press, 1991; reprinted by Mutual Publishing Co., Honolulu, 2009), 41.

2. Ibid., 312.

3. Marion Kikukawa quoted in Mary Cabrini Durkin and Mary Laurence Hanley, *Valiant Woman of Hawai'i: Mother Marianne of Moloka'i* (Syracuse, NY: Sisters of the Third Franciscan Order, 1999), verso page of front cover.

4. Grace Anne Dillenschneider, "A Spiritual View of Mother Marianne Cope," *L'Osservatore Romano* (May 14, 2005): 6.

The Martyrs of Nagasaki (1597), pages 137–142

1. Sigfrid Schneider and Thomas Uyttenbroeck, *The Twenty-Six Martyrs of Japan* (Tokyo: Chuo Shuooansha, 1980), 4.

2. Ibid., 6–7.

3. Ibid., 10.

4. Diego Yuuki, *A Fundaçao do Porto de Nagasaqui* (Maçao: Centro de Estudos Maritimos, 1989).

5. Petra Schmidt, *Capital Punishment in Japan* (Leiden: Brill, 2001), 14.

6. Yuuki, *A Fundaçao do Porto de Nagasaqui.*

7. Peter Baptist, Letters: January 4 and February 2, 1597 in *Archivio Ibero-Americano* 6 (1916): 16–17.

8. Ibid.

Jean-Marie Vianney (1786–1859), pages 143–148

1. John Marie Vianney. *The Little Catechism of The Curé of Ars* (Charlotte, NC: Tan Books, 2009).

2. Ibid.

Matt Talbot (1856–1925), pages 149–162

1. Mary Purcell, *Matt Talbot and His Times* (Westminster, MD: Newman Press, 1955), 247.

2. Ibid.

3. Ibid., 64.

4. Cf. the statements of Pat Doyle, a friend of the Talbots and drinking companion of Matt in ibid., 40–45.

5. Cf. Elizabeth Malcolm, "The Catholic Church and the Irish Temperance Movement 1838–1901," *Irish Historical Studies* 23, no. 89 (May 1982): 1–16.

6. John F. Quinn, "The 'Vagabond Friar': Father Mathew's Difficulties with the Irish Bishops, 1840–1856," *The Catholic Historical Review* 78, no. 4 (1992): 542–56.

7. Ibid.

8. Purcell, *Matt Talbot*, 52–53.

9. Ibid., 53

10. Testimony of Mary in ibid., 88.

11. Cf. testimony of Daniel Manning, in ibid., 127–29.

12. Cf. Joseph A. Glynn, *Life of Matt Talbot* (Dublin: Catholic Truth Society of Ireland, 1928), 24; also the testimonies of his niece, Annie Johnson, and of Pat Doyle in Purcell, *Matt Talbot*, 89, 54–57.

13. Glynn, *Life*, 20.

14. Purcell, *Matt Talbot*, 211–13.

15. Mark Hegener, "Introduction," in ibid., vi.

16. Cf. ibid., 67.

17. There are a number of descriptions of Matt Talbot's working habits and reputation in ibid., 122–33.

18. Ibid., 231.

19. Ibid., 139–40.

20. James Connelly, *Workers' Republic*, 8 April, 1916.

21. For background information, see Mark Tierney, *Croke of Cashel* (Dublin, 1976).

22. Testimony of John Robbins found in Purcell, *Matt Talbot*, 180.

23. Testimony of Br. John Furlong, s.j., found in ibid., 188.

24. Testimony of James Tallon found in ibid., 182.

25. Testimony of Dr. John Henry Moore found in ibid., 218.

26. Testimony of Br. John Furlong, s.j., found in ibid., 228.

27. Testimony of Paddy Laird found in ibid., 161–62.

28. Testimony of Raphael O'Callaghan found in ibid., 159–60.

29. Testimony of Daniel Manning found in ibid., 127–29.

30. Testimony of Mrs. Daniel Manning found in ibid., 129–31.

Bibliography

Franciscan Tradition

Carmody, Maurice. *The Franciscan Story*. London: Athena Press, 2008.
Iriate, Lazaro. *Franciscan History: The Three Orders of St. Francis of Assisi*. Translated by Patricia Ross. Chicago: Franciscan Herald Press, 1982.
Moorman, John. *A History of the Franciscan Order from Its Origins to the Year 1517*. Oxford: Clarendon Press, 1968.

First Order

Monti, Dominic V. *Francis and His Brothers: A Popular History of the Franciscan Friars*. Cincinnati: St. Anthony Messenger Press, 2009.
Nimmo, Duncan. *Reform and Division in the Medieval Franciscan Order (1226–1538)*. Rome: Capuchin Historical Institute, 1987.

Francis of Assisi

Armstrong, Regis J. *St. Francis of Assisi: Writings for a Gospel Life*. New York: Crossroad, 1994.
Green, Julian. *God's Fool: The Life and Times of Francis of Assisi*. Translated by Peter Heinegg. San Francisco: Harper and Row, 1985.
Nguyen-Van-Khanh, Norbert. *Teacher of His Heart: Jesus Christ in the Thought and Writings of St. Francis*. Translated by Ed Hagman. Edited by Louise Hembrecht and Bernard R. Creighton. St. Bonaventure, NY: Franciscan Institute, 1994.
Founder, vol. 2 of *Francis of Assisi: Early Documents*. Edited by Regis J. Armstrong, J. A. Wayne Hellman, and William J. Short. New York: New City Press, 2000.
Prophet, vol. 3 of *Francis of Assisi: Early Documents*. Edited by Regis J. Armstrong, J. A. Wayne Hellman, and William J. Short. New York: New City Press, 2001.

Saint, vol. 1 of *Francis of Assisi: Early Documents.* Edited by Regis J. Armstrong, J. A. Wayne Hellman, and William J. Short. New York: New City Press, 1999.

Anthony of Padua

Jarmak, Claude M. *If You Seek Miracles: Reflections of Saint Anthony of Padua.* Padua, Edizioni Messaggero Padova, 1998.

Rotzetter, Anton. *Saint Anthony of Padua: A Voice from Heaven.* Translated by Sharon Therese Nemeth. Cincinnati: St. Anthony Messenger Press, 1994.

Saint Anthony. Herald of the Good News: A Guide and Light for Today: Excerpts from the Sermons of Saint Anthony. Translated by Claude M. Jarmak. Ellicott City, MD: Conventual Franciscan Friars, 1995.

Seek First His Kingdom: An Anthology of the Sermons of the Saint. Edited by Livio Poloniato. Padua: Edizioni Messaggero Padova, 1988.

Bonaventure of Bagnoregio

Works of Saint Bonaventure. Saint Bonaventure, NY: Franciscan Institute Publications, 1979–.

Bougerol, J. Guy. *Introduction to the Works of Bonaventure.* Translated by José de Vinck. Paterson, NJ: St. Anthony Guild Press, 1964.

Delio, Ilia. *Simply Bonaventure: An Introduction to His Life, Thought, and Writings.* New York: New City Press, 2001.

Ratzinger, Joseph. *The Theology of History in St. Bonaventure.* Translated by Zachary Hayes. Chicago: Franciscan Herald Press, 1971.

Felix of Cantalice

D'Alatri, Mariano. *The Capuchin Way: Lives of Capuchins.* Vol. 1. Translated by Ignatius G. McCormick. Denver: North American Capuchin Conference, 1985.

———, ed. *Processus sixtinus Fratris Felicis a Cantalice cum selectis de eiusdem vita vetustissimis testimoniis.* Vol. 10 of Monumenta Historia Ordinis Minorum Capuccinorum. Rome: Institutum Historicum, 1964.

Junípero Serra

Geiger, Maynard J. *Life and Times of Fray Junípero Serra, O.F.M.: The Man Who Never Turned Back.* 2 vols. Washington, DC: Academy of American Franciscan History, 1959.

King, Kenneth M. *Mission to Paradise: The Story of Junípero Serra and the Missions of California*. Chicago: Franciscan Herald Press, 1956.

Palóu's Life of Fray Junípero Serra. Translated and Annotated by Maynard J. Geiger. Washington, DC: Academy of American Franciscan History, 1955.

Weber, Francis J. *California's Serrana Literature*. Reprinted from *Southern California Quarterly* 51, no. 4 (December 1969).

Maximilian Mary Kolbe

Dewar, Diana. *The Saint of Auschwitz: The Story of Maximilian Kolbe*. San Francisco: Harper & Row, 1982.

Romb, Anselm, ed. *The Kolbe Reader: The Writings of the Saint, Maximilian M. Kolbe, OFM Conv.* Libertyville, IL: Franciscan Marytown Press, 1987.

Treece, Patricia. *A Man for Others: Maximilian Kolbe, Saint of Auschwitz, in the Words of Those Who Knew Him*. San Francisco: Harper & Row, 1982.

Solanus Casey

Crosby, Michael H., ed. *Solanus Casey. The Official Account of a Virtuous American Life*. New York: Crossroad, 2000.

———. *Thank God Ahead of Time: The Life and Spirituality of Solanus Casey*. Chicago: Franciscan Herald Press, 1985.

Derum, James Patrick. *The Porter of St. Bonaventure's: The Life of Father Solanus Casey, Capuchin*. Detroit: Fidelity Press, 1968.

O'Dell, Catherine M. *Solanus Casey: The Story of Father Solanus*. Huntington, IN: Our Sunday Visitor, 2007.

Second Order

Bartolini, P. Rino, Marie Colette Roussey, Marie Pascale Gounon. *Nella Tua Tenda, Per Sempre: Storia delle Clarisse, un'avventura di ottocento anni*. Assisi: Edizioni Porziuncola, 1979–2004.

O'Brien, Celsus. *The Story of the Poor Clares*. Limerick: Franciscan Friary, 1992.

Poor Clares of the Holy Name Federation and the Mother Bentivoglio Federation. *Doing What Is Ours to Do: A Clarian Theology of Life: Poor Clares Reflecting Theologically on the Guiding Images, Foundations, and Insights of Our Life and Lives*. St. Bonaventure, NY: Franciscan Institute, 2000.

Clare of Assisi

Alberzoni, Maria. *Clare and the Poor Sisters of the Thirteenth Century*. St. Bonaventure, NY: Franciscan Institute Publications, 2004.

Armstrong, Regis J. *Clare of Assisi: The Lady: Early Documents.* Hyde Park, NY: New City Press, 2006.

Bartoli, Marco. *Clare of Assisi.* Translated by Sister Frances Teresa. Quincy, IL: Franciscan Press, 1993.

Carney, Margaret. *The First Franciscan Women: Clare of Assisi and Her Form of Life.* Quincy, IL: Franciscan Press, 1993.

Dalarum, Jacques. *Francis of Assisi and the Feminine.* St. Bonaventure: Franciscan Institute Publications, 2006.

Delio, Ilia. *Clare of Assisi: A Heart Full of Love.* Cincinnati: St. Anthony Messenger Press, 2007.

Downing, Frances Teresa. *This Living Mirror: Reflections of Clare of Assisi.* Maryknoll, NY: Orbis Books, 1995.

Knox, Lezlie. "Audacious Nuns: Institutionalizing the Franciscan Order of Saint Clare." *Church History* 69, no. 1 (2000): 41–62.

———. *Creating Clare of Assisi: Female Franciscan Identities in Late Medieval Italy.* Leiden, The Netherlands: Brill, 2006.

Mueller, Joan. *The Privilege of Poverty: Clare of Assisi, Agnes of Prague, and the Struggle for a Franciscan Rule for Women.* University Park, PA: Penn State Press, 2006.

Peterson, Ingrid J. *Clare of Assisi: A Biographical Study.* Quincy, IL: Franciscan Press, 1993.

Van den Goorbergh, Edith, and Theodore Zweerman. *Light Shining Through a Veil: On Saint Clare's Letters to Saint Agnes of Prague.* Translated by Aline Loorman-Graaskamp and Frances Teresa Downing. Leuven: Peeters, 2000.

Colette of Corbie

Bisett, Christopher. "St. Colette of Corbie: Mysticism as a Life of Prayerful Discernment." *The Cord* 49 (1990): 196–203.

Marie-Elizabeth. "Colette of Corbie." *Greyfriars Review* 4, no. 1 (1990): 101–16.

Mother Mary Francis. *The Testament of St. Colette.* Chicago: Franciscan Herald Press, 1987.

Roest, Bert. "A Textual Community in the Making": Translated by Colettine Authorship in the Fifteenth Century"(163-180) in *Seeing and Knowing: Women and Learning in Medieval Europe 1200-1500.* Edited by Anneke B. Mulder-Bakker. Medieval Women: Texts and Contexts Turnhout: Brepols, 2004.

Warren, Nancy Bradley. "Monastic Politics: St. Colette of Corbie, Franciscan Reform, and the House of Burgundy." In *New Medieval Literatures*, no. 5, edited by Rita Copeland, David Lawton, and Wendy Scase, 203–28. Oxford: Oxford University Press, 2001.

————. *Women of God and Arms: Female Spirituality and Political Conflict, 1380–1600.* The Middle Ages Series. Philadelphia: University of Pennsylvania Press, 2005.

Catherine of Bologna

Arthur, Kay G. "Images of Clare and Francis in Caterina Vigri's Personal Breviary." *Franciscan Studies* 62 (2004): 179–92.

Tamayo, Sarita. *Hiddenness and the Imitation of Christ in Caterina Vigri's 'Le sette armi spirituality.'* PhD diss., University of Chicago, 2002.

The Seven Spiritual Weapons. Translated by Hugh Feiss and Daniela Re. Toronto: Peregrina Translation Series, 1998.

Wood, Jeryldene M. "Breaking the Silence: The Poor Clares and the Visual Arts in Fifteenth-Century Italy." *Renaissance Quarterly* 48, no. 2 (1995) 262–86.

————. "Vision and Ecstacy." In *Women, Art, and Spirituality: The Poor Clares of Early Modern Italy*, 121–44. Cambridge: Cambridge University Press, 1996.

Veronica Giuliani

Iriate, Lazaro. "The Franciscan Spirit of St. Veronica Guiliani." *Greyfriars Review* 7, no. 2 (1993): 193–227.

Millane, Pacelli. "The Fire of Love in the Writings of Veronica Guiliani." *The Cord* 49, no. 4 (1999): 188–95.

Picciafuoco, Umberto. "St. Francis in the Piety and Mystical Experience of St. Veronica Giuliani, Based on her Dairy." *Greyfriars Review* 10, no. 1 (1996): 89–106.

Veronica Guiliani. *The Purgatory of Love.* Translated by Oliver Knox. Citta di Castello: Centro Studi Veronichiano, 1943.

Third Order

Third Order Regular

Carney, Margaret, and Thaddeus Horgan. *The Rule and Life of the Brothers and Sisters of the Third Order Regular of St. Francis and Commentary.* Washington, DC: Franciscan Federation, 1997.

Carney, Margaret, Jean-François Godet-Calogeras, and Suzanne M. Kush. *History of the Third Order Regular Rule: A Source Book.* St. Bonaventure, NY: Franciscan Institute Publications, 2008.

Hallack, Cecily, and Peter F. Anson. *These Made Peace: Studies in the Lives of the Beatified and Canonized Members of the Third Order of Saint Francis of Assisi*. Patterson, NJ: St. Anthony Guild Press, 1957.

Pazzelli, Raffaele. *The Franciscan Sisters: Outlines of History and Spirituality.* Translated by Aidan Mullaney. Steubenville, OH: Franciscan University Press, 1993.

Angela of Foligno

Angela of Foligno: Complete Works. Translated by Paul Lachance. Mahwah, NJ: Paulist Press, 1993.

Angela of Foligno: The Passionate Mystic of the Double Abyss. Edited and translated by Paul Lachance. Hyde Park, NY: New City Press, 2006.

Mazzoni, Christina. *Angela of Foligno's Memorial*. Translated by John Cirignano. Rochester, NY: D. S. Brewer Books, 1999.

Mooney, Catherine M. "The Authorial Role of Brother A. in the Composition of Angela of Foligno's *Revelations*." In *Creative Women in Medieval and Early Modern Italy: A Religious and Artistic Renaissance*, edited by E. Ann Matter and John Coakley, 34–63. Philadelphia: University of Pennsylvania Press, 1994.

Mary of the Passion

de Maleissye, Marie Thérèse. *A Short Life of Mary of the Passion*. Paris: Desclee de Brouwer, 1996.

———. *Fifteen Days of Prayer with Mary of the Passion*. Bandra, Mumbai: The Bombay St. Paul Society, 2000.

Goyau, Georges. *Valiant Women: Mother Mary of the Passion and the Franciscan Missionaries of Mary*. Translated by George Telford. London: Sheed and Ward, 1936.

Launey, Marcel. *Héléne de Chappotin and the Franciscan Missionaries of Mary*. Nantes: University de Nantes, 2001.

Mary of the Passion, Foundress of the Franciscan Missionaries of Mary, an Illustrated History. Inspired by *A Short Life of Mary of the Passion* by Marie Thérèse Maleissye. Paris: Desclee de Brouwer, 1996.

Robert, Dana Lee. "The Founding of Foreign Missionary Communities." In *American Women in Mission: A Social History of their Thought and Practice*, 335–38. Macon, GA: Mercer University Press, 1997.

Marianne Cope of Molokai

Dries, Angelyn. "Franciscans in Hawaii: Mother Marianne Cope." In *The Missionary Movement in American Catholic History*, 51–59. Maryknoll, NY: Orbis Books, 1998.

Durkin, Mary Cabrini, with Sister Mary Laurence. *Mother Marianne of Molokai: Heroic Women of Hawaii.* Strasbourg, France: Editions du Signe, 1999.

Gumpel, Peter. *Mother Marianne Cope: Report of the Relator of the Cause.* Vatican City: Congregation for Causes of Saints, 1995.

Hanley, Mary Laurence, and O. A. Bushnell. *Pilgrimage and Exile: Mother Marianne of Molokai.* Chicago: Franciscan Herald Press, 1980. Updated by Honolulu: University of Hawaii Press, 1991. Reprinted by Syracuse Blue Print Co. Inc., 2006. Reprinted by Honolulu: Mutual Publishing Co., 2009.

Mouritz, Arthur A. *The Path of the Destroyer: A History of Leprosy in the Hawaiian Islands and Thirty Years Research into the Means by which It Has Been Spread.* Honolulu: Honolulu Star-Bulletin Press, 1916.

Richardson, Janine. "Keiki O Ka'Aina: Institutional Care for Hawai'i's Dependent Children, 1865–1938." PhD diss., University of Hawaii, 2005.

Third Order Secular

Bach, Lester. *Called to Rebuild the Church: A Spiritual Commentary on the General Constitutions of the Secular Franciscan Order.* SFO Resource Library. Vol. 2. Cincinnati: St. Anthony Messenger Press, 1998.

———. *Called to Build a More Fraternal and Evangelical World: Commentary on the Rule of the Secular Franciscan Order.* SFO Resource Library. Vol. 6. Cincinnati: St. Anthony Messenger Press, 1998.

Foley, Leonard, Jovian Wiegel, and Patti Normile. *To Live as Francis Lived: A Guide for Secular Franciscans.* Cincinnati: St. Anthony Messenger Press, 2000.

McCloskey, Pat, ed. *Day by Day with Followers of Francis and Clare.* Cincinnati: St. Anthony Messenger Press, 1999.

Marquard, Philip. *Called to Live the Dynamic Power of the Gospel. Commentary on the Rule of the Secular Franciscan Order.* SFO Resource Library. Vol. 3. Cincinnati: St. Anthony Messenger Press, 1998.

Stewart, Robert M. *"De Illis Qui Faciunt Penitentiam," The Rule of the Secular Franciscan Order: Origins, Development, Interpretation.* Roma: Instituto Storico dei Cappuccini, 1991.

The Martyrs of Nagasaki

Leon de Clary. *Lives of the Saints and Blessed of the Three Orders of St. Francis.* I. Taunton: Franciscan Convent, 1885.

Uyttenbroeck, Thomas, and Sigfrid Schneider. *The Twenty-Six Martyrs of Japan: Historical Background. Authentic Biographical Stories.* Tokyo: Chuo Shuppansha, 1980.

Jean-Marie Vianney

Ghéon, Henri. *The Secret of the Curé d'Ars.* Translated by F. J. Sheed with a note on the saint by G. K. Chesterton. New York: Sheed and Ward, 1935.

Rutler, George William. *Saint John Vianney: The Curé d'Ars Today.* San Francisco: Ignatius Press, 1988.

Vianney, John Marie. *The Little Catechism of The Curé of Ars.* Charlotte, NC: Tan Books, 2009.

————. *The Sermons of the Curé of Ars.* Translated by Una Morrissy with a special forward to the English edition by Lancelot Sheppard. Chicago: H. Regnery, 1960.

Matt Talbot

Doherty, Edward J. *Matt Talbot.* Milwaukee: Bruce Publishing Company, 1953.

Purcell, Mary. *Matt Talbot and His Times.* Westminster, MD: Newman Press, 1955.